D0884401

the communication of

hate

Howard Giles,
General Editor

Vol. 9

The Language as Social Action series is part of the Peter Lang
Media and Communication list.
Every volume is peer reviewed and meets
the highest quality standards for content and production.

PETER LANG
New York • Washington, D.C./Baltimore • Bern
Frankfurt • Berlin • Brussels • Vienna • Oxford

Michael Waltman & John Haas

the communication of
hate

PETER LANG
New York • Washington, D.C./Baltimore • Bern
Frankfurt • Berlin • Brussels • Vienna • Oxford

Library of Congress Cataloging-in-Publication Data

Waltman, Michael.
The communication of hate / Michael Waltman, John Haas.
p. cm. — (Language as social action; v. 9)
Includes bibliographical references and index.
1. Hate speech—United States. 2. Oral communication—Social aspects—
United States. 3. Freedom of speech—United States. 4. United States—
Social conditions. I. Haas, John. II. Title.
P95.54.W35   364.15'6—dc22   2010040554
ISBN 978-1-4331-0447-3
ISSN 1529-2436

Bibliographic information published by **Die Deutsche Nationalbibliothek**
Die Deutsche Nationalbibliothek lists this publication in the "Deutsche
Nationalbibliografie"; detailed bibliographic data is available
on the Internet at http://dnb.d-nb.de/.

The paper in this book meets the guidelines for permanence and durability
of the Committee on Production Guidelines for Book Longevity
of the Council of Library Resources.

© 2011 Peter Lang Publishing, Inc., New York
29 Broadway, 18th floor, New York, NY 10006
www.peterlang.com

Printed in the United States of America

Contents

Acknowledgements

Various phases of this research received generous support from the University of North Carolina through a Spray-Randleigh Fellowship from the College of Arts and Sciences, a Moister Fellowship from the Institute for the Arts and Humanities, and a Faculty Engaged Scholar Fellowship from the Carolina Center for Public Service.

We want to acknowledge Howie Giles and Mary Savigar for the respect they showed our ideas and for creating a valuable and delightful partnership. Michael wishes to express his appreciation for the Waltmans and Leysieffers whose love and encouragement inspired and sustained this research.

We dedicate our work to the memories of Maria Feldt Haas and Dr. Bill Waltman, parents who taught us our first lessons about the dangers of hate and the importance of genuine respect for social differences.

Chapter 1

Language in Action: Overview of Discursive Constructs Useful for Understanding Hate Speech

Hatred and related constructs, such as tolerance, are controversial and ambiguous for a variety of reasons. First, the many academics working in this area represent several disciplines and often work at the nexus of those disciplines, providing a rich and diverse set of ideas for understanding hate and hate-related issues. This is useful for academic writers but it could hinder the development of a commonly understood core set of constructs and practices that might characterize the work of a single academic discipline.

Second, there is frequently a disconnect between what academics mean by constructs such as "hate" and "tolerance" and how those terms are understood and discussed in our everyday lives. As we have described earlier (Waltman & Haas, 2007), for example, people may claim to hate the boss that bullies them with their power, the former friend who betrayed the secrets of their friendship to a third party, or the colleague who frustrates the accomplishment of their professional goals. A child may claim to hate a classmate who "tattled" on him to a teacher. A politician from one political party may claim that the rhetoric of politicians from another political party constitutes hate speech against the former.

How does one reconcile such everyday understandings and uses of the term "hate" with the more extraordinary hate-motivated actions of the White Supremacist that unleashed automatic weapon fire on a Jewish Day Care Center in an attempt to kill Jewish children before they could mature to become an adult threat to the Aryan race? How do some of the everyday uses of the term "hate" compare with Timothy McVeigh's belief that the Federal Government was infiltrated and controlled by an international Jewish conspiracy (Zionist-Occupied Government) and who viewed his bombing of the Alfred P. Murrah Federal Building in Oklahoma City as a righteous act of self-defense? The use of the term "hate" to describe such a wide range of emotions and actions could certainly interfere with a meaningful academic understanding of the term. Therefore, we define "hate" and describe what we mean by the term.

Hate is generally understood as extreme negative feelings and beliefs held about a group of individuals or a specific representative of that group because of their race, ethnicity, religion, gender, or sexual orientation (Perry, 2001). As he studied hatred, Aristotle felt it important to distinguish hatred from anger. Anger is an emotion that (a) one might have for an individual (not a larger social group), (b) does not prevent one from having sympathy for the objects of one's anger, (c) is usually the result of personal insult or injury, and (d) is likely to promote impetuous action (Olson, 2002; Sokolon, 2006; R. K. Whillock, 1995). Because hatred is an emotion that one feels for a social group, hatred, unlike anger, need not be the result of personal injury or insult and is more likely to prompt deliberate action. Unlike anger, the hateful mind is not capable of sympathy but hopes for evil to befall the hated (Sokolon, 2006). Indeed, the hateful mind would have the objects of its hatred simply perish—the ultimate end for the mind that has learned to hate. Because the hateful mind lacks sympathy, Aristotle viewed hatred as a much more durable emotion than anger, unlikely to dissipate over time or to even be satiated by killing (Sokolon, 2006). So, one is more likely to feel "anger" toward a friend who betrays us. The friendship may never be the same, but the anger is likely to dissipate over time and most of us would not wish that the former friend would "disappear."

It is also important to understand that hatred is an emotion in which one may find pleasure (Hazlitt, 2005). William Hazlitt (2005) suggested a variety of ways that hatred brings us pleasure. First, the fundamentalism and certitude of hatred offers the pleasure and indulgence in self-righteousness. Our hatred of a specific group is enlivened by our construction of that group as an enemy. Inevitably, the enemy is constructed as evil and/or fundamentally flawed. Understanding ourselves as the dual opposite of this evil and flawed enemy allows us to wallow in our own goodness and righteousness. Second, Hazlitt viewed hatred as a destructive, actually primitive, emotion that had to be repressed as humans exchanged their tribal bonds for the bonds of civilized societies (remember, we hate groups/tribes or their representatives); however, we find pleasure in revisiting this darker side of our human nature in our imaginations. Perhaps we revisit this "darker side" when we consume movies and books that vilify old war enemies. Perhaps we even revisit hatred and pantomime this hatred through our allegiances to sports teams and the rivals we love to hate. As we will see in chapter five, it is easy to imagine that ethno-terrorists and perpetrators of hate crimes take great pleasure in the pain that they inflict on the objects of their hatred.

Hate speech may be used for many purposes and may have different intended consequences. Hate speech may be directed to intimidate an out-group. However, hate speech may also be used to influence the behavior of in-group members in a variety of ways (e.g., to recruit members to a hate group, to socialize white people to adopt and understand the proper racist Aryan identity and behaviors, to find pleasure in hatred, or to promote ethnoviolence). Hate speech is used to accomplish a variety of other goals that we discuss in the following chapters. What will become clear is that *hate comes alive in our language and our actions.*

With this understanding of hatred, we will now provide an overview of the remaining chapters in this book. This text is focused on understanding the language of hate in action. How does this language function? What does it accomplish? What are interlocutors attempting to "do" when they appeal to the hatred of an audience? The answers to these questions may be clearly addressed by an examination of the communicative messages produced by those with hateful minds. Hate speech is used to intimidate minorities, to promote ethnoviolence, to contribute to an ideology of hate (and, more generally, a collective memory that constitutes the worldview of racist Aryans), to solidify the in-group against an out-group, and to recruit new members into the organized hate movement.

Chapter two focuses on the discursive nature and organization of hate groups. Hate speech certainly operates in sectors of society beyond the rhetoric of organized hate groups, as we discuss in chapters five and six; however, hate organizations are important for their ideological work that often resonates throughout other societal contexts. Chapter two can be thought of as offering a sociological overview of organized hate groups in the United States. We describe a web of relationships between groups that can be distinguished by the symbols and images that may be observed in their communication and hate speech. Generally, we distinguish between race religion groups (groups that ground their hatred in a specific religious viewpoint) and secular hate groups (groups that primarily ground their hatred in a view of group relations and secular beliefs). Importantly, we discuss the ways that these groups have networked and become more integrated and co-opted one another's symbols and images.

In this chapter, we discuss the most recent incarnation of the ideology of hate. This ideology is important as it provides substance and reason to hatred. This is important work because the ideology of hate has tended to evolve as leaders change and groups fade in significance while other groups grow in importance.

Chapter three addresses the conceptual properties of hate speech. These properties center on the discursive construction of social differences in negative and highly politicized terms. One such discursive construct is the hate stratagem (R. K. Whillock, 1995). The hate stratagem, as described above, is a rhetorical trick that discourages argumentative engagement and reasoning. Instead, the hate stratagem politicizes social differences in order to accomplish some specific social or political goal. We review research on the hate stratagem and extend this work by examining the operation of the hate stratagem in different artifacts of the hate movement (e.g., in the racist novels *Hunter* and *The Turner Diaries*). Other discursive constructs discussed in chapter four include message-induced heuristic processing of hate material. Heuristics are decisional shortcuts that people employ to process social influence messages. Examples of such heuristics include the credibility heuristic (I should comply with this request because the speaker is credible or an expert), the consensus heuristic (I should comply because other people are complying), and the liking heuristic (I should comply because this person is likeable). Several heuristics are discussed in chapter three. Some research indicates that hateful messages are often accompanied by attempts to encourage listeners to process such messages superficially and heuristically.

Social differences are also politicized through the exchanging of myths that constitute the collective memory of the U.S. hate movement. The myths discussed in chapter three functions to teach proper racist Aryan identities, beliefs, and actions (including violence). They also teach Aryans how to think about and treat their enemies. Chapter three extends previous work on racist Aryan myths by illustrating their existence and functions across the most important discursive artifacts in the U.S. hate movement.

Although not a discourse structure, we argue that hate crime often carries important symbolic value. Hate crime has sometimes been referred to as a message crime. A form of terrorism and ethnoviolence, hate-motivated crime and violence communicate a variety of meanings to those who share an identity with the target of the hate crime. Hate crime and ethnoviolence communicates that the other is not welcome and not safe ("this could have been you"). It is this symbolic value that makes hate crimes unlike any other crime, one that tears at the fabric of communities.

Chapter four examines the role the Internet plays in the hate speech produced by hate-mongers. It was not too long ago that if hate-mongers wanted to gather to create congenial environments they would have to travel, often long distances, to secluded compounds in remote areas. Now, for the price of an inexpensive computer, software, and Internet server, they may enter a world where their ideas are normal and respected. It is clear that these congenial environments have played an important role in the radicalization of individuals who go "Lone Wolf" and take it upon themselves to commit horrific acts of hate-motivated violence. This chapter examines several key Web Pages to illustrate how hate speech is used to radicalize readers and promote Lone Wolf terrorism.

Chapters five and six examine samples of hate speech in two mainstream contexts that will resonate with the experiences of readers. In chapter five, we examine hate speech and hate crimes that are directed at immigrants who have entered this country illegally. "Nativism" reflects beliefs and policies that favor established groups in a country and discriminate against "newcomers" or immigrants. In the 19th century, Nativism was a powerful force in American life and politics, as being 100% American meant being white, Protestant, and American-born. American fear of Europeans (and, often, Catholics) fleeing economic and agricultural catastrophes in Europe are widely discussed in American history textbooks. We examine current Nativist discourse that has been used to whip audiences into frenzies by making undocumented immigrants (usually people of color) the repository for all the ills and fears of working-class and middle-class white people. We examine this discourse and identify it as a form of hate speech with important conceptual overlap with the discourse produced by the organized hate movement in the United States. As we note in chapter five, recent years have seen a 40% increase in hate-motivated violence carried out against people in this country without proper documentation. Not surprisingly, this violence has been accompanied by increasingly vitriolic hate speech among politicians and media pundits.

In chapter six, we examine how this Nativism emerged in the discourse produced by the key campaigns of the 2008 presidential election. We describe how the Hillary Clinton campaign gradually devolved into explicit attempts to "otherize" Barack Obama by constructing him as insufficiently American. Over time, this strategy would reveal the production of the hate stratagem and the suggestion that "hard-working, white Americans" would be unwilling to vote for an African American nominee, a suggestion that would be rejected by the voters. In the general election, the McCain campaign would employ rhetoric that resembled that of many hate groups. The McCain campaign employed the hate stratagem and explicitly invoked cultural myths that have been used to vilify African Americans throughout history. This discourse did not fade into the background of our political landscape when Barack Obama was elected President of the United States. Instead, this discourse morphed from simple hate speech that attempted to otherize Barack Obama for his blackness, to otherizing him for both his un-

American attitudes and his "non-American citizenship." Groups such as the Birthers and Tea Party protestors responded to the Obama administration's policies by calling him a Kenyan, Hitler, a Fascist, a Communist, etc. These protests during the summer of 2009 would see the reemergence of militia groups, popular in the 1990s, that cloaked their hatred in suspicion of the government and conspiratorial beliefs that government wishes to take away American's Second Amendment rights in order to take away Americans' liberties. In the summer of 2009, militia groups would coalesce with Birthers and Tea Party protestors to make a potentially violent cocktail of anti-government Nativists (Potok, 2009). We discuss the implications of the return of the militias and their violence that defined so much of the 1990s.

Chapter seven explores the desirable features of anti-hate discourse, discourse designed to respond to hate and promote more humane and tolerant communities. We reconsider the purposes and functions of hate and hate speech in order to articulate the desired functions of anti-hate discourse. Specifically, we argue that anti-hate discourse should reconstruct what was destroyed through hate. Hate crimes represent attempts to destroy the body and identity of its victims. Hate speech vilifies and dehumanizes the identities it targets. So, one important function of anti-hate speech is to re-humanize and revalue the identities destroyed through hate speech. An anti-hate discourse explicitly describes the value and preciousness of the identities demeaned by hate speech. In this chapter, we identify a set of best practices that we gleaned from a close reading of various anti-hate texts such as documentaries, Web Pages, and pamphlets. We warn of potential pitfalls in the construction of messages intended to challenge hate. For example, we note that a community's desire to promote a desired self-image may lead to scapegoating specific hate criminals, making them a vessel into which a community's shortcomings may be poured. Such community identity management strategies may prevent reflection on community characteristics that grow hatred (Williamson, 2002).

The basic thrust of these anti-hate texts is on how one may respond to specific, often interpersonal, encounters with family, friends, and acquaintances. The hateful acts depicted in most of these materials also involve rather explicit acts of hatred. This chapter also focuses on the everyday discourses that support and sustain hatred. While previous chapters addressed the hate, hate crime, and hate speech produced by individual hate-mongers or hate groups, in this chapter we also examine the ways that hatred is manipulated by elements of mainstream society. This Everyday Racism focuses on the ways that broad social discourses produced by police, politicians, and everyday citizens knowingly and unknowingly contribute to a more hateful and fragmented society. These forms of racism may "otherize softly" (Bonilla-Silva, 2006) but still promote hatred. We discuss this Everyday Racism as a form of racism that exists in people's everyday interactions and serves to maintain white privilege. Subsequently, we describe ways that this form of racism may be challenged and confronted.

Finally, chapter eight serves to conclude our discussion of the discursive production of hatred. We consider the implications of the issues discussed and offer suggestions that may shepherd us to more hopeful and humane communities that offer unity in differences.

One important feature of this book is the universality of hatred. Hatred is an international problem that results in isolated acts of murder and more systematic and coordinated genocide. Our writing and our examples are skewed toward American society because that is our focus. We think it is important that readers keep in mind that hatred is a problem that knows no geographical boundaries, and that the American version of hatred must certainly have implications for the hatred experienced by other societies.

We believe the themes discussed in these chapters provide a rather unique view of hate speech in action. The chapters in this book offer a comprehensive examination of how hatred operates in American society. We examine the discourse of various organized hate groups, including the ways that common symbols, images, and icons serve to integrate various groups in the hate movement. We also examine how hatred is manipulated by mainstream politicians, political operatives, and media pundits to pursue the advancement of their own agendas. This analysis allows us to compare the discourse of organized hate groups with these mainstream public voices. This comparison will reveal that these voices are often more alike than they are different. Our analysis of hate-motivated discourse in American society also allows a glimpse at the various technologies that make hate speech available to mass publics (e.g., physical books, television commercials, newspaper and news magazine reports, Internet Web Pages). Another unique feature of this text is our analysis of the desirable features of a discourse that promotes tolerance. We believe this to be a unique attribute among books that examine hatred. The importance of this chapter is given weight by an example of anti-hate discourse, discussed in chapter five, that violated important principles of the anti-hate discourse discussed in chapter seven, resulting in unfortunate consequences for specific individuals and the community they wished to protect.

Chapter 2

Discursive Nature of
Organized Hate Groups

Hatred takes many forms in addition to the forms it takes in organized hate groups. However, a broader understanding of hatred must begin with these groups, and their activities, because organized hate provides an ideology and culture of hatred that inspires, directly and indirectly, hate crimes and ethnoviolence. As we discuss in this chapter, these groups are created discursively. They have articulated their beliefs and ideology through Web Pages, racist novels, and White Power music (Billig, 2001; Daniels, 1997; Davis, 2005; Olson, 2002; Perry, 2001; Waltman & Davis, 2005; Waltman & Haas, 2007; Waltman, 2010-a; R. K. Whillock, 1995). Moreover, these groups pursue their goals (e.g., recruitment of new members and the promotion of ethnoviolence) through discourse (Davis, 2005; Hamm, 1993; Waltman, 2003; Waltman & Davis, 2004).

The challenges of hate are embodied in the violent deeds of those who serve hatred and intolerance. From 1977 to 1989, Joseph Paul Franklin traveled the eastern part of the United States, killing approximately 17 people for posing various threats to his white race. Franklin bombed a Jewish synagogue, killed two black men jogging alone, killed white women who admitted to having sexual congress with black men, and killed couples that he identified as "inter-racial" couples. Over time, Franklin supported his violence through armed robbery.

On April 19, 1995, following procedures described in *The Turner Diaries*, a racist novel that tells the story of a race war in the United States, Timothy McVeigh bombed the Alfred P. Murrah Federal Building in Oklahoma City. He killed 168 people and injured 850 more while leaving a gash across the psyche of the people of Oklahoma City. His purpose was (a) to strike back at the Zionist-Occupied Government (ZOG) of the United States that he perceived as responsible for the unwarranted killing of the Branch Davidians in Waco, Texas; and (b) to try to awaken good white people to the threat of this system.

After years of eluding law enforcement, Eric Rudolph was arrested on May 31, 2003, and charged with the deadly bombings of the 1996 Atlanta Olympic Games, a lesbian nightclub, and abortion clinics. He wanted to strike at the "regime in Washington" that was encouraging race-mixing and diversity, the acceptance of a homosexual agenda, and the murder of unborn white children, respectively (Waltman, 2010-b). Rudolph clearly had additional plans because, after his arrest, he disclosed to authorities where 250 pounds of dynamite could be located.

In June of 1998, Lawrence Brewer, John King, and Shawn Berry tied a black man named James Byrd by the feet to a chain and dragged him to death behind a pickup truck in Jasper, Texas. They left his decapitated body on the lawn of a black church. They believed that the attention drawn to this grizzly hate crime would help them to form their own hate group.

On August 10, 1999, Aryan Nations member Buford Furrow walked into a Los Angeles Jewish community center and began to shoot, leaving a 69-year-old receptionist and four children wounded and traumatized. His purpose was to awaken white people to what he perceived as a Jewish international conspiracy committed to the oppression of white people, and to take some measure of revenge for the Federal Bureau of Investigation's (F.B.I.'s) killing of Robert Matthews, his friend and leader of The Order, a terrorist group affiliated with Aryan Nations.

These examples center on individuals who had a relatively intimate acquaintance with a formal hate group that preached an explicit ideology of hate. However, there are also examples of violence linked to individuals who, though lacking an explicit association with an organized hate group, were familiar with the ideology they preached. On October 6, 1998, Russell Henderson and Aaron McKinney maneuvered a young gay man named Matthew Shepherd to a remote location in order to beat and torture him to death, leaving him tied to a prairie fence just outside of Laramie, Wyoming. They did so because he was gay.

On February 19, 1999, in Sylacauga, Alabama, Steven Mullins and Charles Monroe Butler lured Billy Jack Gaither, a 39-year-old gay man, away from a bar where they were playing pool. They cut his throat and beat him to death with an ax handle. Later, the two men would confess that they killed him because he was gay.

Approximately one week after two airplanes were flown into the World Trade Center, Ali Almansoop, a Yemeni immigrant, was awakened by Brent Seever who, while shouting anti-Arab slogans, shot Almansoop in the back as he tried to escape. Seever had been driving around the neighborhood thinking about the attack on the World Trade Center, and decided to defend the United States by killing someone he perceived to be like those terrorists who attacked the World Trade Center (Levin & McDevitt, 2002).

In January 2009, Keith Luke killed black residents of Brockton, Massachusetts. He claimed that the killings were his attempt to protect the white race from extinction. Luke informed authorities that his racial attitudes were learned entirely from racist Web Sites that "spoke the truth about the demise of the white race" (Keller, 2009a). These sources celebrated ethnoviolence and terrorism as a response to the genocidal threat faced by the white race.

These ethnoterrorists and hate killers are all connected by their commitment to an ideology of hate, informed by their membership in, or contacts with, organized hate groups. Most of these terrorists have been nurtured to believe in a world Jewish conspiracy that Jews are dedicated to controlling world governments, media, and a host of other social institutions. The purpose of this conspiracy is the oppression and eventual genocide of the white race. This genocide is to be accomplished in a variety of ways, including encouraging inter-racial dating and marriage, the growth of Feminism to brainwash women and draw them away from family values, the acceptance of a "homosexual lifestyle," and governmental policies devoted to reducing the significance and influence of white people, such as the Civil Rights Act of 1964, Affirmative Action, and weak immigration laws. Believing in the utter veracity of these conspiracies, the terrorists mentioned above saw themselves in a life and death struggle with Jews and other enemies of the Aryan race. Because they see their struggle as a complete and total race war, there are no innocents, only the enemies of the Aryan race and those white people who are racially unaware and duplicitous in their own oppression.

These ideas have evolved over a long period of time and their sources cannot be framed by geographic boundaries (Timmerman, 2003). Presently, they may be recognized by ordinary people as cultural stereotypes that polite society does not discuss or endorse, at least publicly. However, these ideas are nurtured in a reservoir of hate by groups in the organized hate movement. America's commitment to free speech leads us to permit all forms of hate speech. Many Western democracies have viewed hate speech as too toxic to the social fabric to tolerate, America has not. It is from this reservoir that (a) hate groups spew their hatred when social circumstances are desirable, (b) individuals seek confirmation of their racist ideas, cocooning themselves from beliefs that might challenge their worldview, and (c) domestic terrorists emerge to spread violence after consuming a steady diet of hate.

The Nature of Organized Hate Groups

Hate groups may be regarded as cultures because they may be distinguished by their beliefs, values, goals, and icons that constitute their unique views of race, religion, ethnicity, gender, and sexual orientation (Perry, 2001). The discourse through which these values, icons, and symbols are communicated is a useful way to learn about these subcultures of hate. Beyond the hate movement, the heritage of white supremacy in this country has rendered the white identity as the norm. Dyer (1997) has noted that an identity that is defined as the norm may become taken for granted or relatively "invisible"— perhaps even lacking in cultural content. Indeed, the very power of "whiteness" lies in its ability to be rendered normal and invisible (Gabriel, 1998). One goal of hate groups is to articulate what it means to be White. The rising popularity of folk festivals among White people provides evidence that White people are attempting to connect to the cultures and traditions of their ancestors. Such festivals, themselves usually innocent enough, have become platforms for hate groups' recruitment of White people who may be sympathetic to their unique articulation of a white identity (Waltman, 2010-a).

The present incarnation of hate groups reflects two broad categories that are each composed of distinct subtypes. The first set of hate groups are race religion groups, groups that ground their hatred in a religious doctrine to give ideological substance to their hatred. The second set is secular-based hate groups, groups that ground their goals and activities in social or political beliefs that give substance to their hatred. While secular and religious groups are distinct and separate entities, many racist Aryans participate in the life of a secular group and subscribe to the religious tenets of a race religion. Indeed, as will be argued later, such individuals serve as one marker of the growing permeability in the ideological membranes that separate these subcultures of hate.

Race Religion Groups

There are three primary race religion groups that are currently active in the hate movement. The Identity Church Movement, or Christian Identity, represents a racist version of Christianity and is the oldest of the race religion groups. However, Racist Pre-Christian Paganism and the Creativity Movement, also recognizable as the World Church of the Creator (WCOTC) (prior to a lawsuit in 2003 that forced the group to change its name), are groups that have become popular among younger racist Aryans.

The Identity Church Movement

The Identity Church Movement grounds its hatred in anti-Semitic and racist interpretations of the Christian Bible. Christian Identity is the doctrine that claims that Aryans are the lost tribes of Israel. Adherents to this doctrine believe the Jews to be the literal children of Satan; the offspring of Eve's mating with Satan in the Garden of Eden, and a natural enemy of the Aryan race.

This group was formed by Louis Beam shortly after the F.B.I. botched the arrest of Randy Weaver on charges of possession of illegal weapons in Ruby Ridge, Idaho. (Weaver had been affiliated with Aryan Nations and the government had tried to recruit him to entrap other Aryan Nations members.) Beam preached that the Federal Government views all free-thinking white people as the enemy. This ideology was also advanced by Richard Butler, a Christian Identity reverend in the Church of Jesus Christ Christian, and Pete Peters, reverend in the LaPorte Church of Christ. Beam, Butler, and Peters would minister to individuals who would later become ethnoterrorists (Waltman, 2010-b). Two terrorist groups are associated with the Identity Church Movement: The Phineas Priesthood and The Order.

The Phineas Priesthood is a phantom-like organization that operates through the informal knowledge of the Identity Church Movement. The Phineas Priesthood is not a membership organization that holds regular meetings among individuals who know one another. One claims the title of a Phineas Priest by murdering an inter-racial couple (involving one white partner). The inspiration for the Phineas Priesthood is taken from the Book of Numbers (chapter 25; verses 6–13) in the Old Testament of the Christian Bible. To set the stage, Moses has been wandering the desert with the Children of Israel after leading them out of slavery in Egypt. The Israelites begin to co-mingle with people outside the covenant with God when we are introduced to Phineas:

> And behold, one of the children of Israel came and brought unto his brethren a Midianitish woman in the sight of Moses, and in the sight of all the congregation of the children of Israel, who were weeping before the door of the tabernacle of the congregation. And when Phineas…saw it, he rose up from among the congregation, and took a javelin in his hand; and he went after the man of Israel into the tent, and thrust both of them through, the man of Israel and the woman through her belly.… And the Lord spake unto Moses, saying, Phineas, the son of Eleazar, the son of Aaron the priest, hath turned my wrath away from the children of Israel, while he was zealous for my sake among them, that I consumed not the children of Israel in my jealousy.… Behold I give unto him my covenant of peace; and he shall have it, and his seed after him, even the covenant of an everlasting priesthood; because he was zealous for his God, and made an atonement for the children of Israel.

Another terrorist group that is associated with the Identity Church Movement is The Order. In many ways, The Order serves as a conceptual conduit between the Identity Church Movement and a second race religion, Racist Pre-Christian Paganism. The Order was formed by Robert Matthews, a recruiter for the National Alliance, named after a similar terrorist group in *The Turner Diaries*. Matthews recruited members from National Alliance,

Aryan Nations, and various Ku Klux Klan groups to wage a guerilla war against the Federal Government (the Zionist-Occupied Government). Matthews, a Racist Pre-Christian Pagan, used Pagan rituals to bind together this diverse group of terrorists. To finance their war, and to support other groups, The Order stole millions of dollars from armored vehicles at gunpoint.

Two other important members of the group were the late David Lane and Richard Scutari. The Order would also become famous for the killing of Jewish radio shock jock, Alan Berg, who insulted the group on his radio show. On June 18, 1984, Lane and Scutari would participate in the killing of Alan Berg. The Robberies and this highly visible murder brought the F.B.I. to their door. On December 8, 1984, Matthews was killed in a gun battle with F.B.I. agents. The rest of The Order would be arrested and sent to prison. Once in prison, David Lane converted to Paganism out of respect for Matthews. He would eventually become an intellectual leader among Racist Pre-Christian Pagans.

Alternative race religion groups are growing in popularity among those who view Christian Identity to be insufficiently radical and still fundamentally a Christian system of beliefs. Christianity, with its emphasis on forgiveness, is viewed as a religion of the weak and an outgrowth of Judaism intended to narcotize white people to the growing dominance of the "mud races," subverting the "natural" dominance of the white race. Two main groups have emerged as alternatives to the Identity Church Movement: Racist Pre-Christian Paganism and the World Church of the Creator.

Racist Pre-Christian Paganism

Racist Pre-Christian Paganism is an increasingly important religion in the American hate movement. Racists embracing this religion see it as an "indigenous faith rooted in pre-Christian Anglo-Saxon warrior cultures; and the oneness of the Aryan race with nature" (Gardell, 2003, p. 206). The racist Pagan believes that mainstream Christianity has de-natured white people and separated them from their own "blood." In other words, Christianity and other Jewish conspiracies have taken control of white people's lives and their culture, separating them from their true nature and past. Racist Paganism is intended to reconnect Aryans with their original culture, so that they can re-learn to "think with their blood" (Gardell, 2003, p. 206).

Often referred to as Odinism, this is a religion grounded in the Old Norse pantheon of gods and included (a) Odin, the god of war and the father of all gods and men, (b) Freya, his clairvoyant wife, and (c) Thor, their hammer-wielding son and god of thunder. Odin is known by many names, such as Wotan, his Germanic name. Among White Supremacists, WOTAN is also used as an acronym for Will Of The Aryan Nations. Other lesser-known Norse gods represented various aspects of nature and ideas gifted to humans from the gods (e.g., Tyr, original god of war; Balder, god of light, joy, purity, beauty, innocence, and reconciliation; and a host of other gods constructed to describe the influence of powerful forces on humankind—including the outcomes of war). These characters, themselves, do not provide us with a rich understanding of the racist Pagan mind. To understand this, one must understand the Pagans view of their world, their relationships with their gods, and the end of their world—their apocalypse.

The values of Anglo-Saxon warrior cultures, and their view of their world, will be familiar to anyone who has read *Beowulf* or the *Icelandic Sagas*. Prior to the ascendance of Christianity, Pagans did not believe that humans might transcend the physical, human world to any kind of spiritual world approximating a Christian understanding of heaven or hell. The possibilities they saw for a life beyond the present were limited, almost exclusively, to the stories that might be told of them following their death, ideally a death that was noteworthy and in defense of King, kinsmen, and companions. The most glorious name would be earned in the Wael-raes, the rush of the battle-slaughter, thereby bearing tangible witness to one's commitment to his king and the venerable bond between one and his battle companions (Heaney, 2000, p. xv). Such noble action was rewarded in times of peace, for those who lived through the Wael-raes, and was essential to establishing one's place in the social hierarchy. In other words, commitment to kinsmen (and king) and courage in battle are values that are at the hub of this warrior culture. This is part of the consciousness that White Supremacists are trying to return to in their embracement of racist Odinism. Hate-motivated murder is viewed as analogous to killing for Odin in battle or making a human sacrifice to Odin (Waltman, 2010-a).

The pre-Christian Pagan imagination did conceive of an afterlife for the bravest of warriors—but it was not an eternal afterlife. Those warriors who demonstrated exemplary bravery in battle might be selected by the Valkyrie, the blond, fair-skinned demigoddesses of death. These select dead warriors are lifted by the Valkyrie to Valhalla, Odin's great hall, a monument to male bravery and the honor of war. It is said that the rafters of Valhalla are spears and the roof is constructed from the shields of fallen warriors. The warriors fight during the day and feast at night in Valhalla. The warriors live, thusly, in Valhalla until Ragnarok, the final day of battle when all the world will be scorched from battle and the earth will sink into the sea. In this final battle, men fight beside and against the Pagan gods. However, a new earthly world will arise from this destruction in which re-born gods live peacefully with humankind in a new and better world. It is this power of Paganism that Racist Pre-Christian Pagans hope to draw from to fuel their hatred and ethnoviolence.

Racist Odinists take Ragnarok as a metaphor for RAHOWA (RAcial HOly WAr), and they draw on the traditions of bravery in battle and the legends of the Valkyrie and Valhalla to add a religious fervor to their hate. The Web Site TightRope weaves the images and icons of Old Norse Pagan traditions into stories and cartoons that celebrate the Aryan race and depict ethnoviolence as a natural part of the life of the true Aryan. To reach a cartoon called "Son of Har," the reader must click on images depicting a skinhead youth making gestures that signify various Old Norse gods (Odin, Balder, Tyr, and Thor). The young man is wearing an amulet of Thor's battle hammer around his neck. The young man removes an automatic pistol from an alter, adorned with a swastika and pictures of Hitler and Robert Matthews. As he proceeds to the eventual assassination of a prominent Jew in his community, his car is followed by two ravens, as if the Valkyrie (symbolized by the ravens) has designated the upcoming assassination and "warrior" as worthy of Valhalla.

The TightRope Web Site portrays ethnoviolence as part and parcel of a normal Racist Pre-Christian Pagan life. Such images tell us something very important about the racist Pagan view of violence. Violence, itself, is a cultural totem, tied closely to the racist Pagan's identity. As such, the racist Pagan feels most "natural" and most closely connected to his community when committing violence.

Odinism shares with Nazism, and Fascism more generally, a social Darwinist philosophy, that views the survival of the white race as a goal of their religion. This "might is right" worldview is found in the belief that all racially aware white people are preparing for the inevitable racial holy war by becoming self-sufficient and taking on the responsibility to live healthy lives, avoiding narcotics and alcohol, and becoming physically fit (Davis, 2005; Waltman & Davis, 2005). This certainly resembles Hitler's belief in the possibility of a race of Aryan supermen. So, it is not too surprising that Odinism has been very appealing to neo-Nazis and young, racist skinheads. The fact that many in Hitler's Third Reich subscribed to a similar occult-like religion to inform their beliefs in a re-born Germanic identity is a fact that is not lost on many pupils of Nazism. So, the blending of fascist hatreds with Odinism provides many neo-Nazis with an ideology that is deeply and historically familiar.

As noted earlier, David Lane and Richard Scutari, former members of The Order, are responsible for founding Odinism as an influential prison religion. According to an SPLC Intelligence Report (2000), Odinism is the fastest growing and most violent religion behind prison walls. Only very recently, Lane passed away in prison as the result of a heart attack. Already, he has been treated as a martyr by those in the hate movement. Even behind prison walls, Lane influenced White Supremacists through a publishing operation established by his wife in the mid-1990s. Indeed, Lane is revered as the publisher of the racist credo known as 14 words: "We must secure the existence of our people and a future for white children." This mission statement has been adopted by a host of groups within the larger hate movement. In a Web Page maintained by a group calling themselves White Revolution (see http://www.whiterevolution.com), Lane was memorialized as a Prisoner of War and a man of action. The reader is encouraged to "join these men of action before we [white people] become an extinct species."

Creativity Movement

Creativity, known as the World Church of the Creator (WCOTC) during the 1990s, is a religion that grounds its philosophy in white supremacy. The religion is the advancement of the white race. WCOTC was initially founded by Ben Klassen, a religion he termed Creativity, on the belief that it is the natural destiny of the white race to rule over all others; Creativity sees white people's social ascension as predetermined by a "creator" who fashioned the other races before he created the white race. Afterward, the creator made its finest creation, the white race, and gave it dominion over all others (Hamm, 1993, p. 203). It should be noted that the Creator is not an omnipotent being in the sky (Klassen viewed Christianity as superstition). According to Klassen, the white race has a soul, an intuitive feeling or desire to create (music, literature, law and order, architecture, etc.). The "inferior" souls of other races are said to lack this impulse. Klassen believed that anything that threatens the white race threatens this impulse toward creation and, therefore, threatens the world. Consequently, what is good for the white race is good, and what is bad for the white race is, by definition, bad (Waltman, 2010-c). Although Klassen encouraged his followers to pursue their "religious" beliefs through peaceful means, he did believe that a race war between the white race and the other "mud" races would be inevitable.

These ideas are enumerated in a book Klassen authored called *The White Man's Bible,* a text that has influenced not simply those who subscribe to Creativity but also a variety of racists and hate-mongers. Therefore, this text is examined more closely in chapter four.

When Klassen passed away, Matt Hale took charge of the Creativity Movement and renamed it the World Church of the Creator. Under Hale's leadership, WCOTC would become one of the largest hate groups in the United States with affiliations in 27 states organized through 30 Web Sites (Anti-Defamation League-a). Hale would become a charismatic leader and the most visible face of the hate movement during the 1990s and early part of the 21st century. During this time, he would appear on network news programming, serve as a mentor to a vicious racist spree killer, draw a significant proportion of racist skinheads to Creativity, and ultimately be convicted of conspiring to kill a federal judge.

From his home in East Peoria, Illinois, Hale conducted caustic and hateful attacks against Jews, Christians, and people of color through his Web Site and various speeches. Creativity's "cold" racial holy war turned hot in July of 1999 when Benjamin Nathaniel Smith began a spree killing of African Americans, Jews, and Asian Americans that began in Chicago, and included the murder of Northwestern basketball coach, Ricky Birdsong. Smith's stated purpose was to jump-start the racial holy war that Klassen predicted. Smith's killing spree ended when he killed himself, surrounded by police, in Indiana. Smith had been mentored by Matt Hale, although there was no firm evidence that Hale was legally culpable in Smith's murders. Hale subsequently portrayed Benjamin Smith as a martyr for his race.

Hale's fortunes began to unravel when he and his World Church of the Creator were sued for the rights to that name by an Oregon-based, non-racist church also using the name Church of the Creator. Because the Oregon church was the first to register the trademark, a federal judge ruled against Hale and his church. Hale would conspire to have this federal judge murdered when he encouraged his members to wage war on the federal judiciary (Waltman, 2010-c). The only other time that Hale had employed this violent rhetoric was when he was ultimately denied a license to practice law in Illinois—immediately before Benjamin Smith's two-state rampage. Waltman (2010-c) described how Hale's discourse encouraged individuals to strike out at the enemies of the Aryan race while temporarily insulating his organization from the violence he fostered. In the end, F.B.I. informants and undercover agents infiltrated his organization and revealed him to be a builder of terrorists. Although Hale is in prison, he has served as a symbol of one who was willing to give up his freedom for his race. Since his imprisonment, Creativity is attempting to return to its place of prominence in the hate movement.

In the end, all race religions operate similar to Creativity. They are not groups whose main purpose is to build membership roles. Rather, their purpose is to build terrorists by providing a set of cultural beliefs and practices that create enemies and provide a rationale for the killing of those enemies.

The idea is the creation of a terrorist like Benjamin Smith, Buford Furrow, or Timothy McVeigh who kill on their own (or with one or two partners) while providing the leaders and formal group plausible deniability.

Secular Race Groups

Neo-Nazi groups

Neo-Nazi groups, such as the National Alliance, have drawn on the Fascism of Adolph Hitler and the Third Reich to inform their "White Power" rhetoric. Their deification of Hitler and the Third Reich provides them with a rich, symbolic heritage that grounds their hate in a historical struggle for Aryan purity. Many numerical racist symbols explicitly link the neo-Nazi identity with Adolph Hitler. Hitler's birthday, April 20, is celebrated through the numerical symbols "420," "4/20," or "4:20." Neo-Nazis identify themselves to one another through the "88" numerical symbol ("Heil Hitler"—"H" is the eighth letter of the alphabet) or, more recently, "18" ("Adolph Hitler"—"A" is the first letter of the alphabet and "H" is the eighth letter of the alphabet). Such symbols may appear in public as graffiti, placards, or individual tattoos (Anti-Defamation League-b).

Most neo-Nazis, or neo-Nazi-like groups, reject any kind of religious philosophy. Tom Metzger, founder of White Aryan Resistance (WAR), says of religion: "We better solve the problems by ourselves because there's nobody going to come here and magically do it for us" (Ezekiel, 1995, p. 73). Metzger's remark provides insight into more than his view of religion. Metzger's comment also emphasizes the neo-Nazi value of action over thought, a value that is drawn from the Fascism that followed World War I. The neo-Nazi embracement of violence as a means to political ends flows directly from 20th-century Fascism. Mussolini (1932) wrote:

> Fascism, the more it considers and observes the future and the development of humanity quite apart from political considerations of the moment, believes neither in the possibility nor the utility of perpetual peace. It thus repudiates the doctrine of Pacifism—born of a renunciation of the struggle and an act of cowardice in the face of sacrifice. War alone brings up to its highest tension all human energy and puts the stamp of nobility upon the peoples who have courage to meet it. All other trials are substitutes, which never really put men into the position where they have to make the great decision—the alternative of life or death. (*Internet Modern History Sourcebook*, 2007)

The fascist embracement of violence is, rather naturally, expressed by fascist artists. The Futurists, an artistic and literary movement in Italy during the early part of the 20th century declared in their manifesto:

We want to sing the love of danger.... The essential elements of our poetry will be courage, audacity, and revolt. We want to exalt movements of aggression...the slap and blow of the fist. We want to glorify war—the only cure for the world—and militarism...the beautiful ideas which kill. (Marinetti, 1909)

Hitler gave the fascist view of violence and war a focus and purpose when he blended it with his interpretation of Social Darwinism (also known as natural law or biological determinism). This philosophy asserts that stronger nations and people possess a natural right to dominate or exterminate weaker nations (Von Maltitz, 1973). From this point of view, war and conquest are not immoral, but merely the fulfilling of a predestined mission (Hamm, 1993). This view of violence and conquest is explicitly translated into the practices of modern neo-Nazis.

Within the American neo-Nazi movement, the value of action and violence is manifested in William Pierce's *The Turner Diaries* (published under the pseudonym of Andrew McDonald). Pierce, founder of National Alliance, tells the story of the racial holy war in his "novel." Pierce depicts a struggle pitting racially aware white people against a government organized for the oppression of white people. Pierce describes the counter-insurgency of the revolutionaries in great detail, providing models for the making of bombs, potential targets, and the logistics for carrying out successful bombings. *The Turner Diaries* has, indeed, served as a "how to" manual and inspiration for many extremists. The novel was found in the possession of the ultra-violent group, The Order (led by Robert Matthews), and of Timothy McVeigh, the infamous Oklahoma City bomber. McVeigh is thought to have selected his target, and executed his mission, in Oklahoma City based on a bombing described in *The Turner Diaries*.

Racist skinheads

Racist skinheads, somewhat neo-Nazi in character, tend to be more loosely organized but highly violent youth. Anti-racists have argued that members tend to be disaffected and troubled working-class youth with no real agenda but hate (Hamm, 1993). The Anti-Defamation League (ADL) went so far as to claim that skinheads were disintegrating before our eyes. But that was in 1988 and the racist skinhead subculture is still an ominous presence on the extremist landscape.

Skinheads are recognized by their shaved heads, steel-toed Doc Martens, and "Donkey" jackets, artifacts of the urban, working-class background that nurtured this youth subculture (Hamm, 1993). Racist skinheads have occasionally added to the symbolism of this uniform by painting the toes of their boots red (to reflect the blood shed in battle for the Aryan race), interweaving red and white shoestrings in their Doc Martens (to represent their sacrificed blood and the purity of the Aryan race, respectively), or wearing red and white suspenders (D. E. Whillock, 1995).

Hamm (1993) distinguishes between terrorist and non-terrorist racist skinheads. Terrorist skinheads tend to subscribe to neo-Nazi beliefs and/or the values of Odinism described earlier but, in Hamm's study, they were more likely to grow their hair to the norm, dress in mainstream clothing, and pursue a college education while working. The concept of "beserking," a term that has been used to describe skinhead attacks on minorities, is taken from the fighting style of Viking warriors who went into battle in a crazed state, preferring death to retreat. Skinhead beserking is fueled by beer and White Power music, two central elements of skinhead culture. Indeed, Hamm (1993) argues that White Power music, with its celebration of neo-Nazi beliefs and Nordic Aryan ideas, provides an ongoing infusion of their ideology into the life world of the skinhead. Because terrorists listen to White Power music daily, this infusion occurs on a regular basis. Non-terrorists are less inclined to hold neo-Nazi beliefs and are also less likely to participate in ethnoviolence. Violence may or may not be a part of their lives, but non-terrorists are more likely to become involved in fights against other white people (or anti-racist skinheads, specifically). Unlike their terrorist counterparts, non-terrorist skinheads tend to dress in the skinhead "uniform."

The American skinhead movement received an additional injection of neo-Nazi beliefs from Tom Metzger of White Aryan Resistance (WAR). Metzger encountered a newsletter that was produced by Ian Stuart (founder of the White Power band, Skrewdriver) in London. Metzger set out to create, through WAR, an organizational structure that would permit him to distribute his ideas to skinheads, providing them with more ideological grounding than they possessed in the past. By mentoring skinhead groups across California, he hoped to create a cadre of young racist warriors who would take the racial holy war to individual Jews and minorities across California (Hamm, 1993; Langer, 1990). Metzger is reported to have said of his foot soldiers, "If you're going to do anything, you need to have somebody with you who's going to stand their ground, and most conservatives won't. The skinheads have already got the main thing, and that's guts" (Hamm, 1993, p. 53). On October 21, 1990, the Southern Poverty Law Center and Morris Dees won a civil suit against Metzger and his organization for conspiring with skinheads in the death of Mulugeta Seraw, who was killed in November 1988 by three racist skinheads. This forced Metzger into bankruptcy. The bankruptcy and the belief among many skinheads that they were being "used" and exploited by Metzger contributed to his diminishing influence on racist skinheads.

Although Metzger's influence on skinheads was removed by the Seraw suit, there was someone who was ready to fill the vacuum, Matt Hale and the World Church of the Creator. Prior to his conviction, increasing numbers of skinheads were turning to the Creativity Movement to provide them a more substantive race ideology. Hamm (1993) interviewed a number of skinheads who reported being "reverends" in the World Church of the Creator and who claimed that Creativity is core to skinhead beliefs.

The Ku Klux Klan

The Ku Klux Klan (the KKK or the Klan) is a truly American-grown hate group. The Klan grew from the reconstruction that followed America's Civil War. Fearful of the loss of a Southern white identity, and presumably violent former slaves, the Klan arose as one of America's first terrorist organizations, grounded principally in a belief of white supremacy. The Klan was wed to the American film industry in America's first silent film, *Birth of a Nation*. This film glamorized the Klan as the protector of white womanhood and white virtue from predatory and marauding freed slaves during reconstruction. The film actually became a powerful recruiting tool for the Klan in the second decade of the 20th century. The Klan's self-avowed purpose was to protect the virtue of Southern white women from supposedly marauding bands of former slaves. This ongoing narrative of the "black rapist" has become a virtual proverb that justifies white hate and white fear. The idea of the Klansman as a white knight-like defender of white womanhood was given physical form in a cartoon entitled Knight of the Cross (see http://www.tightrope.cc/). The ritual slayings of former slaves are so brutal and well known that they do not require repeating here, but Markovitz (2004) provides a thoughtful treatment of the role lynching has played in the collective memory that shapes contemporary racial politics.

Once highly violent in the 1920s and 1930s, the Klan has become less violent and has moved into mainstream politics, as evidenced by David Duke's emergence as a white activist and Louisiana politician. Presently fragmented and often fighting among themselves, Klan groups advance their agenda by talking about social issues that are often a part of American political life, such as crime, AIDs, and immigration (Perry, 2001). That is, rather than railing against blacks, Hispanics, and gay men and women, they are more likely to rail against crime, immigration, and AIDs.

Racist militia groups

Racist militia groups represent a subculture that, operationally, has faded into the background of the American Hate Movement. However, their ideas and commitments remain a part of organized hate. Moreover, the reemergence of the militia during the summer of 2009 (Potok, 2009) demands their inclusion here. Militia groups ground their worldview in a focus on the protection of an individual's "right" to own, store, and trade guns in sufficient quantity that individual citizens will be in a position to protect themselves from a shadow government determined to continually reduce individual liberties, an event that militia groups prepare for through regular paramilitary training exercises.

Militia groups see any attempt to control individual citizens' ability to purchase and own guns as evidence that the Federal Government has the nefarious intent to disarm Americans and to impose a New World Order. Some militia groups reject racism and terrorist activities; however, news coverage of militia activities throughout the 1990s also reveals a sinister and evil element in the militia movement whose ideology blends anti-statist beliefs with racism to create a rather unique, radical nationalist philosophy that views the Federal Government as a structure that has been co-opted by Jewish interests and is bent on subverting the "natural" white American identity (e.g., Crothers, 2003).

Racist militia groups believe that only a portion of the citizenry constitutes America's "sovereign citizens," citizens who have the right to assess, reject, or endorse government decisions. Sovereign citizens are those whose forbearers signed the original Constitution, creating the original social contract Americans made with their government (Crothers, 2003). According to Crothers (2003), the militia movement was born in Ruby Ridge, Idaho, when the F.B.I. attempted to arrest Randy Weaver, sparking a gun battle that resulted in the accidental killing of his wife. It gained steam in Waco, Texas, when the F.B.I. accidentally burned to death David Koresh and the Branch Davidians, who were suspected of warehousing illegal weapons. The crescendo came in Oklahoma City when Timothy McVeigh bombed the Alfred P. Murrah Federal Building. The Oklahoma City bombing was such an extreme act that it caused the militia movement to burn itself out (Crothers, 2003)

Integration and Bricolage within the Hate Movement

These subcultures of hate can, and should, be understood as distinct. However, there is tangible evidence that hate groups are becoming more integrated at both an organizational level and at a conceptual level. At an organizational level, it has long been possible for hate group members to commune, share ideas, and reinforce their hatred. This has typically taken the form of national and regional rallies where individuals would travel to a particular location. However, the growth of the Internet has permitted a degree of integration between unique groups that has not been previously witnessed. A number of individual groups provide Web links to one another on their organizations' Web Pages. Moreover, white supremacy groups are making themselves available to the general public through Web Pages devoted to political issues outside the mainstream of American political life (Waltman & Haas, 2007). Within the past few years, however, hate-oriented search engines and Internet-based newspapers have made it possible for Internet users to not only remain connected to one another (Hamm, 1993; Langer, 1990) but to sample the ideologies of a variety of different white supremacy groups. As a result, hate groups have become most effective in their bricolage. Literally, bricolage means to tinker with something. Bricolage is an intellectual construct that emerges from the neo-Marxist, British sociological tradition, and it is a method used by scholars to describe and understand how the meaning of cultural symbols and artifacts may be transferred from one culture to another.

Hate group members are proving to be workman-like bricoleurs. As noted earlier, during the 1990s many American skinheads "rounded out" their secular ideology with the religious commitments of the World Church of the Creator. Indeed, many skinheads also became ministers in WCOTC. Originally, RAHOWA was not a construct that was central to American skinheads. That construct has been incorporated into skinhead ideology (Hamm, 1993) and one skinhead group has taken the name "Skinheads of the Racial Holy War," and they explicitly blend their skinhead secularism with Creativity (see http://www.rahowa.com). An electronic news organization, the Vanguard News Network (VNN), reports news and social events from a white racialist perspective. It claims to draw its readership from White Supremacists from a variety of backgrounds, and it incorporates the signs and artifacts of different hate communities into its publication with meticulous care. Another Internet organization, TightRope, blends images of the Anglo-Saxon, Germanic warriors with the artifacts of neo-Nazism to provide drama and inspiration to readers as they celebrate a white warrior ethic in stories that are intended to teach readers how to kill the major threats to the white race: Jews (i.e., the Zionist-Occupied Government, or ZOG) and the morally inferior "mud races." Perhaps the hate movement has not yet achieved Tom and John Metzger's vision of a Pan-Aryan Nationalist Movement (Hamm,

1993), but there is growing evidence of ideological integration and strategic cooperation among different communities in the hate movement.

Recent writers have divined an overall ideology of hate from the Web Pages maintained by different hate communities (Perry, 2001). The increasing cultural integration of different hate communities provides even more coherence to a common ideology that transcends differences and permits organized social action within the hate movement. Perhaps it is this increasing cultural integration that has changed and differentiated the ideology of hate suggested by Perry in 2001. This new ideology of hate is described in the following section.

The Ideology of Hate

An ideology may be understood as any system of ideas underlying and informing social and political action. But an ideology is more than a common belief system or definition of reality. Berger and Luckman (1966) argue that an ideology is a definition of reality attached to a power interest. So, an ideology becomes a system of ideas that legitimates the subordination of one group by another group. This form of collective memory emerges from the dominant discourses operating within a culture. A variety of cultural ideologies are readily identifiable—race ideologies, gender ideologies, and right-wing and left-wing ideologies, to name but a few. Identities are used to advance ideologies and motivate the emergence and maintenance of hegemony, a system of power structures that is established to maintain the power of the privileged group. Hegemony is often perpetuated by communication and persuasion. An example of this form of persuasion may be seen in the Duisberg group's work (a group of German critical discourse analysts) that focuses on "collective symbols" that are used to represent foreigners in media-produced racism, or what has been termed "everyday racism," in Germany (Reisigl & Wodak, 2001). From their analysis of German newspapers, they report that German alleged perpetrators of crime were singularized and individualized but "foreign" alleged perpetrators were collectivized by the prioritization of their ethnicity in newspaper reports (Reisigl & Wodak, 2001). Consequently, minorities and foreigners often appeared to be more significant threats to the social order than members of the majority.

Various hate groups see the Civil Rights Movement as a key moment in American history when white people became the true minority in America and in the world. They feel that they are oppressed by other social groups and they view themselves as a counterinsurgent-hegemonic force that is determined to rearticulate racial and gender dynamics in America (Perry, 2001). They see the new hegemony as such a destabilizing force in social relations that a racial holy war (RAHOWA) is the only means by which America may, again, become a white America. Such conspiracies result in a persecution paranoia that permits these groups to identify enemies wherever they perceive a threat to a white American identity. Arguably, this paranoia feeds what Meyer (2001) called *identity mania,* a social condition in which differences between groups are politicized and the confirmation of one's own identity is the primary goal of social and group interactions.

As a counter-hegemonic force, hate groups have espoused an ideology of hate that defines their own identity as the norm. Identities outside the norm are, by virtue, different and inferior. Consequently, difference is seen in moralized terms (e.g., white = wholesome; non-white = alien) and reflective of a "natural" social hierarchy where racial and ethnic identities are situated. Thus, difference is understood to be a threat to the norm. Naturally, hate speech and hate crimes become a way of "policing" difference to maintain the natural social order (Johnson, 1997; Perry, 2001). Naturally, too, the "American identity" becomes the battleground in the clash between hegemonic and counter-hegemonic forces.

Perry (2001) identified six principles that constitute the ideology of hate (Christian Identity, White Supremacy, Xenophobia, Sexism/Heterosexism, Anti-Statism, Racial Holy War [RAHOWA]). Those principles are discussed below. However, in the present, these six principles constitute an incomplete accounting of the hate ideology, due to the ways that hate groups have morphed and changed over the past seven years. Consequently, we introduce two additional concepts—Lone Wolf Terrorism and Neo-Paganism—that provide a more complete accounting of the hate ideology.

Christian Identity

The racism and anti-statism in the hate movement is traced to the principle of Christian Identity. This principle takes as dogma that the white race is the true covenant race described in the Christian Bible. Just as white people are understood to be the children of God, the racially aware white person also understands that Jews are the children spawned from Eve's mating with Satan (Jews are often depicted as serpents in racist literature and images) and are an ongoing threat and the "natural" enemy of white people (God's chosen). Thus, the struggle between Aryans and Jews is an earthly manifestation of the ultimate conflict between God and Satan. Specific conspiratorial beliefs within the dogma of Christian Identity are all too familiar: Jews control the banks and are financing a black revolution in America, Jews control the Federal Government (the Zionist-Occupied Government) to oppress white people, Jews are pornographers determined to perpetuate interracial mixing in order to extinguish the white race (Waltman & Davis, 2004, 2005).

White Supremacy

The ideology of the hate movement is also grounded in the notion of white supremacy. Racist Aryans understand their race to be responsible for building everything good in the world (e.g., Daniels, 1997). Race categories are organized hierarchically to reflect differences that are inherent in the essences of the categories. These differences justify and underlie the hostility that is expressed toward inferior groups. This hostility further fuels the drive for racial purity. "Race-mixing" is treated as genocide and is understood to be the goal of all non-whites. This genocidal threat vilifies the Other and makes violence an acceptable and desirable response to the new hegemony.

Xenophobia

The ideology of the hate movement is also grounded in Xenophobia—the exaggerated hostility directed toward foreigners, especially non-white immigrants. Many hate groups are expanding the scope of their hate to immigrants. In their rhetoric, they use the term "alien" instead of illegal immigrant, though one can imagine that the hate movement does not distinguish between legal and illegal immigrants. Immigrants are understood to be in America for two reasons: (a) to exploit the welfare system and (b) to take jobs from real Americans. The contradiction inherent in these beliefs typically goes unaddressed by those who hate.

Sexism/Heterosexism

The ideology of the hate movement is also grounded in Sexism/Heterosexism. Hate groups see natural distinctions between men and women, much as they see natural distinctions between races and ethnicities. In general, women are essentialized as breeders and caretakers. However, women, specifically the wombs of white women, are viewed as the frontline in the genocidal threat to the white race. Good women are the key to protecting the white American identity. Good white women raise children (to be racially aware) and support white men. Bad white women work outside the home, have priorities other than children, mix with men who are not white, and have abortions.

Feminists are viewed as a threat to the white race because they have deemphasized the traditional role of women. Violence against the Other is justified because the purity of the white woman's womb must be protected.

Homosexuals reject the traditional relationship between men and women. Consequently, such "gender traitors" represent a threat to the white race. Because homosexuality represents a voluntary rejection of traditional sex roles, it is equated with "other perversions," such as pedophilia. One of the more vitriolic images reflecting these beliefs may be found on a Web Site maintained by Westboro Baptist Church, http://www.godhatesfags.com/home.html, that depicts Matthew Shepherd, a gay man murdered in Laramie, Wyoming burning in hell. A previous version of this Web Site maintained a count of the number of days that Matthew Shepherd had been burning in hell.

Anti-Statism

The ideology of the hate movement is also grounded in Anti-Statism. The ultimate threat to white America is the Zionist-Occupied Government (ZOG). The New World Order, represented by advances in civil rights, would make those of European descent minor players in American social and political life. ZOG represents all elements of the State: the media, the Federal Government, law enforcement agencies of all kinds, and the like.

Racial Holy War

The ideology of the hate movement is also grounded in the RAHOWA (RAcial HOly WAr) construct adopted by members of the Identity Church Movement, racist skinheads, neo-Nazis, and Racist Pre-Christian Pagans. This concept imbues the ideology of hate with apocalypticism and millennialism. For Christian Identity adherents, this belief flows rather naturally from the Armageddon myth advanced by mainstream Christianity. Thus, it is only logical, because Jews and other "mud races" are the literal offspring of Satan, that the final battle between good and evil should become manifest in a Racial Holy War pitting Aryans (God's children) against the Jews (Satan's offspring) and their minions (African Americans, Arabs, Latinos, etc.). Thus, Christian Identity adherents are pre-millinealists; they believe that Christ will return only after Christians have imposed Christian values and law on the entire earth. Christian Identity adherents argue that this inevitable Racial Holy War is ultimately an act of Christian love, albeit a love of white Christians, because it will facilitate the coming of the Kingdom of Heaven (Crothers, 2003).

Lone Wolf Terrorism and Neo-Paganism

From a more recent reading of Web Pages, Internet postings, and racist novels, we see two additional constructs that constitute the ideology of hate. First, a complementary construct to RAHOWA has recently emerged in the American hate culture: Lone Wolfism (Davis, 2005; Guttentag & DiPersio, 2003; Waltman & Davis, 2005). A Lone Wolf is a terrorist who follows the principle of leaderless resistance. Rather than following the explicit orders of the leadership of a specific hate group, lone wolf terrorists see a wrong (e.g., mixed-race couples, the oppression of ZOG) and take it upon themselves to strike at the problem through violent action.

Lone Wolfism represents a conscious shift in the organization and operation of many hate groups. Leaders of hate groups are becoming the intellectual arm of the hate movement and they spread their ideas through Internet sources. Potential Lone Wolves are encouraged to avoid membership and association with an organized hate group. Potential Lone Wolves are also counseled to avoid making racist remarks or jokes in public or with anyone but their closest associates. Potential Lone Wolves are told that their conscience will tell them when to "act." Several physical and Internet texts tell readers how to prepare themselves to be a Lone Wolf. Timothy McVeigh and the other terrorists mentioned at the beginning of this chapter are examples of Lone Wolf terrorists.

Second, Neo-Paganism is replacing Christian Identity as a religious doctrine among many of the younger members of the hate movement. The basic beliefs of Neo-Paganism, or Odinism, have been described in our discussion of the hate movement's race religions. By way of summary, many younger people in the hate movement are reconnecting with an ancient Norse polytheistic religion that they believe to be culturally and spiritually wed to the soul of the Aryan people. They draw upon the ethos of these ancient warrior cultures to legitimize and encourage hate crime, hate murder, and ethnoviolence against the enemies of the Aryan race (Waltman, in press-a).

This preceding discussion provides a description of the substance of the hate movement. However, the ideology of the hate movement must also be understood for its form as well as its substance. This ideology represents a form of Fundamentalism. Fundamentalists intend to create among adherents a closed system of thinking and action that "artificially excludes differences, doubts, and alternatives" (Meyer, 2001, p. 21). The fundamentalist form of ideology results in the refusal to respect cultural differences in a fair, peaceful, and open-minded way. According to Meyer, Fundamentalism, across a range of geopolitical perspectives, causes identity to degenerate into identity-mania, a social condition in which difference is politicized and moralized.

Difference that could challenge the in-group identity must be policed, undermined, and subjugated; thus, purging the social environment of all cultural differences. Ultimately, that which is different is defined as undesirable, a "drag on society," a threat to the in-group, scapegoated, and situated in the heart of conspiracy theories that articulate a threat matrix to the in-group identity (Crothers, 2003).

A discussion of the hate ideology would be less than complete without a discussion of social forces that make this an ideology that is compelling to those who would hate. Most Americans would claim to reject the ideology of hate as it has been articulated here. But it must be remembered that this ideology did not emerge in a social vacuum. It sprang forth from a larger culture with a specific history that made this ideology seem reasonable to members of the various groups discussed in this chapter. After all, these groups emerged from a culture and built a new nation, largely, on the purchase and enslavement of human beings from Africa. This was justified in a variety of ways that all centered on the assumption that Africans were not fully human. This kind of hatred is still capable of appearing through the cracks, of what Hazlitt (2005) might refer to as "civilization." In Jena, Louisiana, a noose appears in a tree when African American high school students sit under a tree that is understood to be a "white-only" tree. Subsequently, this symbol of hatred (Markovitz, 2004) would appear in a variety of other places, including an African American professor's office door at a prestigious university. The various beliefs and fears expressed in the ideology of hate are shared by many in mainstream American society. One need not be a White Supremacist to oppress women or to believe that homosexuals, "seeking special rights," represent a threat to traditional American values. One need not be a card-carrying White Supremacist to vilify illegal immigrants or to describe them as a disease-carrying threat to America (Potok, 2007). One need not be a White Supremacist to mistake an Indian American for someone from Saudi Arabia and attack that person on September 12, 2001. Likewise, one need not be a White Supremacist to believe that, following the destruction of the World Trade Center, people who "look like" a terrorist should be profiled, investigated, and detained, so that "we" may be safer. One need not be a White Supremacist to oppose or to feel uncomfortable with inter-racial marriages. In part, then, the ideology of hate is compelling to the hate-monger because it is similar to the beliefs and fears of a larger society. As discussed in chapter four, this makes hatred a useful tool to accomplish a variety of social and political goals in the everyday discourse of people who do not self-identify as a hate-monger or a member of an organized hate group.

Conclusion

Numerous examples of domestic terrorists demonstrate that these individuals have had close contact with various hate groups. Their numbers illustrate that individual acts of ethnoterrorism are not freakish novelties but are common enough that both F.B.I. and hate groups have developed a name for such actors: Lone Wolves. The hate groups that influence these individuals take the form of race religion groups, secular hate groups, or blends between the two. The diversity of these groups provides followers and readers of hate texts a broad and rich set of beliefs, ideas, messages, and cultures from which to choose—a smorgasbord of hate.

Hate groups are an important part of hatred in American life. As we have discussed, they lay the foundation for hatred through the maintenance and refinement of an ideology of hate that provides a rationale for the oppression and subordination of a wide range of "enemies" that they believe white people must defeat to ensure their own survival. They represent the most extreme forms of hatred and are most likely to produce America's most violent hate-mongers and domestic terrorists. As we have made clear, America has seen significant death and trauma that have been dealt by domestic terrorists with connections to organized hate groups. We also know that the hate movement has leaders that have been responsible for creating terrorists. These "idea" people have been responsible for articulating and spreading the ideology of hate. In addition, they have been responsible for creating in their followers, listeners, and readers the motivations and intentions to kill. The emergence of race religion groups is associated with a movement that is more violent, better armed, and more apocalyptic in their thinking than before (Perry, 2001; Potok, 2009). They are becoming more integrated and better networked through the Internet, drawing on one another's work and coming closer and closer to a kind of Pan-Aryan Nationalism envisioned by Tom Metzger (Hamm, 1993; Waltman & Davis, 2004).

Following the 2008 Presidential election of Barack Obama, America's first African American President, hate groups have grown to their largest numbers in history: 962 (Holthouse, 2009-a). As we discuss in chapter six, discourse and events following the election illustrate that ordinary white Americans drew on the ideology of hate to express their frustrations and fears over what the election of Barack Obama means to them and their view of America. It appears that in their frustration many are turning to the extremists to make sense of their changing country. The narratives that extremists will share to make sense of this change have been well documented in this chapter. We know what kind of "medicine" these "medicine men" will prescribe (Burke, 1995). Will future Lone Wolves emerge from those frus-

trated Americans who have purchased guns and ammunition in record numbers since the 2008 Presidential election?

Chapter 3

Conceptual Properties of Hate-Motivated Speech

I hate all Frenchmen without distinction, in the name of God and of my people, I teach this hatred to my son. I teach it to the sons of my people.... I shall work all my life that the contempt and hatred for this people strike the deepest roots in German hearts.

Ernest Arndt, 1802
(Chirot & McCauley, 2006, p. 85)

In this chapter we discuss the nature of hate speech and provide a range of examples of this unique form of discourse. We have noted that a widely accepted definition of hate is extreme negative feelings and beliefs held about a group (or individual representative of that group) because of their race, ethnicity, religion, gender, or sexual orientation (Perry, 2001). It is important to remember what distinguishes hatred from anger: Anger is an emotion that (a) one might have for an individual (not a larger social group), (b) does not prevent one from having sympathy for the objects of one's anger, (c) is usually the result of personal insult or injury, and (d) is likely to promote impetuous action (Olson, 2002; Sokolon, 2006; R. K. Whillock, 1995). Because hatred is an emotion that one feels for a social group, hatred, unlike anger, need not be the result of personal injury or insult and is more likely to prompt deliberative action. Unlike anger, the hateful mind is not capable of sympathy but hopes for evil to befall the hated (Sokolon, 2006). Indeed, the hateful mind would have the objects of its hatred simply perish—the ultimate end for the mind that has learned to hate. Because the hateful mind lacks sympathy, Aristotle viewed hatred as a much more durable emotion than anger, unlikely to dissipate over time or to even be satiated by killing (Sokolon, 2006). In fact, it seems doubtful that hate murderers and ethnoterrorists are attempting to satiate their hate through their violence.

It is also important to recall that hatred is an emotion in which one may find pleasure (Hazlitt, 2005). Hazlitt (2005) suggested a variety of ways that hatred brings us pleasure. First, the fundamentalism and certitude of hatred offers the pleasure and indulgence of self-righteousness. Our hatred of a specific group is enlivened by our construction of that group as an enemy. Inevitably, the enemy is constructed as evil and/or fundamentally flawed.

Understanding ourselves in terms of this enemy, who is evil or flawed, allows us to wallow in our own goodness and righteousness. Second, Hazlitt views hatred as a destructive, actually primitive, emotion that had to be repressed as humans exchanged their tribal bonds for the bonds of civilized societies. But we find pleasure in revisiting this darker side of our human nature in our imaginations. Indeed, it is easy to imagine that ethnoterrorists and perpetrators of hate crimes take great pleasure in the pain that they inflict on the objects of their hatred. This is likely to contribute to the durability of hatred.

Hate speech may be used for many purposes and has different intended consequences. Hate speech may be directed toward specific out-group person(s) in order to intimidate. However, hate speech may also be used to influence the behavior of fellow in-group members in a variety of ways (e.g., to recruit members to a hate group, to socialize white people to adopt and understand the proper racist Aryan identity and behaviors, to find pleasure in hatred, or to promote ethnoviolence).

Mindful of this definition of hate and the diverse forms of hate speech, we argue that hate speech is characterized by four important features. These features are not mutually exclusive and may each be manifested in the same hateful message. We also understand that discourse need not possess all of these characteristics to constitute hate speech. First, hate speech is discourse that seeks to politicize social differences (e.g., race, ethnicity, religion, sexual orientation). Clearly, the politicization of difference is not a neutral act. Often, the purpose of such speech is a persuasive one. The politicization of social difference is accomplished by constructing relevant in-group and out-group identities. The rhetor differentiates the in-group from the out-group by polarizing the two groups employing some rather familiar tactics. The in-group is differentiated from the out-group by constructing the out-group in flawed, negative, even vile, terms. Often, the ultimate goal may be to evoke disgust so that the in-group may view the out-group as a disease or a contaminant (Chirot & McCauley, 2006). Of course, the in-group is constructed in positive, highly valued terms. But the differentiation of groups often involves more than the constructing of a positive in-group identity and negative out-group identity. Indeed, hate speech often involves the normalization of the in-group identity. That is, the in-group is seen as the norm and the out-group is seen as a departure from the norm. Of course, departures from the norm are understood as undesirable. The departure is understood to be undesirable because of our tendency to totalize and essentialize social differences (Chirot & McCauley, 2006; Wood, 1998). Totalizing is defined by Wood (1998) as the practice of defining someone or something by a single quality, as if that quality were the whole of the person; for example, thinking about a gay man only in terms of his sexuality while allowing his brilliance as a writer, his compassion as a friend, or his sense of humor to fade from awareness. We essentialize when we assume that a characteristic or set of characteristics is the essence of all members of a social group. For example, we essentialize by assuming that all gay men may be recognized by a somewhat flamboyant and effeminate speaking style and penchant for fashion. It is important to recognize that these are not simply cognitive processes but are labels that can be put into practice through social discourse. Indeed, it is public discourse, public hate speech, that stabilize prejudice and bigotry. Tsesis (2002) elaborates:

> Culturally accepted images of the other reassure individuals who adopt them. They play out like a puppet show with clearly defined evil and good characters. Each succeeding generation receives its indoctrination into the cult of racial and ethnic superiority.... The cognitive foundations of bigotry are found in cultural discourse. (p. 86)

Second, hate speech is characterized by attempts to construct the out-group in negative and dehumanized terms, often while praising the in-group and constructing them in positive terms. The motivation for these constructions is clear. In writing about intergroup conflict many years ago, Tajfel (1981) noted that groups often denigrate other groups in order to increase their own status by comparison. This would involve attempts to verbally construct the out-group as all alike. This dehumanizing activity is also accomplished by expressing dominance over the out-group. This verbal domination might take the form of racist jokes and cartoons (Billig, 2001; Meyer, 2001; Waltman & Davis, 2004). This kind of domination may be found in physical artifacts that, due to their cultural meaning, have come to take symbolic value, such as a burning cross, a swastika, or a noose. Of course, the use of such artifacts is not only intended to dominate but is also intended to instill fear in the out-group.

It is important to note that the construction of an out-group can be a rhetorically sophisticated activity. When the in-group distinguishes themselves from an out-group, they often do so in ways that would be counter-intuitive to an outsider. An out-group identity may be attached to a group that is very similar to the in-group, perhaps dangerously similar (Chirot & McCauley, 2006). It is especially important to distinguish out-groups that may be close to the in-group essence but still outside that essence. For example, recent history illustrates that many Shiites and Sunny Muslims hold as much enmity for one another as they do for any other out-group. Nazis viewed Jews as especially dangerous because many Jews were "passing" as German. Under Pol Pot, one quarter of all Cambodians were killed by other Cambodians because they had been "infected" with "foreign" ideas (Chirot & McCauley, 2006). We discuss the Sleeping White Man Myth in this chapter. This is a set of beliefs that distinguish racially conscious Aryans from Aryans who have been brainwashed by the Jewish media, multi-culturalism, and consumerism. The Sleeping White Man is treated and viewed as a non-white to be conquered along with the other enemies of racist Aryans. Indeed, the Sleeping White Man is discussed, explicitly, as a race-traitor. This tendency to otherize those who are similar to us based on the presence or absence of some perceived group essence illustrates the powerful role of discourse and communication in the creation and expression of hate.

We believe an important, but not necessary, third feature of hate speech is the context in which it is produced. Hate speech is most easily identifiable as such when the objects of hatred belong to a historically oppressed social group, a group that has been oppressed because of their race, ethnicity, religion, or sexual orientation. Hate speech capitalizes on these out-group experiences and attempts to marginalize and strike fear in their hearts. A swastika painted on a white, Christian, heterosexual professor's office door does not carry the same message as a noose hanging on a black professor's office door handle. The former might be confused or even assume that the swastika represented a case of mistaken identity. The latter would make no such assumption.

This discussion has focused on very broad characteristics of hate speech, which may take a variety of forms. The following section addresses a specific form of hate speech that has proven to be a useful concept for understanding and interpreting hate speech in a variety of contexts and channels: the hate stratagem.

The Hate Stratagem

R. K. Whillock (1995) first introduced the hate stratagem in her analysis of a political flyer that was described as "talking points" for the supporters of a specific gubernatorial candidate in Alabama. Whillock found that these talking points constituted a series of hate appeals designed to manipulate voters' prejudices and encourage their support of a particular political candidate. Whillock distinguished the terms "strategy" and "stratagem," arguing that an argumentative strategy is a form of discourse involved in the clash of reasoning, supported by emotional appeals and fairly presented evidence intended to induce compliance. She conceived an argumentative strategy as an influence technique commensurate with Habermas's (Bernstein, 1978) notion of the ideal communicative climate in which actors might only be influenced by the argumentative force of the better idea. A stratagem, however, she recognized as a "trick" for deceiving another in order to gain his or her compliance. The "proof" that supports the hate stratagem is found in cultural stereotypes that are easily accessible to those processing the hate stratagem. Because this form of cultural knowledge is commonly accepted, it often goes unexamined by those processing the hate stratagem. Essentially, the use of the hate stratagem should be understood as an attempt to discourage thoughtful reflection on an issue and to encourage the reliance on cultural stereotypes and fear that appeal to our baser nature. Next, we discuss the following characteristics of the hate stratagem that will help us to understand how rhetors may manipulate our hate in order to achieve our compliance.

R. K. Whillock (1995) argued that the hate stratagem possesses four characteristics. The hate stratagem attempts to (a) inflame the emotions of individuals by encouraging them to view themselves as members of a significant and important group, (b) denigrate a specified out-group and individuals who belong to that out-group, (c) inflict permanent harm on the out-group by suggesting that they possess highly undesirable characteristics and attributes that isolate them from other social groups, particularly the in-group, and (d) rhetorically conquer the out-group. Whillock found that the hate stratagem was a useful part of the normal political process that strategists use to win elections. Waltman (2003) found that the hate stratagem plays an important role in the Knights of the Ku Klux Klan's attempts to recruit children into their Youth Corps through their "Just for Kids" Web Page. In the following sections, we provide examples of discourse that instantiate each characteristic of the hate stratagem.

Inflaming Emotions

The inflaming of emotions is intended to coalesce the intended audience members into an important and valued in-group. R. K. Whillock (1995) argued that the above-mentioned flyer attempted to "suggest a conspiracy" designed to harm the gubernatorial candidates and their supporters, "We learn that *they* 'have been working for months trying to soil' 'our' candidate's character and reputation." Once that stage has been set, specific examples are provided as evidence of a conspiracy." Examples cited by Whillock included (a) "A candidate responsible for the appointment of the gang of five who took a nomination away from Graddick," (b) "The State Democratic Executive Committee...responsible for purging conservative and moderate legislators in 1983...liberal teachers and blacks would control not only the Democratic party, but also the legislature," and (c) the opposition and his cronies will "control the state education budget and use their power to force institutions to give feedback in return for their appropriation." Readers of this flyer are told that the only way they may stop these evils is to come together as a group to oppose them by supporting their candidate (R. K. Whillock, 1995, p. 39).

Waltman (2003) found that in-group solidarity was created among young readers of the Just for Kid's Web Site maintained by the Knights of the Ku Klux Klan by emphasizing the importance of a specific in-group, white Christians:

> We want to have a White Christian America again…then we can help look after the other people in the world. The bible says that if we can take care of our Christian brothers and sisters and live a good Christian life, then our country will be blessed. …and there aren't terrible things happening in America to White Christians…then we can be a blessing to all the children of the world. (p. 27)

Here, the writer makes very clear that white people are favored by God and that, ultimately, white people have the ability to make the world a better place for everyone. So, what is good for white people is good for the world.

The children learn that, as white Christian children, they can contribute to the Knights immediately:

> The truth is that there are women and kids in the KKK. Women are in The Knights because they care about their country, they care about their race, and they care about kids. Kids are in the KKK because they want to learn about their heritage and they want to make the world a better place. (Waltman, 2003, p. 27)

By emphasizing the role that children play in the KKK, the child learns that they can play a significant role in an already significant organization and the child's identification with the in-group is enhanced. Then, the Knights are able to suggest a threat that simultaneously looms over this "important organization" and the child. The child is even given a deceptively positive label for their preference of white Christians over out-groups when they are told, "It's love not hate," love of one's own group and not hate of another group.

Denigrating the Out-Group

This characteristic of the hate stratagem involves the construction of the out-group as vile and a terrible threat to the in-group. Indeed, the tactic of providing reasons to oppose a candidate has proven to be more effective than providing reasons to vote for a candidate. This is often most effective when the rhetor is able to identify in-group values that are defiled by the out-group. Whillock suggests an example from the flyer: "Hubert hired a Montgomery lawyer to fight the dismissal of a junior high school teacher in Huntsville who had been convicted of sodomy with three young boys." So, one of the opposing candidates is so vile as to defend someone who would rape children, a community's most precious resource. Additionally, black leaders are depicted as "carpetbaggers" who aided in the purge of conservatives and moderates and "who routinely abuse power to get lucrative land deals and other perks and rip-offs" (R. K. Whillock, 1995, p. 41). This denigration of the out-group, the portrayal of them as extreme, isolates members of the out-group. Once isolated with a negative label, a label grounded in a cultural stereotype, the out-group is even more vulnerable to attack.

Waltman (2003) reports several examples of the Knight's discourse that denigrates different out-group members in order to recruit children to their Youth Corps. Children visiting this Web Page learn that, following reconstruction, a Jewish cabal of bankers and politicians sympathetic with newly freed slaves attempted to destroy white people. Children learn, "White people had to salute black people on the street. Whiskey sellers sold liquor to blacks who excited about no longer having a curfew would roam the countryside hurting men, women, and children" (p. 29). Additionally children are told, "Troops of armed men would not allow the white people to defend themselves" (p. 29). The Knights tell children that this sort of persecution continues today as a "liberal media" conspires to vilify the KKK:

> Usually the programs that they make about the KKK on TV just show really mean acting men. Sometimes the men they show are made to act really dumb.... That's because the very rich people who own the TV shows and newspapers and movies don't like white Christians.... The politicians do almost everything they say—even pass laws that hurt white Christians. (p. 29)

The children learn that this even includes their own pastors because "the preachers and church leaders...don't want to say anything about gays or racemixers.... Most of the preachers today deceive the people who trust them" (p. 29). This goes so far that the Knights attempt to inoculate children against arguments that their teachers might raise about the KKK:

> Your teacher might be a very nice man or woman, but that doesn't mean they haven't learned the wrong history about the KKK.... There are many Atheists who teach in teacher colleges.... *Your teacher will most likely give you wrong information against the KKK.* (p. 29, emphasis added)

In sum, this second characteristic of the hate stratagem involves attempts to denigrate the out-group by linking the out-group's identity with highly undesirable qualities and attributes. It is also clear from these examples that such tactics rely on negative cultural stereotypes that are familiar to message recipients.

Inflicting Permanent and Irreparable Harm on the Out-Group

The out-group is denigrated in the second characteristic of the hate stratagem. The third characteristic of the hate stratagem involves attacking and destroying those characteristics the out-group uses to construct its identity. This is the discursive equivalent to a swastika on a synagogue door or a noose hanging from a black professor's office door (R. K. Whillock, 1995). R. K. Whillock offers several examples from the hate letter to instantiate this characteristic. We are told in the letter that Siegelman claims to be a Christian but we are also told that his wife is Jewish. This attack is made against her to vandalize her worth as a human being and this is made clear in the question, "Do you think the people of Alabama want a Jew family living in the Governor's mansion?" (R. K. Whillock, 1995, p. 42). As Whillock notes, this also serves as an attack on Siegelman, questioning his status as a "good Christian."

This characteristic of the hate stratagem is often seen in attempts to construct the out-group as a threat to the in-group. Similar tactics are noted in Waltman's (2003) study of the Knights of the KKK discourse. Children learn that it is the nature of black people to engage in violence against white people:

> The founders of America didn't want slaves to keep coming to America. They were afraid because in some small islands in the Tropics where there was slavery—when there became so many black people—they all got together and murdered all the white people—moms, dads, and kids.... They killed them all. (p. 30)

Subsequently, children would learn that this did happen in this country:

> When there would start to be bigger groups of black people in different towns . . . they would start to riot and steal or kill.... Yes, there were still nice black people, but the more there were the more they would hate white people. Today there are many black people in America. (p. 30)

This is a clever tactic. By linking black violence toward white people to a kind of mob mentality that takes over when blacks find themselves in large groups, the rhetor anticipates and explains away any personal experience with individual blacks a child might have that contradicts the negative group stereotype.

Rhetorical Conquering of the Out-Group

The fourth characteristic of the hate stratagem is the conquering of the out-group. This, of course, is the ultimate goal of the hate stratagem. This conquering ultimately serves to negate the out-group's existence. The Knights argue that their warranted fear of violent black people should lead them to voluntarily segregate themselves from African Americans:

> Just because a person is black or another race doesn't make them bad people. But you should always be careful where you go and who your friends are. Young girls should be extra careful. Many black boys feel extra cool if they hurt a white girl. Some kids don't learn until its [sic] too late. (Waltman, 2003, p. 30)

This voluntary segregation from potential out-groups removes them from the everyday consciousness of white people. In Aristotle's terms, they would cease to exist for white people. Moreover, the use of hate appeals unleashes a set of forces in message recipients that is difficult to control (R. K. Whillock, 1995). That is, once people give expression to their hatred they continue to give full vent to this hatred (Ellul, 1965; R. K. Whillock, 1995).

Hate Speech and Heuristics

Heuristics are decision-making rules that we employ to reduce the burden of many decisions. They operate primarily below our level of awareness and we are often not aware that we are employing such decisional shortcuts. Heuristics have been studied by a variety of researchers in several disciplines (e.g., Kahneman & Tversky, 1972; Petty & Cacioppo, 1986; Srull & Wyer, 1980; Waltman & Burleson, 1997). Those who study people's use of persuasive heuristics have generally distinguished between two forms of information processing: a contemplative and deliberative process (the central route to persuasion) and a non-deliberative and uncritical process, the heuristic route to persuasion (Petty & Cacioppo, 1986). While not strictly mutually exclusive, the use of one route tends to diminish the operation of the other. While heuristics are useful in their ability to reduce the cognitive burden of many persuasive decisions, they can lead to errors in judgment and are often treated as a form of bias. Indeed, we are more likely to fall victim to heuristics if we do not have a great deal of knowledge on the persuasive topic or if the persuasive tasks are difficult and burdensome.

Petty and Cacioppo (1986) and Cialdini (2001) have described several heuristics that people may fall victim to when processing persuasive messages. For example, people may intuitively rely on (a) the authority and expertise of the message producer, the credibility heuristic, (b) the degree to which other people support the message, the consensus heuristic, (c) the degree to which one feels affinity for the message producer, the liking heuristic, and (d) the degree to which the message producer appears to be similar to the message recipient, the similarity heuristic.

Recall our claim that the hate stratagem is characterized as a tactic that encourages superficial message processing. Waltman (2003) argued that this tactic was well suited to the persuasion of children who lack the ability to process persuasive messages with the sophistication of the typical adult. In fact, Waltman found that the Knight's of the Ku Klux Klan employed such persuasive heuristics to influence the children targeted by their hate stratagem. He found that the Knights made use of the credibility heuristic (I should agree with the KKK because they are an expert/authority). For example, this Web Page made liberal use of quotations by Abraham Lincoln, who the children have learned to think of as the "great emancipator" and a respected historical figure, to suggest that Lincoln was indifferent and/or contemptuous to the enslaved Africans. So, the child learns that the KKK's views of African slaves were shared with Lincoln, a highly credible figure.

Waltman (2003) also reported that the Knights made effective use of the consensus heuristic (I should agree with the KKK because many other people also agree with them). He argued that many children would find the Knight's message to be influential simply because it was on the Internet. However, the Knights also encouraged the children to view the Knight's message as widely accepted: "We want to make known that we are the largest, oldest, and most powerful Klan organization" (Waltman, 2003, p. 32).

The Knights also encouraged children to rely on a liking heuristic (I should agree with the KKK because they are a likable group). The Knights take great pains to present themselves as a likable and admirable organization. The child learns in several sections of the Web Page that their organization is about "love" not "hate." Rather than present the violent history of the KKK, they present the Klan's actions during Reconstruction void of any violence:

> One night when the club was meeting they accidentally came across an outlaw band of negroes. But this time instead of the white people getting murdered, the negroes ran away screaming. They thought the men in their costumes were the ghosts of dead soldiers who had died during the Civil war [sic] just a couple of years earlier.... These deeply religious men felt that God had given them a great gift in disguise—a peaceful way to defend themselves. (Waltman, 2003, p. 32)

Note the use of words like "club" and "costumes" that make the KKK appear to be an organization on par with the Elks or the Masons as opposed to an organization that has been historically associated with lynchings and the op-pression of African Americans, Jews, and Catholics.

As part of a larger study, Waltman and Haas (2007) reported that the Na-tional Socialist Movement (NSM, "America's largest Nazi organization") employed a photo gallery in rather sophisticated ways to (a) create the im-pression that the leaders of NSM were authoritative leaders, the credibility heuristic, (b) enhance the likeability of members of NSM, the liking heuris-tic, and (c) to suggest that large numbers of individuals share the values of NSM, the consensus heuristic. We have come to believe that the heuristics discussed in this chapter are easily understood by those who manipulate hate to influence others and are, consequently, employed by such rhetors rather naturally.

Having discussed constructs that are useful for conceptualizing the na-ture of hate speech, we turn to an important means by which hate-mongers have distributed hate discourse among large groups of individuals in the hate movement: racist novels. We discuss two racist novels that have had a par-ticularly significant influence on the violence within the hate movement and have changed the way that those in the hate movement have come to think about their individual and collective identities.

Hate Speech and the Novels of William Pierce

Racist novels have become an important vehicle through which the ideology of hate is expressed and through which new members are recruited, social-ized, and educated in the hate community. Several novels of minimal literary value are circulated through the Internet and interpersonal contacts. How-ever, there are only two novels that have had meaningful impact on the col-lective imagination of the hate movement (and the individual imaginations of individual members), both of which were written by the late William Pierce under the pseudonym of Andrew Macdonald. William Pierce was the leader of National Alliance and an architect of the American hate community. Mor-ris Dees of the Southern Poverty Law Center summed up his role in the hate community in a documentary entitled *Hate.com: Extremists on the Internet*: "He is not a builder of bombs. He is a builder of bombers" (cited in Gutten-tag & DiPersio, 2003). Without a doubt, he is an icon that inspires a broad swatch of people in the American hate community.

The Turner Diaries

Originally published in 1978, *The Turner Diaries* depicts a racial holy war from the perspective of one terrorist, Earl Turner. The war is described as a revolution led by a group of Aryan rebels against a corrupt government that is controlled by Jewish interests (ZOG—Zionist-Occupied Government), labeled The System. In the text, The System chips away at the rights of Aryans by outlawing individual possession of firearms and promoting violence against white people, and is the vanguard in the genocidal attack on the Aryan race. *The Turner Diaries* depicts white people as America's true minority and the revolutionaries see themselves as a counter-hegemonic force to The System. The novel, functioning almost as a declaration of Aryan independence, details a list of Aryan grievances against the social order.

The Turner Diaries has been found in the possession of a number of hate-motivated killers, including Timothy McVeigh (the bomber of the Alfred P. Murrah Federal Building in Oklahoma City). While in the Army, McVeigh became an avid reader of *The Turner Diaries* (Crothers, 2003). When McVeigh encountered fellow soldiers who he believed might be sympathetic to his racist views, he would loan them the book, describe it as an "interesting read," and suggest that they talk about the book when they were finished. In fact, *The Turner Diaries* served as McVeigh's blueprint for the planning and execution of his bombing. In the first pages of *The Turner Diaries,* William Pierce describes how Earl Turner combined gasoline and fertilizer in barrels in the back of a truck to make the entire vehicle a bomb. The aftermath of the Oklahoma City bombing is eerily similar to the aftermath described by Pierce.

Perhaps for this reason, it is understandable that so many writers have described *The Turner Diaries* as a "how to" manual for the commission of ethnoviolence. But *The Turner Diaries* is truly far more to the American hate community than a "how to" manual. As Turner bombs and kills his way through an ultimately successful revolution, the reader is taken through a series of events that portray the desirable characteristics and attributes of an Aryan revolutionary. So, *The Turner Diaries* serves as a primer on what constitutes a proper racist Aryan identity and how one may lead a proper racist Aryan lifestyle (Waltman & Davis, 2005). Recently, *The Turner Diaries* has appeared in digital form on YouTube, as read by Pierce (see *The Turner Diaries Audio Book*). Now the White Supremacist need go no further than their computer to have access to this important artifact.

Hunter

Buoyed by the success of the *The Turner Diaries*, Pierce's second novel, *Hunter*, introduced readers to Oscar Yeager. Yeager has come to understand the Federal Government of the United States to be the same kind of Zionist-Occupied Government as that described in *The Turner Diaries*. Yeager sees this immoral government as such an evil that he can not, in good conscience, ignore this state of affairs. The tangible evidence of this evil is found in inter-racial couples and gay men and women living unashamed public lives. He begins this journey with an uncomplicated and undifferentiated understanding of his own hatred as he plots, tracks, and kills the enemies of the Aryan race. However, his understanding of this "evil" becomes more sophisticated the more he kills. Eventually, a highly placed F.B.I. agent, sympathetic with Yeager's cause, becomes aware of his ethnoviolence and becomes his mentor, slowly exposing him to the extensiveness of the corrupt status quo. Eventually, Yeager becomes fully aware of the extent to which his government is controlled by an international Jewish conspiracy that is plotting the slow genocide of Aryan Americans (and Aryans worldwide).

There are three noteworthy points to attend to in this basic synopsis. First, ethnoviolence is portrayed not simply as a means of destroying evil but as a path of Aryan enlightenment (the more violence Yeager commits, the more he learns). This is fully consonant with the point made in chapter two that violence is treated as a cultural totem of the American hate community. Second, strategically, Pierce allows new readers and potential racist Aryans to learn about the Jewish hegemonic structures that oppress Aryan Americans by following Yeager's path to enlightenment (Davis, 2005). Pierce has said about his intention in writing *Hunter*:

> Fiction or drama...gets much more inside the head of the person experiencing it because the reader or viewer identifies with the character. Seeing the reaction to *The Turner Diaries*, I then wrote a second novel, *Hunter*, so that I could carry my readers through a process of development. I tried to make hunter much more of an educational novel. (Guttentag & DiPersio, 2003; see also Davis, 2005, p. v)

Third, Yeager is the literary embodiment of the Lone Wolf discussed in chapter two, an individual terrorist who plans and executes individual hate killings independent of a hate group or hate group leader. The rise of the Lone Wolf in the American hate community appears to correspond with the emergence of *Hunter*. So, it appears that *Hunter*, like *The Turner Diaries*, has contributed to the actions and collective knowledge of racist Aryans.

Research that has examined these novels has attempted to identify the myths that are employed to shape and influence readers. Myths have been described as the content of a given culture (Hart, 1997). More specifically, myths are master narratives that describe exceptional people doing exceptional things and serve as moral guides that may influence the actions of those in that culture (Burke, 1995; Hart, 1997; Waltman & Davis, 2005). Myths do not emanate from a single narrative; rather, myths emerge from clusters of cultural narratives that express a common thread, theme, or idea. As important discourse structures, myths may be a useful means by which cultures are understood (Balthrop, 1984; Barthes, 1972).

Myths may be further understood by examining specific subtypes with instantiations of each subtype. Hart (1997) identifies four types of myths: (a) Identity myths, (b) Eschatological myths, (c) Sociological myths, and (d) Cosmological myths. Identity myths are focused on what makes one cultural group(ing) different from another. We teach our children that Abraham Lincoln was born to meager means in a log cabin but rose to positions of influence through hard work. We all learned that Andrew Johnson came from and represented common Americans. Such identity myths are used to encourage young people to believe that we live in an egalitarian society in which people are limited only by their ambitions and personal skills.

Eschatological myths are master narratives that help people to know where the status quo is taking them. (Eschatology is the branch of theology concerned with the end of world.) Christian parents employ such myths when they teach that a Christian life, and acceptance of Jesus Christ as their personal savior, will result in heavenly rewards. Conservative politicians employ eschatological myths when they argue that reduced government and decreased government spending is the path to a strong economy.

Sociological myths are narratives that teach one the proper way to live. Teachers and parents employ such myths when they teach children that Abraham Lincoln trekked through the woods to return a penny accidentally left behind by a customer in the store in which he worked. Similarly, we teach children that George Washington was so honest "he could not tell a lie." Such master narratives communicate to members of a society the values they should emulate in action and deed.

Cosmological myths are master narratives that describe why we are here and what our ancestors were like. Such myths serve to communicate from where "we" come. Cosmological myths are invoked when we teach children that (a) we are a nation born of people who valued freedom and liberty, (b) the U. S. is a Christian nation, (c) America was freed by farmer-soldiers who fought off the British Army with their own muskets, or (d) Great Grandfather Conrad came to America and worked several jobs to provide his family a better life and finally became an engineer.

When one teaches a child a particular set of myths, they are saying, "This is who we are." When a rhetor invokes particular myths when attempting to influence others, they are saying, "You should do as I suggest because it is consistent with who we are." There are a number of reasons that myths have persuasive value (Hart, 1997). Myths provide the rhetor with authority by associating the rhetor's claims with historical "truths." We "know" that George Washington was so honest he could not tell a lie. Over time, members of a family may take for granted that Great Grandfather Conrad was a heroic figure, responsible for the betterment of his entire family. For example, think about instances in which politicians have attempted to persuade us to favor a particular policy. Second, myths give meaning to the present by connecting it with the past. Third, myths provide a heightened sense of community by focusing attention on a shared, collective memory. Fourth, myths dramatize individual decision making by depicting struggles between "good" and "evil." When language may create the cohesion of the in-group, it simultaneously differentiates the in-group from potential out-groups. Fifth, myths are ideological in that they legitimize collective action through social discourse (Burke, 1995; Doty, 1986; Smith, 1984). The power of mythology lies in the images myths evoke and may serve to buttress ideology by giving individuals a concrete means of identification and participation in a collective form of memory (Balthrop, 1984; Waltman & Davis, 2004). Sixth, myths provide a sense of coherence to an argument as plot lines and characters are brought together in narratives that provide logic or a "truth." Perhaps this coherence is achieved because narratives are often presented, not only as "a truth" but as "*the* truth." Hart (1997) describes this function of myths as drawing on the "ancestral ghosts" in our shared memories to bring together "diverse parts of an audience's emotional life" (p. 243).

A Reinterpretation of *Hunter*: The Hate Stratagem

Waltman and Davis (2005) and Davis (2005) provided a close reading of *The Turner Diaries* and *Hunter*, respectively. Certainly, Davis (2005) built on the work of Waltman and Davis (2005) and there is a degree of important "replication" and unique important insights in Davis's analysis. Some of the myths emerging from *The Turner Diaries* also appear in *Hunter*. So, we employ examples from *The Turner Diaries* where they may add important insights into the myths and how they are used to construct a hate stratagem.

Waltman and Davis (2005) employed the constant comparative analysis of Grounded Theory to identify a total of 12 myths used to construct a view of the racist Aryan identity and a view of the Other. These myths with corresponding definitions can be found in Appendix A. Davis employed the same constant comparative analysis to identify 17 myths that are used to construct views of the racist Aryan identity, African American identity, and Jewish identity (these myths with corresponding definitions can be found in Appendix B).

Perusal of the myths in Appendixes A and B reveals that, superficially, racially aware Aryans are viewed positively, almost god-like. It should be noted that racially unaware Aryans are viewed as the Other. The authors argue that these myths constitute a collective memory that justifies an ideology of hate and the promotion of ethnoviolence. Initially, this constellation of myths was viewed as providing a rich set of characters, proclivities, and plot lines that provided important insights into the American culture of hate. The writers treated ethnoviolence as something hate-mongers "did" to accomplish their hateful goals and was a natural consequence of their tendency to glorify their own group and to demonize out-groups they saw as a threat. In retrospect, it appears that violence is not simply something that racist Aryan's "do" to accomplish their political and social goals, but it is an important cultural artifact in much the same way that one may think of *Hunter* or *The Turner Diaries* as cultural artifacts (Waltman, 2010-a). Ethnoviolence becomes an important form of action and behavior that allows the racist Aryan a tangible way of participating in the collective life of the group. This has important implications and suggests, among other things, that a Racist Pre-Christian Pagan feels most like a Pre-Christian Pagan when they are fighting or killing the enemies their race (Waltman, 2010-a). In the following pages, we reinterpret the arguments and analysis of Waltman & Davis (2005) and Davis (2005) to highlight violence as the central cultural artifact that emerges from an examination of their mythologies.

First, we reexamine the myths and other discourse evident in *Hunter* to determine how the use of the hate stratagem makes ethnoviolence not only a natural consequence of hate speech, but how it also integrates explicit calls for violence within the logic of the hate stratagem. To date, researchers have examined the hate stratagem's operation on audiences very different than the intended audience of *Hunter*. R. K. Whillock (1995) studied a hate stratagem intended for adult, presumably white, voters in Alabama. Waltman (2003) studied a hate stratagem intended for young children who might be doing research for a school report on the Klan. Pierce's intended audience is the Aryan who has elected to read this book. The bulk of readers are likely racist Aryans, or someone sympathetic to Pierce's racist views, who might be radicalized enough to be sympathetic with a Lone Wolf terrorist. Indeed, Pierce dedicated *Hunter* to a Lone Wolf terrorist mentioned in chapter two, Joseph Paul Franklin, "who knew his duty as a white man and did what a responsible son of his race must do, to the best of his ability and without regard for the personal consequences." This dedication makes very clear what readers should be learning from this book: How and why to kill the enemies of the Aryan race. Morris Dees confirms that Pierce is really only trying to influence that small percentage of people disaffected enough to find his message compelling (see Guttentag & DiPersio, 2003). Moreover, the goals pursued by Pierce are clearly different than the goals pursued by the rhetors in Whillock's and Waltman's research. This will certainly shape the substance of tactics pursued in Pierce's hate stratagem. We see evidence of this when we examine the novel through the lens of the hate stratagem.

Inflaming the emotions of readers by creating in-group identification

The first feature of the hate stratagem involves inflaming the emotions of the reader by creating in-group identification and encouraging the reader to feel pride in their race. Because Pierce can assume the reader will prefer their own race, he goes about the process of helping the reader to understand that this is natural and desirable. Pierce views this as necessary because he believes Aryans are living in a world that emphasizes tolerance and diversity and that discourages them from seeing what is special about their own race. Pierce uses the protagonist's thoughts to convey this to readers. Early in the book, the reader follows Yeager in the killing of inter-racial couples who disgust him and threaten the existence of the Aryan race. Pierce uses this internal monologue to explain his views of race. Yeager reflects that his understanding of race emerged when he was fighting in the Vietnam War where he learned about blacks, Jews, and the Vietnamese:

> One other thing his Vietnam experience had given him was a deeper appreciation for people of his own kind...and Oscar could not help contrasting them with...the Black GIs in the heavily integrated U.S. ground forces. It was not just his instinctive xenophobia responding to differences in appearance and speech. It was something deeper and more fundamental. (p. 9)

But the reader learns that the Aryan's preference for his own group is not only natural but spiritual and noble (p. 17): "The Blacks felt it and used the word 'soul' to express the individual's spiritual roots to all past and future generations of his race" (p. 9). Race, he argues, gives a person roots that determine his entire relationship to the world (pp. 9-10). Yeager explains the concrete implications when he asks readers to consider the word "pride." He says that, to whites, this word means self-respect and a sense of accomplishment that follows the successful completion of a task. However, he claims, for blacks, pride equates with a swaggering arrogance (p. 10). Through this and other examples, the reader is provided "evidence" of Aryan superiority and justifications for Aryans' preferences for their own race.

We know from previous research that one aspect of the white race, in particular, is used to personify the beautiful, the good, and the threat to the white race: the Female Aryan Ideal Myth. All kinds of atrocities against black men have been "justified" by constructing them as a threat to white women during America's long and varied history of racial hatred. This was an image that was explicitly manipulated in the film *Birth of a Nation* when a newly freed slave in South Carolina attempts to force himself on a beautiful young white woman who has been chased into a forest. She jumps from a cliff in order to not "defile her race" by succumbing to the sexual advances of this black man (Roach, 2006). This image, and others like it, was an important part of the Klan's use of this film as a recruitment tool (Roach, 2006). Pierce and his contemporaries have treated white women as the front line of the racial conflict in America. Essentially, protecting the wombs of white women is equated with protecting the white race (Perry, 2001). The Other's violation of the white womb becomes a genocidal assault on the white race.

Pierce articulates this Female Aryan Ideal Myth to explain Yeager's hate-motivated killings and to inflame the emotions of his readers. First, he describes Yeager's girlfriend, Adelaide, as possessing attributes that his readers will recognize as a standard European view of beauty:

> Long and lean and lithe, with silky smooth skin, perfect thighs...a flat belly, so lovely, so pure... it...made his heart ache with desire the way it ached when he watched an unusually spectacular sunset. (p. 15)

This is the vision that the racist Aryan is trying to protect and defend by committing acts of ethnoterrorism. The readers' emotions are further inflamed by descriptions of other desirable attributes that are worth protecting. Adelaide is portrayed as having a heightened sexual desire for Yeager because she loves him (pp. 14, 121). However, this sexual desire is understood to be a means to ultimately serve her race. As Yeager notes: "We need to think seriously about getting you pregnant. It's really a crime against Nature for someone with your genes not to have five or six kids" (p. 53). Adelaide is also an ideal white woman because she is also willing to be a help-mate by performing a variety of mundane activities, such as typing, for Yeager and his mission. This is expressed most emphatically by Adelaide after Yeager has explained his "battle" to her:

> I just want you to know…that if you decide to go to war against the whole world, I'll be your camp follower, if you'll have me. And if you charge unarmed into the gate of Hell, I'll be running along behind you as fast as I can, if I believe you still love me. (p. 56)

In summary, Pierce inflames the emotions of his readers and creates identification with the in-group by constructing a rationale that justifies the readers' preference for their own race and by personifying a Female Aryan Ideal in Adelaide that is used to justify the protection of the white race. Together, these arguments create strong in-group identification with their racial group.

Denigrating the out-group

The second characteristic of the hate stratagem involves the denigration of the Other. Waltman (2003) found that this characteristic was exemplified through the development of conspiracy theories. Such conspiracy theories are evident in the myths communicated in *Hunter*. These conspiracies are portrayed in the Zionist-Occupied Government Myth and the Jewish-Controlled Media Myth. Initially, Yeager comes to view his terrorism as a way to "wake up" his race. Eventually, he will encounter people who add sophistication to his hatred by inviting him to see this threat as a conspiracy carried out by Jewish interests who control the Federal Government (ZOG Myth) and the various forms of media (Jewish-Controlled Media Myth). These myths denigrate Jews by constructing them in familiar stereotypical terms. They are understood to be (a) money hungry, (b) hyper-craving of power and influence, (c) seeking only their own narrow self-interests, (d) possessing a lack of self-control in the pursuit of power, (e) treacherous, and (f) possessing undesirable and unattractive physical attributes that coincide with these behavioral and psychological characteristics.

These myths not only denigrate Jews, but they also position Jews as a danger to Aryans. The ZOG Myth asserts that Jews have acquired control of the Federal Government. Racist Aryans see evidence of ZOG in the success of the Civil Rights Movement and programs such as Affirmative Action that have disadvantaged white people. This is evident in references to the "governments minority-coddling programs" (p. 35) or government programs that "stipulate triple reimbursement of all losses suffered by any member of an identifiable minority group as a result of a racist act" (p. 255). Of course, there is a more pernicious side to ZOG that uses elements of the government to act as thugs. An F.B.I. agent sympathetic to Yeager's mission tells him: "We may be secretly glad when you waste some race-mixer in a parking lot, but we'll fall all over ourselves to be the first to nail you for it. We're the Jews' mercenaries, and we earn our keep" (p. 65). This agent later describes the F.B.I. as an American version of the K.G.B. (p. 90). An example of the history of ZOG is seen when this same agent informs Yeager that a cabal of Jewish presidential advisors planned the Japanese surprise attack on Pearl Harbor to pull the United States into the Second World War (p. 74).

ZOG is also seen as a destroyer of good Aryan morals:

> The National Education Association [an arm of ZOG]…endorsed a model bill which would require the schools in those states where the bill became law to have a course titled "Alternative Sexual Orientation" for all students.… The purpose of the bill, which had been drawn up by a coalition of homosexual groups working with the Anti-Defamation League…to "combat bigotry" and…help young people to understand that persons with a sexual orientation different from their own are just as normal as anyone else, and that no specific "orientation" is more moral or more desirable than any other. (p. 207)

So, the goals of ZOG are differentiated and extensive. ZOG wishes to (a) promote minority interests, (b) promote Jewish interests, (c) police and attack Aryans, and (d) coordinate the promotion of a homosexual agenda. All of these are perceived to be corrupting influences that are designed to make America less "Aryan" and more "Jewish."

A second conspiracy theory is found in the Jewish-Controlled Media Myth. This myth explains how Jews have gained control of a variety of media ranging from newspapers to the entertainment industry in Hollywood. It is by controlling news stories and by distracting white people with entertainment that ZOG is able to control white people. One character, in the process of educating Yeager about the extent of the Jewish conspiracy, blurts out: "Virtually all the media are controlled by Jews, and they call the tune for everyone else in the media" (p. 41). Elsewhere, the Jews are described as "the masters of the controlled news" (p. 9). Moreover, the media is able to function as an agent of ZOG. Racist Aryans see the operation of the Jewish-Controlled Media Myth when television shows young African Americans and young white people living integrated social lives or when an inter-racial couple is portrayed positively on a television show. By continually portraying such images as "normal," they see a Jewish-controlled television industry attempting to turn young Aryans against their race (p. 71). To illustrate the importance of this Jewish-Controlled Media Myth, we learn that this conspiracy has been operating for years and has even caused the spread of Communism during the first part of the 20th century (pp. 125, 138).

The ZOG Myth and the Jewish-Controlled Media Myth denigrate Jews by constructing conspiracy theories that imbue Jews with undesirable motives—controlling the lives of white people. Another myth achieves this same purpose for African Americans, the Black Savage Myth. This is an all-too-familiar narrative among racists of all stripes. This myth constructs African Americans as personally and culturally inferior to Aryans. This myth frequently draws on metaphors that suggest that African Americans are sub-human. They are understood to be creatures (p. 21), tribal (p. 73), and jungle inhabitants (p. 90).

Inflicting permanent harm on the out-group

Permanent harm is inflicted on the out-group by destroying the validity of the group's identity. This involves constructing the out-group as a more immediate threat to Aryans (not simply a distant threat posed by a vague conspiracy). In *Hunter*, this is accomplished when Jews and African Americans are not constructed simply as an Other, but rather, they are constructed as an inherent threat to Aryans.

The Black Predator Myth constructs African Americans as having an almost genetic predisposition to harm white people. This myth takes many forms. Early in the text we learn that the desire to rape white women is inherent in the African American male character. Adelaide comments:

> I haven't had another proposition from a Black in more than a year. The other White girls were pestered by them all the time.... They simply won't take "no" for an answer.... Besides, it was general knowledge that girls who did date them [African Americans] usually got raped if they didn't give in voluntarily. They called it "date rape," but it was still rape—very often gang rape. (p. 52)

This image is portrayed many times throughout *Hunter:*

> There was that rape of the jogger in Rock Creek Park last week, for example, in which more than 20 teen-aged Blacks grabbed the girl and spent nearly two hours raping her repeatedly, right on the jogging path. Then they cut her throat and left her to die. It wouldn't have made such a splash in the media if she hadn't been a Senator's niece. (p. 55)

The "savage" nature of African Americans is often emphasized when they engage in violent predatory action. During a "black revolt" Pierce describes their violence in an office:

> Blood-spattered Blacks with blood-dripping knives, ice picks, cleavers, or hatchets in their hands, running from desk to desk, from counter to counter, from work station to work station, stabbing, hacking, slicing, chopping amid the screams and groans of the [Aryan] victims. (pp. 251–252)

During this uprising, Pierce describes gangs of armed Blacks roaming the countryside (p. 258), smashing store windows and stealing (p. 255), wholesale burning, looting, and raping (p. 247), and as Black "wolf packs" roaming out of control (p. 90).

So, the Black Predator Myth constructs African Americans as an inherent threat to the safety and lives of Aryans. When this myth is coupled with an understanding of the Female Aryan Ideal Myth, the reader is to understand that black predators pose a genocidal threat to the Aryan race. Similar myths construct Jews as an immediate threat to Aryans.

The Jewish Pornographer Myth depicts Jews as producers, distributors, and addicts of pornography. This is a threat to Aryans in more than one way. First, pornography is an attempt to pervert Aryans into many forms of degeneracy and to force miscegenation down America's throat (p. 68) and to "pump their poison into the minds and hearts of the White population" (p. 244). The Jewish Pornographer Myth also has a second meaning. Jews are pornographers when they attempt to promote cultures that are non-Aryan (p. 97) and promote race-mixing (p. 84). Such actions are genocidal attempts to invade the Aryan imagination (Davis, 2005).

The Treacherous/Violent Jew Myth also constructs Jews as a threat to Aryan survival. This is roughly the equivalent of the Black Predator Myth:

> And what if the Jews' origins in the Middle East and their subsequent history gave them a significantly different genetic heritage from Whites of European ancestry? Keller and Ryan had suggested that the Jews possessed a special sort of inborn malevolence, a genetically based hatred of the world, which expressed itself in an all-encompassing, though cleverly concealed campaign against their White neighbors. (p. 81)

Yeager reflects that his experience led him to recall the Jews he knew as especially treacherous (p. 83), at war with whites (p. 73), Soviet spies (p. 74), dirty tricks specialists (p. 86), and hucksters and illusion builders (p. 106). Pierce uses Yeager's reflections to portray Jews as innately deceitful, vengeful, and violent toward the Aryan race (Davis, 2005).

The Jewish Vampire Myth constructs a Jewish identity that survives by infiltrating and "feeding" on other cultures. According to this myth, Jews have no culture to contribute to the world around them (Waltman & Davis, 2005):

> In Nature there are…parasites…which might reasonably be compared with the rabies-carrying vampire bat…. [Jews] have a record spanning thousands of years, during which they have infiltrated and destroyed one society after another while living as a privileged minority among their potential victims. (p. 104)

This parasitism is said to be fundamental to Judaism, based on the exploitation of Gentiles (p. 99). So, the Jewish Vampire Myth constructs Jews as not only subhuman but as a historically continuous parasite that feeds on white nations. Understood as a conflict inherent in group relations, the Jewish Vampire Myth, if accepted, ensures that Jews and Aryans may never peacefully co-exist and situates race relations as an epic struggle between good (Aryans) and evil (Jews).

Rhetorical conquering the out-group

The fourth characteristic of the hate stratagem is the conquering of the out-group. Previous work on the hate stratagem describes how one might verbally conquer the out-group. In the case of *Hunter,* out-groups are conquered by calling for out-group members' actual deaths. There are several myths discussed by Waltman and Davis (2005) and Davis (2005) that describe how the Aryan (Lone Wolf) should experience the murdering of the Other: the Dispassionate Aryan Myth, the Pleasure of Murder Myth, and the Terrorist's Burden Myth.

The Dispassionate Aryan Myth describes how the racially conscious Aryan should be unemotional and detached while killing the enemy. Pierce writes of Yeager:

> He could hardly believe how easy it had been.... He had done the whole thing as calmly—one might say casually—as if he had been delivering a pizza instead of carrying out a daylight assassination. (p. 25)

Being emotionally detached certainly allows the Lone Wolf to kill without being touched by the taking of a life. However, the value of this form of violence is described by Pierce in *The Turner Diaries.* During the Day of the Rope, a day following the Aryan-won race war, when all race traitors are hung by the neck, the protagonist, Earl Turner, describes the actions of the terrorists against the doomed race traitor:

> He was jerked off his feet with the same impartiality they had shown those who accepted their fate in silence. They were ordered not to argue with anyone or explain anything. (p. 168)

This dispassionate attitude holds symbolic value for the racist Aryan. Like the early fascists (Mussolini, 1932), these racists revere violence as a means to political ends. So, it is not surprising that they would fetishize violence. Pierce explains further in *The Turner Diaries:*

> Above all else we must show ourselves as disciplined, since we will be demanding strict discipline on the part of the population. We must never give vent to our feelings or frustration or our personal hatreds but must show by our behavior…that what we are doing is serving a higher purpose. (p. 164)

The Dispassionate Aryan Myth informs potential Lone Wolves how they should act while murdering the Other. The Pleasure of Murder Myth tells potential Lone Wolves what they will feel during and after murder. This myth teaches potential Lone Wolves that they should feel pride in their work and gratification in murder:

> There definitely had been more satisfaction for Oscar in Killing [one particular African American] than the other Blacks. Partly it was because this one had publicly declared himself an enemy of the White race by his actions against Whites in South Africa, and partly it was because he was such an arrogant, swaggering, uppity [n-word].[1] (p. 20)

Yeager also observes: "[He] could not help feel a little pride when he considered how essential his own efforts had been" (p. 130) and how it is "satisfying to teach these uppity aliens [Jews] a little humility" (p. 173).

Pierce creates a Terrorist's Burden Myth to describe the conflict that the Lone Wolf will experience as a result of his terrorist activities. Part of the terrorist's burden is the loss of a normal life with normal relationships. Yeager ponders:

> Where was he headed? What sort of ultimate outcome was he seeking? …perhaps he should quit while the quitting was good and marry Adelaide. He sighed at the prospect. (p. 26)

Another feature of the terrorist's burden is the recognition that his terrorism will certainly result in the death of some innocent Aryans. This dissonance is resolved by recognizing that non-combatants will always be killed in any war (p. 179). This rationalization allows the terrorist to know that the killing of Aryans serves a worthy cause (p. 230).

These righteous killings are possible to the extent that the Lone Wolf possess two attributes: being moral (the Moral Aryan Myth) and vigilant (the Vigilant Aryan Myth). By the time Pierce has written *Hunter*, the moral Ar-

---

[1] Throughout the book, we use the euphemism "n-word" to substitute for the racial epithet. This word has played an especially significant role in the maintenance of white supremacy in American life and has been a great source of pain and suffering among African Americans. We do not use the euphemism to comfort ourselves. We are sympathetic with the NAACP position that it is time to "bury" that word and remove it from public discourse.

yan is treated, almost exclusively, as someone who is willing to kill the enemies of the Aryan race. Indeed, Davis (2005) notes: "The Moral Aryan Myth
situates action, or ethnoviolence, as a ritual symbolic of one's morality" (p.
10). In *Hunter*, Yeager provides the reader with a number of rationalizations
for his terrorist killings that equate his murders with the protection of the Aryan race. Just as action is moral, inaction makes one immoral. Yeager poses
a hypothetical situation to illustrate his commitment as a moral Aryan:

> Suppose you and I were walking through the park...while the raping was in pro-
> gress. Suppose I were unarmed, and it was a good mile to the nearest telephone.
> Some men, I suppose, could tell themselves there was nothing they could do, except
> start running for the telephone, in the hope they could get the cops there in 20 or 30
> minutes. But for me there would be no choice. If the girl were a member of my race
> I would have to charge right in there and do what was humanly possible to rescue
> her. If I ran away I would not be able to live with myself. I would feel dirty and dis-
> honorable forever afterward. (p. 56)

Through these myths, violence against the Other makes one a moral Aryan,
with the Moral Aryan Myth reduced to action and violence. Readers learn
more about the proper Aryan identity through the Vigilant Aryan Myth.

The vigilant Aryan is one who is always prepared to view the events of
his world through their hateful and White Supremacist ideology. To the racially conscious Aryan, this ideology is not a biasing perspective; rather, it is
a tool that allows the Aryan to notice the conspiracy of the Zionist-Occupied
Government that goes unnoticed by so many white people who have been
seduced by the benefits of capitalism. Vigilance involves being disciplined
(p. 196), planning terrorist actions carefully (pp. 65, 93), understanding one's
prey (pp. 102, 138, 254), and studying so that one can protect one's self from
brainwashing and manipulation (pp. 83, 252).

In summary, the myths that constitute *Hunter*, an important textual artifact of the hate movement, cohere in a way that suggests the presence of a
hate stratagem. The Moral Aryan and the Female Aryan Ideal Myths help to
inflame the emotions of readers by enhancing identification with the Aryan
race and suggest that preference for one's own race is a natural and desirable
way to orient toward one's world. The Black Savage, Zionist-Occupied Government, and Jewish-Controlled Media Myths suggest conspiracy theories
that denigrate the out-group. The Black Predator, Jewish Pornography,
Treacherous/Violent Jew, and Jewish Vampire Myths suggest the third characteristic of the hate stratagem as they inflict permanent harm on the out-
group by destroying the validity of the group's identity. The fourth characteristic of the hate stratagem is the verbal conquering of the in-group. The Dis-

passionate Aryan, Pleasure of Murder, and Terrorists Burden Myths focus on the satisfaction that the Lone Wolf terrorist will feel while killing the Other.

The Symbolism of Hate Crime

We have argued that hate speech is used to denigrate, dehumanize, and rhetorically dominate another due to their race, ethnicity, religion, gender, or sexual orientation. One of the important things about hate crime and ethnoviolence is the symbolic value of such violence. Hate crimes are a means by which the identities of the offender and target are constructed relative to one another (Perry, 2001). Hate crimes are directed against identities that are already marginalized by interlocking hierarchies of oppression (e.g., racial, gender, or heterosexist hierarchies) that privilege whiteness, maleness, and heterosexuality. Hate crimes become one way of policing difference (Perry, 2001, 2003). When white men beat a young African American male with bats as they shouted insults against President Obama following the 2008 Presidential election, they were policing differences and identities they believed to be advancing "beyond their place." When someone placed a noose on the doorknob of a female, African American Professor, that person was policing difference that was challenging a hierarchy that privileged whiteness and maleness. Thus, there is a symbolic convergence between hate speech and ethnoviolence (and hate crimes more broadly) that is important to address.

Hate-motivated violence is certainly used to construct the identities of the target and perpetrator. In a sense, however, the crime is more than a crime against an individual. It is also meant to intimidate and terrorize entire groups in a community (Herek, Cogan, & Gillis, 2003; Iganski, 2003). Hate crimes and ethnoviolence instill fear in a targeted group that other crimes do not (Iganski, 2003). They communicate to other members of the group, "This could have been you. You are not welcome nor wanted here." Hate-motivated violence and criminal activity constitutes one form of hegemony that the dominant group uses to oppress other groups. Perry (2001) explains:

> The target audience is not so much the victim as it is others like him or her. Richard Wright's words come easily to mind in this context: 'The things that influenced my conduct as a Negro did not have to happen to me directly. I needed but to hear of them to feel their full effects in the deepest layers of my consciousness. (Wright, cited in Perry, 2001, p. 10)

The lynching ritual in the United States serves as an historical exemplar of ethnoviolence as a means of maintaining white supremacy and the dominant power relationships in the United States: "Historically, such crimes have been actively encouraged, passively condoned, or simply ignored by systems of governance, especially the criminal justice systems" (Maroney, 1998, p. 565). For years, gay men and lesbians failed to report hate-motivated violence because doing so often brought another round of violence or harassment from the police (Clark, 2010; Perry 2001). Next we examine the nature of hate crimes and hate-motivated violence, and the procedures for reporting them that contribute to their symbolic value and their usefulness as a form of oppression.

The nature of hate crime statutes and the procedures associated with their reporting to the F.B.I. contribute to their symbolic value as a means of oppression. Hate crime statutes are diverse and vary from state to state. At the national level, the F.B.I. is prohibited from investigating crime motivated by gender, disability, or sexual orientation. It would only be logical, therefore, that gay men and lesbians, for example, would conclude that their government had little interest in protecting them.

The way that hate crime statistics are reported to the F.B.I. may inadvertently contribute to the oppression of vulnerable minorities. Reports compiled by the F.B.I. rely on local law enforcement agencies to voluntarily submit data via Uniform Crime Reports (UCRs) that include hate crime reporting categories. Those who have reason to fear hate crime and ethnoviolence are aware of this system. The system itself appears to be established to encourage the underreporting of hate crimes. The clearest indication that hate crimes are underreported can be found in the data included in the 2008 report (F.B.I., 2009). This report included the largest number of participating law enforcement agencies in the history of the act. However, only 15.6% (2,145) of the 13,690 participating law enforcement agencies reported even a single hate crime to the F.B.I. That is, 84.4% reported zero hate crimes within their jurisdiction in 2008.

Why would law enforcement agencies fail to report these statistics? There are likely multiple answers to this question. Perhaps some local law enforcers believe that all assaults or murders are hate crimes because "one must hate in order to murder." Perhaps some local law enforcement agencies do not report hate crimes because they are populated by people who condone prejudice and ethnoviolence. Perhaps law enforcement agencies do not want their communities to be known as places where hate crimes occur. Following the hate-motivated murder of Matthew Shepherd in Laramie, signs were placed in windows around town for national media that proclaimed: "Hate is not a Laramie value." As we discuss in chapter five, some law enforcement agencies fail to report murder as a hate crime even when, for example, perpetrators were reported by witnesses to have shouted racial epithets while assailants beat a man to death.

Ethnoviolence itself is often identifiable by characteristics that contribute to their symbolic value. First, hate-motivated violence is often excessively brutal (Levin & McDevitt, 2002). The excessive brutality of a hate-motivated attack is often the feature of the crime that first brings public attention to the crime. One thinks of the murder of James Byrd in Jasper, Texas. After being dragged behind a pickup truck, his bloody and dismembered body was left in front of an African American church. In the case of James Byrd, we know that the brutality of the crime was intended to be political. His killers wanted to draw the imagination of the public in order to start a chapter of their own hate group (Guttentag & DiPersio, 2003). In Laramie, Matthew Shepherd was barely recognizable following his beating.

Sometimes the excessive brutality of hate-motivated violence is associated with the motives that animate such violence. Perpetrators of hate-motivated violence may be at the margins of the community or be economically vulnerable. Seeing themselves as victims, their violence may come from feelings of resentment and scapegoating. Sometimes hate-motivated violence may be animated from feeling personally threatened by the invasion of the out-group. Such a "defensive hate crime" (Levin & McDevitt, 2002) is intended to communicate that "you don't belong." As teenagers in Shenandoah, Pennsylvania, beat an undocumented worker to death, they shouted, Get the f--- out of Shenandoah."

Second, while targets of hate crime are chosen because of their membership in a vulnerable out-group, the crime itself is usually perpetrated at random (Levin & McDevitt, 2002). In fact, the specific victim is immaterial to the perpetrator (Perry, 2001). A specific member of the out-group is attacked because the victim is present when the opportunity for the attack is present. Perpetrators of hate-motivated attacks are typically unknown by their victims. This random nature of the attack makes the victim interchangeable with other group members (Perry, 2001). For the attacker, one African American or Jew is as good as any other African American or Jew. The interchangeable nature of victims communicates to other members of the group that they, too, are not safe. This also serves to further terrorize the victims of hate crimes because they can't rationalize their future safety. They know that they were targeted because of their membership in a group they cannot leave.

Third, hate-motivated violence is often perpetrated by multiple attackers (Levin & McDevitt, 2002). This probably is a factor in the brutality of hate-motivated attacks as individuals lose their inhibitions as they are encouraged by the group. The group may also provide individuals with security and anonymity. Hamm (1993) and others have described these highly violent attacks as "beserking." Still others have referred to these attacks as "wilding."

Fourth, hate-motivated violence may be a product of a specific hate group (Hamm, 1993) but it is more likely that the perpetrators of hate-motivated crime are not members of a hate group. The fact that a hate crime may be perpetrated by an ordinary person adds to the terror that targeted communities may feel. This suggests that almost anyone could be a potential assailant.

Of course, we distinguish between hate speech and hate crime. To equate the two would be to equate discourse and violence. However, we should not ignore the symbolic value of hate-motivated violence as a form of hegemony that maintains the power and privilege of whiteness, maleness, and heterosexuality.

Conclusion

We have focused our attention on two constructs that offer important insights into the nature of hate speech produced by individuals in the organized hate movement: Myth and the hate stratagem. In so doing, we have offered a thorough exploration of these constructs by examining their operation across physical and Internet texts. We have argued that the Myths constitute building blocks of a racist Aryan collective memory. Moreover, we have demonstrated that these myths play an important role in the operation of the hate stratagem. For example, we demonstrated that a Black Savage Myth and a Treacherous Jew Myth played an important role in the rhetorical attempt to inflict permanent harm on these out-groups (the third characteristic of the hate stratagem). Similarly, the Pleasure of Murder Myth and the Lone Wolf Myth have played an important role in the accomplishment of the fourth characteristic of the hate stratagem, the rhetorical conquering of the out-group.

This chapter has demonstrated that hate speech is increasingly used to call for violence against the enemies of the Aryan race. In the next chapter, we discuss hate crime and the relationship between hate speech and hate crime in more detail.

Chapter 4

Hate Speech and the Internet

The Internet has changed the way people live their lives. This change has often been for the good, and it has often been for the bad. For example, in recent years, politicians have made revolutionary use of the Internet to raise funds, network supporters, and communicate with their constituents. Much has also been written about the growth of advertising on the Internet (Schumann & Thorson, 2007). Unfortunately, the Internet also has played a role in the radicalization of individuals in the hate movement.

The Internet has become the lifeblood of the organized hate movement. A Web Site associated with hate groups and hate issues first appeared in March 1995. That Web Site was created by Don Black, the leader of Stormfront. Black also introduced Web Pages devoted to the recruitment of children. His young son, Derek, produced and edited a section of the Stormfront Web Page that adapted Black's racist message to the interests and reading and cognitive abilities of children.

In the past, many of the individuals and hate groups operated in relative isolation from one another. When individuals did gather, they were required to travel, often long distances, to meet at some physical compound or location. Now, for the cost of a phone line, inexpensive computer, and software, individual White Supremacists are able to go to the Internet and find a potentially anonymous but congenial environment where they can openly express many of their beliefs that would be rejected in their more public life (Kessler, 1999). Many leaders have used these inexpensive tools to produce Web Pages that rival the quality of any university Web Page. It is probably not a coincidence that during this same period of time (1995 to the present), hate groups have become more integrated, violent, and apocalyptic in their thinking (Perry, 2001; Waltman, 2010-c).

Many Lone Wolf terrorists sequestered themselves away from other people and cocooned themselves within the Internet and their hateful discourse for long periods of time to reinforce their hateful views prior to committing ethnoviolence (Crothers, 2003; Guttentag & Di Persio, 2003). This suggests that, among other things, the Internet has served an important mechanism for self-persuasion to reinforce extreme views (Petty & Cacioppo, 1986).

Today there are approximately 4,000 Web Sites devoted to the expression of hate, and the Southern Poverty Law Center estimates that there are 962 active hate groups in the United States. In the following pages, we discuss Web Pages that help us to understand some important features of these texts.

Hate Speech and the Internet

Hate group Web Pages typically fall into one of the following categories: Web Pages that represent the views of a specific hate group (e.g., National Alliance) in the form of online newspapers (e.g., Vanguard News Network) or newsletters (e.g., TightRope), or Web Pages that are devoted to giving hatred its ideological substance (e.g., Women for Aryan Unity; The Insurgent). In this chapter, we describe four Web Pages whose primary purpose is to contribute to the ideological development of the U.S. hate movement: (a) Vanguard News Network, an online news source for Aryans, (b) The Lone Wolf Survivalist, a Web Page intended to be a resource for the education of potential terrorists, (c) Women for Aryan Unity, a Web Page devoted to carving out a substantive niche for women in the hate movement, and (d) The Insurgent, Tom Metzger's comprehensive Web Page that offers readers access to almost every important writer who has contributed to the ideological substance of the hate movement (one important exception being the writings of William Pierce, discussed in chapter three). The Insurgent also offers games, artwork, and other material that allows readers to find diverse pleasures in their hatred. Because of its comprehensive nature, we devote most of our critique to The Insurgent. Together, these four Web Pages permit insight into the history and aspirations of the hate movement.

The Vanguard News Network

Past research has examined the online newspaper the Vanguard News Network (VNN). We described this page in less detail elsewhere (Waltman & Haas, 2007). There are at least two forms of VNN readers may access. We describe the more user-friendly version of this site (see references). A reader first entering the site encounters a vivid red banner with the title of the newsletter in bold and black letters. Under the title of the newspaper are two sentences: *"No Jews. Just Right."* In the "Who We Are" section, the reader will find the names of the editor and 22 writers. The reader is also informed of the following:

> We are a group of disgusted and disaffected writers driven out of academia and journalism by the Semitrical Correctness that has denatured our culture. [Recall the Jewish Vampire Myth.] We have come together on the Internet to reclaim the American mind from the Jews. In short, we are the antibodies, and our advent heralds the day a White political force rises and reasserts civilization. [Recall the RAHOWA Myth.]

It is here where the reader is informed that VNN means that "probably for the first time in your life, you get news spun accurately. For once you are getting *news from people who look and act like you*, and who share your beliefs." This claim reflects the Jewish-Controlled Media Myth and the belief in the Zionist-Occupied Government, also referred to by the racist acronym ZOG. The Jewish-controlled media is also reflected in the Department section of VNN called *"Between the Lines."* This section of VNN is devoted to teaching readers to decode the real meaning of articles and stories found in the popular media. Between the Lines contains several transcripts of articles written by popular writers and pundits. VNN has inserted editorial comments that are intended to help the reader understand the author's (ZOG's) real goals. In the examples that follow, insertions and changes made by VNN are italicized.

In a speech delivered by George Bush on October 8, 2002 in Cincinnati, VNN vandalized the President's remarks as noted in their italicized commentary:

> Tonight I want to take a few minutes to discuss a grave threat to peace, and *America's determination to confront the world by leading that threat—oops, shouldn't've said that;* lead the world in confronting that threat.... The threat comes from Iraq. It arises directly from the Iraqi regime's own actions—its history of aggression, *its insistence upon existing,* and its drive toward an arsenal of terror *to counter the one we've armed Israel with....* We resolved then, and we are resolved today, to confront any and every *opponent to mass immigration* threat, from any source, that could bring sudden terror and suffering to America.

This example illustrates the Zionist-Occupied Government Myth discussed in this chapter and elsewhere (Waltman & Davis, 2005). VNN is attempting to make the point that ZOG wants us to fear the terrorists while diminishing the danger that illegal immigration poses (from VNN's perspective, a more immediate threat).

VNN also interprets what they called David Horowitz's American Conservatism: An argument with the Radical Right. This example illustrates that the hate movement, while somewhat conservative in nature, views conservatives as no less a part of ZOG than any liberal element of government:

On July 16 of this year (2002), my website *www.frontpagemagazine.com* ran a story about the "Wichita Massacre," the brutal execution of four white youth by two criminal brothers who happened to be black. *Note the wording "just happened to be black." Yes, indeed, Mr. Horowitz may want us to believe it could have "been anyone." Just like the scores of Bolshevik commissars who slaughtered tens of millions of Eastern Europeans just "happened to be Jewish."* This hypocrisy regards the murder of blacks by whites as an indication of the existence of a characteristically American racism and therefore banner news, while the far more prevalent murder of whites by blacks is routinely considered to be without racial overtones and—as in the Wichita case—not to be newsworthy at all. *Mr. Horowitz, isn't it also a bit hypocritical to talk about media bias without mentioning which group predominantly owns and controls the media in this country? How about mentioning WHY this media bias exists?*

So, VNN would waste no time attempting to invalidate Horowitz's argument by invalidating *him*. A further example:

In the commentary I wrote to accompany our feature, I described Taylor as "a man who has surrendered to the multicultural miasma that has overtaken this nation and is busily building a movement devoted to white identity and community," agendas we "did not share." *Well, yes, I am not surprised that a Jew is opposed to the notion of "white identity." Can't have those pesky goyim fooling around with the same sort of cohesive in-group identification that has allowed Jews to survive and prosper for centuries, can we? ... Instead, demonize white ethnoracial identity politics by equating it with "multiculturalism"...that'll scare away all the kosher conservative lemmings. After all, why read AR [American Renaissance, a white racialist publication] when you can instead vote for the "conservative" George Bush, the man who'll sell our birthright to illegal alien Mexicans in order to garner a few votes.*

These examples, and many others, illustrate the belief that these authors operate in concert to produce broad social discourses that are designed to distract white Americans from ZOG's oppression and control of their lives. It also reflects the belief that the media produces a veil that can be deconstructed, allowing readers to ascertain ZOG's true message. By pouring over the broad range of stories, readers will eventually teach themselves how to decode the news of the day. Eventually, readers will learn to decode the news on their own.

VNN's Multi-Media Center section offers a range of slick promotional materials and cartoons that advance VNN's racist agenda. Through the manipulation of digital and non-digital images, Jewish, African American, and Latino identities are vilified and dehumanized. Because this is done through "humor," the Multi-Media Center becomes a place where White Supremacists may go to find pleasure in their hatred.

Other "departments" include book, movie, music, and television reviews, from a white racist perspective—everything is viewed through a racist lens. One example is a review of the movie, *Harry Potter and the Sorcerer's Stone*. The writer gets to the heart of his concerns in his first paragraph:

> *Harry Potter and the Sorcerer's Stone* is the best movie of the year (and you know I'm not one given to superlatives). There are a few negroes within, but they are very obviously just part of the backdrop, and contribute little to the film. It looks as though the filmmakers just threw them in so they wouldn't be accused of racism. (http://www.vanguardnewsnetwork.com/movie.htm)

In a review of Michael Moore's *Stupid White Men*, a writer for VNN laments his loss of respect for Michael Moore, who he once viewed as a "neo-Marxist folk hero" to the American middle class. The writer explains that in the chapter entitled "Kill Whitey," Moore "demeans his own race" by accusing white people of inventing slavery, the nuclear bomb, and other social ills:

> Moore is inadvertently conceding the moral superiority of whites over other races by his standards of moral goodness. That is to say, Moore obviously feels this is the correct moral position to adopt; and by doing so, he's espousing a morality that is shared only by whites. Other groups have been responsible for atrocities equally as reprehensible as those of whites.

These and other book reviews contribute to a social cocoon in which readers may envelop themselves and encounter ideas in a congenial White Supremacist environment.

The Departments section illustrates that one goal of VNN is to cultivate a white racist way of life—a white racist culture. This culture is an inclusive one. VNN is self-conscious in the way it incorporates the symbols and mythology of both secular and religious hate groups into its online newspaper (e.g., Confederate battle flags, swastikas and other neo-Nazi symbols, and Pagan symbols). Obviously, this enhances the credibility and attractiveness of VNN to a broad range of groups and potential subscribers.

Lone Wolf Survivalist

Lone Wolf Survivalist is an electronic educational newsletter that draws on Amazon.com to provide potential Lone Wolves with information, tools, and manuals to ply their trade. The subtitle of this newsletter reads, "The Hour of Redemption is Near." At the top of the home page, the potential Lone Wolf may click on Sniper Training/Silencers, Retreats/Wilderness, Artillery, Tools, and Underground Economy. Most new visitors probably click first on the Lone Wolf Creed, featured prominently below a snarling wolf.

The Lone Wolf Creed begins, "I am the Lone Wolf; I am covert. I conduct surveillance...and intelligence on my opponents. I do not join groups and/or organizations due to informants, agents, provocateurs, and trouble-makers. I avoid being on a list. [Recall the Terrorist's Burden Myth.] Even if I am on a list, I have a list...on my opponents. I know where they live, where they go shopping, where their kids go to school, where their spouse works...who their friends are, their habits and even their birth dates. [Recall the Pleasure of Murder Myth.] I have studied and researched Lone Wolf tactics.... I am prepared when I am arrested...to insist on 5 words, I HAVE NOTHING TO SAY.... [Recall the Dispassionate Aryan Myth.] I am the Lone Wolf! I am always listening."

This Web Page tries to cover exactly who they are, remaining understandable only to those "in the know." But the reference to five words gives them away. The five words were coined by San Diego White Supremacist Alex Curtis, who believed White Supremacists should use this "code of silence" with law enforcement as an expression of solidarity with racists throughout the United States (see Anti-Defamation League-c).

The balance of Lone Wolf Survivalist is a narrative that is organized around products (e.g., camouflage, boots, homemade silencers, cross bows), manuals (e.g., Ultimate Sniper, Building a Log Cabin, Fighting in the Streets), and information about how to create a resistance movement (Spy & Counterspy). As noted previously, this narrative is organized around the myths that emerged from our analysis of *Hunter*. Readers learn how to become a Lone Wolf but they also learn to identify with the role of Lone Wolf. Readers learn that this is a valuable identity that can "secure the well being" of one's family. Several manuals are prepared by the Army, Marines, and Special Forces—organizations that someone drawn to the Lone Wolf lifestyle is likely to find credible. By taking on the Lone Wolf identity, potential Lone Wolves may cloak themselves in the credibility of these forces.

Women for Aryan Unity

Women for Aryan Unity (WAU) is a Web Page devoted to creating a "new Feminism" among racist Pagans that will allow men and women to work co-operatively and meaningfully for the protection and promotion of the Aryan race:

> At this time in the Movement's history, when the great task of redefining a Woman's role in the cause is posed; of reinventing the concept of *feminism* within the parameters of Race and Revolution, WAU can only be a group of equals, a staff of educators and disseminators, not hangers on, joiners, or pseudo soldiers.

WAU is explicitly reinterpreting and differentiating the Female Aryan Ideal Myth described in *Hunter*. This statement also places WAU in the category of White Supremacist publications (and publishers). They claim that 90% of the women who belong to WAU are Odinists. A portion of their Web Page is devoted to sharing information about Odinism: religious blots and their meanings (including suggested rituals and meditations), Pagan meanings behind specific days of the week and months of the year, names of goddesses from various Aryan traditions (e.g., Celtic, Germanic), ways of living cooperatively with nature and the environment (including environmental friendly practices and suggestions for a vegetarian diet that does not tread on animals or the earth). As they note, they are trying to create a new way of thinking and living that will add ideological substance to Aryan hatred:

> From the most ancient times of our Folk, a body of spiritual teaching known as the ageless wisdom has been handed down, Mother to Child, Generation to Generation. A systematic and comprehensive account of the evolution of consciousness in Woman and Nature, it describes how the worldsoul came to exist, how it functions, and Aryanity's place within it.... Women and their Folk, in turn, are "Sparks of the Goddess," spiritual entities expressing a Folksoul through a physical Race. Each of us is essentially a divine ray of this Folksoul, but compared to the greatest adepts of our ancestry, most individual women today recognize and embody this divinity to a limited degree.

WAU is a well-organized Web Page with far-flung interests. One important project undertaken by WAU is the publication of the writings of the late David Lane, the charismatic and articulate leader of the racist Odinist movement in the United States, and other members of The Order. Our analysis will not focus on this portion of their discourse but on the thing that is really unique about this group: the education of women into Odinism. The ideas of David Lane are addressed in the next section of this chapter.

There are additional sections that help women to apply Odinist values in their home. These include games and activities that mothers may share with their children and health advice that will help women to have happier and healthier pregnancies, such as tips that will help women remain vegetarians while also caring for all the nutritional needs of their unborn children. Like most Americans, they see pedophilia as a horror in its own right. Protect Our Children is a section devoted to teaching parents how to recognize pedophiles and the signs of sexual child abuse.

The group promotes a variety of projects that further racist Odinist causes. Other important sections include information on the dangers of abortion and pedophilia. As with other groups alluded to in chapter two, WAU opposes the abortion of white babies because white people need to populate their communities because non-whites are "arriving in our country already pregnant." So, giving birth to white children who will join their cause is an important contribution that women can make to the hate movement. (Recall the Female Aryan Ideal Myth.) The writer comments:

> Abortion is an issue not often addressed within our movement, I cannot actually ever recall coming across pro-life/anti-abortion facts and information on any racially based website. Most use the reason, "But what about non-whites who have abortions etc.?" All I have to say is Why would I as a white racialist even care what non-whites get up to, they are not my priority or even my concern, my concern is focused on the amount of young white women murdering/aborting white babies at an average of 2000 per day in the USA.

Another important project undertaken by WAU is Adopt a Bruder. This link connects the reader with a page entitled Free The Order. This page is devoted to connecting women with members of The Order still in prison. One goal is for readers to contribute money each month to a specific prisoner while also staying in contact with their assigned prisoner.

Free The Order also allows members of the order to continue to publish their ideas as racist Odinists. The page also serves to memorialize the late David Lane. Up to this point, the rhetoric of WAU appears pretty benign. There is very little that would be noticeable as hate speech. Instead, the focus really is on educating readers about the nature and essence of Odinism. The images of women on this page reflect traditional European standards of beauty. The first such image that appears on this Web Page's banner is of a woman with long red hair dancing in the wind. Her skin is alabaster in hue and she wears clothing reminiscent of the kind of finery we might expect of a Lady at a Renaissance festival, clearly representing the kinds of ideas to which WAU would like to see Aryans return.

Most of the other images of women are presented with children and depict other situations that would emphasize traditional maternal roles (an important part of the Female Aryan Ideal Myth). Another important part of this myth is the Aryan woman's role as a helper for the men to whom she is committed. This role is evident in the projects undertaken by WAU. The Adopt a Bruder campaign involves women working to provide imprisoned men with various forms of social support. While WAU has many of their own writing projects, the Pen of the Proud basically places WAU as a publisher of the words of men. The WAU view of Aryan womanhood, however, is different from the objectified stereotype presented in *Hunter*. These are women of substance doing substantial work.

The Insurgent

The Insurgent is a Web Page constructed and maintained by Tom Metzger, the head of White Aryan Resistance (WAR). Metzger has been a highly visible figure in the hate movement since the early 1980s (Hamm, 1993). Against a black backdrop, the reader first notices "Tom Metzger Available for Interviews and Lectures" in bright blue lettering outlined in flames. Below this message is a menacing wolf baring its teeth and poised for attack. WAR has long used this image to project an identity that is powerful and threatening to its enemies. Below this image is a picture of a powerful, sexually provocative white woman gripping the face of a black man with a look of malice on her face. Beside this image appears the lettering, "White is coming." This is followed by a memorial to David Lane and a variety of links to hate-centered Internet sites, WAR-produced videos featuring Metzger, and YouTube videos that support features of Metzger's beliefs.

On the left of the page is an extensive navigation bar consisting of, but not limited to, headings that allow the reader access to (a) WAR's radio club, (b) Tom Metzger's positions, (c) David Lane's extensive writings that lay the intellectual foundation for Racist Pre-Christian Paganism, (d) Ben Klassen's writings that lay a foundation for the race religion of Creativity (including *The White Man's Bible*), (e) information about white prisoners of war, (f) racist computer games, (g) racist artwork, (h) racist jokes, (i) racist cartoons, (j) books and articles useful for understanding Tom Metzger's White Separatist position, and (k) merchandise that may be purchased from WAR. As this suggests, The Insurgent is complicated in a variety of ways. First, The Insurgent contains as much information as any racist Web Page that we have encountered. Second, this Web Page presents information through a variety of channels (articles, position statements, the publications of past leaders in the hate movement, videos, cartoons, and artwork, to name only a few). Third, the Web Page allows readers to satisfy a variety of pleasures through their hate. For example, readers may play games that permit them to enact their hate against their enemies. Readers may find humor through the racist jokes and cartoons. Readers may admire artwork that represents cherished values and identities (e.g., Pagan heroes). Readers may view the email messages of others that reinforce their own racist views, providing what Haslett described as the pleasure of certitude (see chapter two). Finally, readers may experience the pleasure of learning because this site effectively presents readers with the intellectual underpinnings of the hate movement. Potential White Separatists may read Metzger's relatively brief positions to become acclimated to this worldview. Those with more extensive knowledge of Metzger's White Separatist position may delve into the extensive writings of Lane and

Klassen. For these reasons, our analysis of The Insurgent Web Page will provide significant and extensive insights into the intellectual/ideological foundation of the broader hate movement.

In the coming pages, we argue that the discourse of The Insurgent pursues the hate stratagem described throughout this chapter. As we do so, we make note of the use of the myths that constitute a significant part of the collective memory of the U.S. hate movement.

Inflaming of the emotions of the in-group

We begin our discussion of the hate stratagem with a reference to Ben Klassen's *White Man's Bible*. Because we will draw on this text several times in our discussion, it is appropriate to say a few things about the religion known as Creativity. The *White Man's Bible* consists of 73 chapters, or "Credos." This religion is described by Klassen as "a truly all-inclusive religion, a four dimensional religion based upon the philosophy of a Sound Mind in a Sound Body in a Sound Society in a Sound Environment." Consequently, Klassen writes extensively about proper diet (primarily the consumption of raw vegetables) and medicine. He believes that a sound environment means that white people should dedicate themselves to the protection of the environment. A sound society means primarily a homogenous and white society. Klassen uses these four philosophical commitments to make his hatred seem more reasonable and logical. For example, after he discusses the toxin of meat and disease, he turns to the "toxin and disease of Jews, Blacks, and the other mud races."

It should not be surprising that a religion dedicated to the advancement of the white race would spend a good deal of time praising the white race. This is, indeed, so. Klassen explains in his foreword:

> Our insignia was designed to reflect our emphasis on racial polarization. The "W," of course, stands for the great and noble White Race. The crown indicates that we are the *aristocrats* of Nature's creation. The halo reaffirms our vow to guard and sanctify our *precious blood lines as the most sacred* value on the face of the earth. (emphasis added)

In his position statement on "Rights," Metzger echoes this when he claims that WAR believes in a natural (white) Aristocracy. Later in the foreword, Klassen explains:

> The White Man has made astounding, yes fabulous, progress in the field of science and technology in the last few centuries and especially so in the last few decades, all due to the process of "experiment," that is, probing Nature with set questions and

accepting her answers, and then using reason and common sense in fitting together those answers into an ever widening mosaic of knowledge.

In Credo 1, Klassen presents the Golden Rule of Creativity: "What is good for the White Race is the highest virtue; what is the bad for the White Race is the ultimate sin." Because white people are "responsible for all civilization" and are the "summit of nature's scheme" (Credo 22), it is logically extended that what is good for the white race is good for the world because even Hindu and Chinese civilizations "are the result of White invaders" (Credo 2).

While Klassen believes that the present generation of white people have stalled, due to the infiltration of Jews into white cultures, he is confident that white people, organized around a religion intended to advance white interests, can reverse this situation: "With our present-day knowledge, with the program of Creativity, and with 500 million White people as the basis of our gene pool, we can build a world that would bedazzle the early Americans and the ancient Romans alike" (Credo 17).

This myth of whites as the builders of civilization is also reflected in some of the artwork in The Insurgent. The art available on The Insurgent reminds us of posters that one can imagine on a White Separatist's wall. One such poster presents the image of a strong, good-looking white man wearing a hard hat and work shirt. In the background is the skyline of a city, a bridge resembling the Golden Gate Bridge, and an airplane in ascent. At the top of the poster are the words, "White Men Built this Nation," and at the bottom of the poster, "White Men *are* this Nation!!" So, this poster proffers that not only are white men responsible for building our society, but the appropriate American identity is a white identity (this discussion suggests a myth not identified in previous work, the White Man as Society Builder Myth).

Also within the art section are several posters that portray Aryans as the inheritors of a grand and glorious Pagan, Viking tradition. As discussed in chapter two, the initiated "reader" of these posters will understand that these posters connect the reader to this glorious past by "blood" that is pure, regal, and makes one a part of a community (or folk) superior to all others (Gardell, 2003). These posters provide readers with a more visual and tangible way of identifying with this Anglo-Saxon past. One such poster depicts a Viking warrior leaning against the head of a Viking ship. The top of the poster is bordered in Celtic knots. At the feet of the Viking ship is a representation of Mjolnir, Thor's hammer, long understood as a symbol of power among racist and non-racist Pagans. Above the Viking's head the reader finds the message: "As Our Ancestors Before Us, Our Kinsmen Must Always be Prepared to Fight—For There is Nothing More Horrible than Cultural or National Obliteration." It should be noted that for each "t" in this comment stands an upward pointing arrow. This upward pointing arrow, the Tyre rune, is the racist Pagan symbol for warfare and battle (Waltman, 2010-a).

Another such example can be found in a poster with two shirtless Aryan men. The man in the background is a Viking specter holding a battle-ax in his left hand. The man in the foreground is a modern man wearing a Mjolnir pendant. Throughout the poster, racist Pagan symbols are situated in highly visible ways. A Celtic cross is evident on the modern Aryan's hammer. A Norse rune is placed in the bottom left-hand corner (this rune expresses faith in Odinism and was later adopted by the German Nazis). Above and beside the men is the message, "If one day we can visualize and create a new yet very old white awareness who, conscious of soul, race, and history, unhesitatingly proclaims the old yet new values, then around this nucleus will gather all who stumble in darkness though rooted in ancient soil of our European homeland." Here again we have the image of White Man as Builder of Society against this backdrop of the "superior" Aryan Pagan bloodlines.

Within the art section are several posters of Viking warriors with similar messages supplementing the visual imagery and written messages with various runes. One rune that is frequently present is the Volknot, the knot of the slain, represented by three interlinking triangles. This symbol is often worn, or tattooed into the skin (Waltman, 2010-a), as a symbol of one's willingness to give their life to Odin in battle.

Readers of The Insurgent learn to view Aryans as regal, precious builders of high culture, and superior to all other races. Readers also will see more explicit denigration of those defined as the out-group.

Denigration of out-group identity

The enemies of the Aryan race are denigrated and dehumanized in many and varied ways in order to encourage readers to view them as different and more like objects than people. This is accomplished effectively through the use of humor in the Jokes and Cartoons sections of The Insurgent.

While humor may be enjoyable, it is far from being a simple construct. Meyer (2000) argues that humor serves four social functions. Humor enhances group identification by promoting a sense of belonging and commonality among group members. While humor may unite a group, it may also promote group differentiation by contrasting the in-group with an out-group (the object of humor). Communicators may use humor to encapsulate their views into memorable phrases or anecdotes, thus clarifying their position. Finally, humor may serve to enforce social or group norms by "making fun of" behaviors or attitudes that deviate from the group's expectations. As this suggests, humor often may be used for strategic and political reasons

(Waltman & Davis, 2004). We argue that The Insurgent uses humor quite strategically.

Numerous cartoons depict Mexicans as exclusively dirty, unkempt, lacking in personal responsibility, and a drag on society. One such unkempt Mexican is presented holding an outline of the United States that is labeled "United States of Mexico." The artist has posed the question: "Hey, White man. Where will you go when *this* happens?" The artist is drawing on a reality that many white people fear, specifically, that within a generation, white people will be in the minority in the United States (Roberts, 2008). Other cartoons explain this by alluding to the large number of illegal immigrants coming into the United States. When Mexican women are represented in cartoons, they are almost always shown as being pregnant. Such images depict Mexicans as a drain on public resources and as taking jobs from Americans. One cartoon presents a drawing of a naked, pregnant Mexican woman with the message: "This remarkable medical information just in! Finally, an answer to the age-old scientific mystery. How do Mexicans reproduce so rapidly? Research has revealed their female offspring are actually born pregnant!"

Interestingly, a writer in the "Women" heading of The Insurgent's Position section denigrates minorities in order to appeal to racist men to treat the women of the hate movement in less demeaning ways. The writer explains:

> It has come to the attention of several White racist females that there are some "conservative, Christian, right-wingers" amongst us who want NOT the survival of the White race, but for a return to the days when women were submissive and silent and tolerant of the intolerable. While I agree the feminist movement has done severe damage to our race, it disgusts me that you (they?) would use our movement as a means of *muddying* White women by urging them to act like mindless breeders with the brains of a sub-Saharan n-word. (emphasis added)

The writer explains that sexist white men are acting like their enemies and would have white women act like the enemies of the Aryan race:

> Those who expect White women to act like muds have insulted our honor.... Even the thought of being treated like a mud insults us! We are not tortillas. Perish the thought that we'll be White on the outside, but non-white on the inside.... Our fighting spirit prevents us from acting in such a despicable manner.... Stop whining about strong White women and look to them as partners in the Struggle, rather than just ovaries with tits who provide meals, sex, house cleaning, and child care for you.

Why would sexism be a non-white attribute? The writer has explained that the inequality of women is directly linked to the actions of Jews:

> The invasion of Rome by occult Judaism, and the later evolution of occult Christian-
> ity, perpetuated some of the worst stereotypes of women. The Judeo basis for Chris-
> tianity, through the writings of the Old and the New Testaments, are very negative
> towards women. Jews in particular, operating in western society, brought in the very
> worst oppression of women. Christianity simply promoted the same negative regard
> for women.... These attitudes have had a strong influence on White European and
> American civilization.

While the writer does not make this link, it is entirely consistent with this
ideology to claim that this sexism was created by Jews in order to sow the
seeds of discontent among Aryan couples in order to create a fertile ground
for the growth of Feminism, a conspiracy that distracts white women from
the need to reproduce white children (Perry, 2001; Waltman & Davis, 2005).

In a game entitled Watch Out Behind You Hunter, the reader may play
the role of a hunter in the woods. The object of the game is to hunt down and
kill naked gay men before the gay men sneak up behind and sodomize the
hunter. The game graphically portrays the rape, complete with screams. The
player wins points by moving the hunter with arrow keys and using the space
bar to shoot potential rapists. The game certainly essentializes gay men as
driven by sexual urges and as sexual predators. This is consistent with the
observation that the hate movement has equated gay men with child predators (Perry, 2001).

Perhaps the most vitriolic denigrating of non-whites may be found in
Klassen's *White Man's Bible*. Throughout this bible, non-whites are referenced with demeaning terms with determined regularity. African Americans
are always referred to as the n-word. Klassen uses the term "muds" to refer
to any group other than Aryans. In the second Credo, the enemies of the
white race are equated with a nest of snakes under a child's bed. Klassan
asks: "How should these snakes be dealt with?" He suggests that they should
be killed immediately. One would not consider the Mother snake's perspective or feelings but only the perspective of her children.

In Credo 17, Klassen argues that only a completely white homogenous
society is acceptable to the Creativity Movement. He refers to the rich diversity of America as a "slop pail." He is disgusted by "a multi-racial society
where the 'N-word' and the scum are proud to be 'Americans' and the
Whites are ashamed to be White" (Credo 18). We see from this quotation,
once again, that many in the hate movement are motivated by defining the
American identity as a white identity.

Credo 71 involves a question-and-answer session with Klassen. The 25th
question posed reads: "Why do you use the term 'n-word' in your book instead of showing some respect for the blacks and calling them 'negroes' instead?" Klassen is stunningly honest in his response, "This is a deliberate

choice of words. As we state on page 49 in *Nature's Eternal Religion*, if we are for White racial supremacy then we must stop giving them credit and respect which they did not earn, do not deserve, and never did."

How might writers of The Insurgent deal with the very visible successes of African Americans that would seem to contradict claims that they are subhuman and intellectually, emotionally, and morally inferior to whites? Certainly, they would point to Affirmative Action programs and ZOG interference in the lives of Aryans. In the Race section of The Insurgent's Positions, the writers claim that this success is largely due to race mixing and "gene piracy." The claim is that white genes are responsible for minority social and economic progress:

Find the latest *Newsweek* magazine and examine its cover, which displays "The New Black Power" and a photograph of three "black," corporate leaders [see picture in top-right corner in this Newsweek Web Site, which had featured three mixed-race "blacks" if picture is not displayed]: http://www.msnbc.com/news/NW-front_Front.asp. "blacks" are climbing the ladder of corporate America on the genes of their white ancestors, as Marxian Jews' affirmative-action quotas force whites to elevate the negroid gene pool throughout whites' civilization. To identify the race of any mixed-race person by the racial type of just one of his/her parents is racist.

This argument allows the writers to denigrate African Americans while also praising the in-group "gene pool." From this point, the writers are able to pivot and write about the genocidal threat this poses to the Aryans. This, of course, takes us to the third characteristic of the hate stratagem.

Inflicting permanent harm on the out-group

When employing a hate stratagem, rhetors inflict permanent harm on the out-group by articulating the dangerous, immediate, and catastrophic threat they pose to the in-group. The Insurgent uses David Lane's writings in a very clever way. The Insurgent is able to use his writings to teach racist Pagan principles while simultaneously using Lane's incarceration as a concrete example of the devious and pernicious threat of ZOG and the Jewish conspiracy to destroy Aryans. Lane argues that because he was distributing a pamphlet, *The Death of the White Race*, the Jews attempted to attack him personally:

The Jewish media forced the Colorado Real Estate Commission to take away my Broker's license because I refused to sell homes to coloreds in White areas.... a White man is forced to commit Race Treason in order to be allowed to work in America.

Lane claims that this persecution extended to his trial following his arrest for the crimes he committed with Robert Matthews and The Order: "I would advise anyone in Federal custody to assume the lawyer assigned to him by the court is actually a Fed.... They are masters at making one believe they...care about one's fate." Lane described Judges as "highly skilled actors."

The Jewish-planned genocide of the Aryan race is the quintessential threat Aryans face. As alluded to previously, this threat comes, in part, from race mixing. Lane saw Jews and minorities as a source of this threat but he also blamed white women for this imminent threat:

> When Black Panthers went to prison, thousands of beautiful, young White women pledged their love. Sitting in my cell I can observe May Britt (Mrs. Sammy Davis Jr.), Nicole Brown (Mrs. O. J. Simpson), Lisa Presley (ex-Mrs. Michael Jackson), and the crème de la crème of our young White women across the country, by the millions, as they desert their race.... The women of our race by and large will not return by verbal persuasion.... Women will again have to become prizes, treasures, and possessions. White men will have to...reacquire a barbarian spirit, arm themselves and seize women, territory, power, and the needs of life, or the race will die.

Clearly, this threat is so immediate and Aryan enemies so committed to genocide that violence and the expression of power is the only real and logical response.

Klassen also describes this threat in Credo 2 of the *White Man's Bible:*

> Working towards the n-word-erization of America is the Jewish race. Pushing, clawing, propagandizing with a fury unparalleled in history, the Jews are working towards their ultimate historical goal—total enslavement of all the races of the world—and every Jew a king. Why do they want to reduce the White Man down to a mongrelized moron in order to rule the world? The question almost answers itself. Morons are easier to control than an intelligent, aggressive and belligerent opposition, such as the White Race has always been.

In the History chapter of *Revolution by Number 14,*[2] Lane describes how ZOG uses taxation to discourage large white families:

> The White race comprises about 8% of earth's population. Due to abusive taxation we have had to curtail family sizes and now we average far less than replacement. Meanwhile, our taxes are used to breed Colored families of a dozen or more children.... The relevant statistic to survival is the number of White women of childbearing age or younger. About 2% of earth's population is young White female. In addition, our masters force us to accept immigration by millions of Coloreds each year into the once White countries. Finally, the propaganda promoting inter-racial mating, particularly between White women and Colored males, is unceasing.

Lane argues that white genocide also is due to Jewish control of the idea of America and the imposition of what he terms "Counterfeit Culture":

> You can no more be both White and American than you can stop the motion of the planets. The singular intent of America in all its facets is to mix, overrun, and exterminate the White race.... If you support the aims or the continued existence of the entity known as America, then your treason cannot be calculated in the words of mortals.

In Counterfeit Culture, Lane argues that Jews have changed American U.S. culture from one of order to a culture of confusion. Therefore, he argues that the folk, members of the race, constitute what Aryans should think of as nation. Consequently, racial loyalty must supersede geographical and national boundaries.

In the Positions section of The Insurgent, under government, this distrust of the government is described in more detail by Metzger. Metzger argues that governments are basically gangs and thieves. They use taxes to steal the people's money without providing services of similar value to the money that is collected. The government is the tool that controls naive white "sheep." Governments are inherently evil because they possess an inherent desire to conquer other nations. This often creates wars in which one group of white men is pitted against another group of white men, creating another source of white genocide. The Insurgent sees all wars as "practice" for the eventual racial holy war when the military will inevitably be used against Aryans.

In Credo 29, Klassen reminds readers that this genocidal threat, while institutionalized in government and media, is fundamentally understood in group terms:

> Thus, historically, through mongrelization the "n-word" has been able to destroy every race and civilization that has been stupid enough to drag him into their midst. The Jew is utilizing every financial, legal, or propaganda means today to mongrelize White America, to pump the black blood of Africa into the veins of White America. The Jew is pushing this program with a vengeance and a fury unparalleled in history, and we might add, with astounding success. Race-mixing in America has become his supreme holy cause.

Readers of The Insurgent find an enemy and a threat to Aryans in the Jews and their minions. With this threat comes the justification for the righteous conquering of these enemies.

Rhetorically conquer the out-group

The out-group is rhetorically conquered, in part, when the rhetor expresses pleasure in the domination of the out-group. This was accomplished earlier in chapter three through what was described as the Pleasure of Murder Myth. This is accomplished in a variety of ways in The Insurgent. One interesting place in this Web Page to identify the operation of this characteristic is in the Games section. Earlier, it was argued that the game "Watch Out Behind You, Hunter" served to essentialize gays as rapists. However, the game also allows the game player to symbolically conquer gay men by hunting and killing the predatory rapists.

Another game is called Border Patrol. Unlike the hunter game just described, this game gives the game player the "shooter's perspective," and allows players to "hunt" Mexicans "jumping" the U.S./Mexican border. The Mexicans run across the computer screen at a quickened pace. The player is able to score points by shooting the "border jumpers" who explode with blood and screams when shot.

A similar game, entitled Bin Laden Liquors, also offers the game player the shooter's perspective. Players are able to manipulate a gun in a liquor store that has been ransacked. The image of Bin Laden periodically peeks from behind a liquor store counter. Again, the player is able to score points by shooting this image with a shot gun. Like the other games described above, the game is bloody and grizzly.

These games allow the players to find pleasure in their hatred by enacting the Pleasure of Murder Myth. These games also take potential Lone Wolves one step closer to actually killing minorities. By playing these games, one is able to look down the barrel of a gun and see non-Aryans explode as they fire the gun. Arguably, when the game is repeated time after time, a kind of routinization may take place in the mind of the game players, and the players may eventually come to see themselves killing their enemies. We don't want to oversimplify or suggest a causal relationship between video games and murder. Even if these video games do not lead to real murder, they do allow the player to symbolically dominate those they hate.

A cartoon found in the Stickers section of The Insurgent advocates the murder of illegal Mexican immigrants and functions to rhetorically conquer Mexicans and take pleasure in their imagined deaths. A group of Mexican immigrants look on in horror when they encounter the decapitated head of a "border jumper" stuck on a spike. The caption reads: "Hey America, want to know a way to stop the flow of illegal immigrants from Mexico? Just post a few of these along the border." A similar sticker shows American tanks, soldiers, and helicopters positioned along the U.S./Mexican border. The caption reads: "The only way to stop the flood is to cut off the flow." All of these examples rhetorically conquer the out-group by constructing an identity of Mexicans that is alienated from the rest of society. The last two cartoons explicitly portray violence against Mexicans as righteous.

Another feature of The Insurgent that allows the rhetor to symbolically conquer the Other is found in the Art section. A number of posters glorify the killing of the Aryan's enemies. A poster on page three (of four) of the Art section depicts three figures and two SS lightning bolts. The first figure is a fallen Aryan man. Kneeling beside the man is a woman holding her baby in one arm (the logical assumption is that the three are a family). In the other hand she is pointing an automatic handgun at those who have killed her husband. The woman is portraying a highly differentiated role available to women in the hate movement (Blee, 2002). She is Mother, nurturer, and a soldier for her race.

In a cartoon entitled Klan Man, the question is asked: "How do you keep the N-word off your front porch, and away from your daughter?" The second frame of the cartoon shows a frightened African American male with a handgun pointed at his face. The third frame of the cartoon simply contains the word "Kaboom."

A poster entitled "Race-Mixing" presents the image of an African American man and an attractive white woman. The white woman is holding a baby that is drawn to look almost disfigured. In the bottom left-hand corner of the poster is the figure of man with a ski mask covering his face and holding an M16. Three questions are written beside this man: "Make you wanna puke? Or, maybe cry? *How about kill?*"

Certainly, these last two poster present "race-mixing," "gene raiding," or "genocide" as the ultimate justification for the killing of Aryans' racial enemies. This is a narrative that we have seen repeated across a variety of racist texts. This Art section contains many similar examples in which the artist depicts the symbolic domination of the other.

Klassen claimed that he never advocated violence or killing. This is technically (and legally) true. However, he said a number of things that would lead his followers (such as Matt Hale and Benjamin Nathaniel Smith) to believe that the killing of the white man's enemies was justifiable and necessary. So, he does, indeed, produce discourse that symbolically dominates the Other. In Klassen's view, the only acceptable society (and eventually world) is a homogenously white world:

> I have stated in the beginning of this chapter that only a homogenous society can be stable and survive. Homogenous means one kind, the same race, and more or less the same level of intelligence, similar moral standards, similar basic goals, ideals, re-

ligion and culture.... Do we want a world populated with primitive African n-word? Of Chinese? Jews?... No, indeed, we want none of these. Our religion is not designed for n-word or mongrels, nor any of the mud races.... For us it is either all, or nothing. (Credo 17)

Where would everyone who is not white go? Klassen knows exactly what he is calling for. He simply refuses to write or speak about it, explicitly:

First of all, stop the wild influx of freeloading mud races into our midst. Today, under Jewish promotion, the illegal Mexicans are invading the United States by the millions and the government is not lifting a finger to stop them.... The Second Step we must take simultaneously with the first, is to cut off all aid.... The Third Step we must take after stopping mud migration into White countries is to expel those coloreds already here.... The Fourth Step must be one of aggression.... We will not rest until the entire world is the home of the White Race. *The rest of the procedure need not be spelled out. We will know what to do once we get started.* (Credo 21, emphasis added)

It does not take a lot of imagination, or speculation, to see that Klassen understands that "what to do" involves genocide. After all, Aryans are involved in a struggle for literal survival.

Our analysis reveals that the Web Pages examined here employ a hate stratagem to move readers from pride in their own race to ethnoviolence and murder of those who would threaten the white race. This analysis may be joined with previous work on the hate stratagem (Waltman, 2001; Waltman & Haas, 2007; R. K. Whillock, 1995) and allows us to now claim that the hate stratagem appears to be a tactic that has been used in a variety of contexts (with a variety of audiences) to encourage the oppression and murder of the Other.

Conclusion

Our analysis of hate speech on the Internet also allows us to draw broader conclusions about the nature of hate speech in that venue. We have argued that one of the defining features of myth is that it constitutes a broad social discourse that can be found in a broad range of cultural artifacts. That is, it is a form of narrative that may be encountered in a variety of places and spaces within a culture. Our analysis, when coupled with previous research on the myths that constitute a collective Aryan memory (Davis, 2005; Waltman & Davis, 2004; Waltman & Davis, 2005), illustrates the operation of overlapping myths that may be found in jokes, cartoons, novels, YouTube videos, and numerous Internet Web Pages. These ever-present myths teach that non-Aryans are less than human, a threat to the existence of the Aryan race, and that violence is an acceptable and righteous solution to Jewish contamination of their culture. Consumers of these various artifacts learn that ethnoviolence is not only justified but rather it is also an action that defines the validity of one's racist Aryan identity and is a path to self-fulfillment.

We have argued that the myths constitute the building blocks of a racist Aryan collective memory. Moreover, we have demonstrated that these myths play an important role in the operation of the hate stratagem. For example, we demonstrated that a Black Savage Myth and a Treacherous/Violent Jew Myth played an important role in the rhetorical attempt to inflict permanent harm on the out-group (the third characteristic of the hate stratagem). Similarly, the Pleasure of Murder Myth and the Independent Aryan (Lone Wolf) Myth have played important roles in the accomplishment of the fourth characteristic of the hate stratagem—the rhetorical conquering of the out-group.

Chapter 5

Nativism and Nativist Discourse

In this chapter, we examine Nativist discourse in politics and the press that seeks to vilify immigrants as hopelessly un-American, cultural pollutants, and threats to the American way of life. This discussion will remind us of claims made earlier. First, hatred is not an unusual state of mind found in abnormal individuals. We will find that hatred is far too normal and it can be a persuasive resource that many access on a daily basis. Second, this discussion will illustrate that the hatred of hate groups is consonant with the hatred of the broader society. Indeed, the reader will have the opportunity to compare the rhetoric of David Duke with the rhetoric of politicians and to observe the homology between the two. First, we discuss Nativism as a concept.

Nativist Discourse: Constructing Immigrants as a Cultural Threat

On April 14, 2009, Tom Tancredo was brought to the University of North Carolina (UNC) at Chapel Hill by the student chapter of Youth for Western Civilization (YWC) to deliver a speech about why "illegals" should be denied in-state tuition to public universities. Student and non-student protestors converged on the campus to protest the speech. Protestors successfully disrupted the speech through shouting, chants, and the breaking of one window pane. The vast majority of students, faculty, and administrators were shocked by the protestor's actions, due in no small part to UNC's historic commitment to free speech and respect for divergent views; however, this shock may have been due to ignorance of YWC's goals and rhetoric. Analysis of the previous and subsequent discourse produced by Tancredo and YWC reveals a Nativist influence that seeks to demean and vilify undocumented workers and contributes virtually nothing to a discussion of a rationally reformed immigration policy. As noted in chapter one, Tancredo and YWC are the inheritors of a rich American rhetorical tradition that has vilified and demeaned European, Chinese, Jewish, and Catholic immigrants in order to privilege American-born, white, Protestant, mostly male citizens.

In this chapter, two cases that illustrate and reflect a rising Nativism in the United States are explored: (a) a Web Page and blog maintained by YWC, including the rhetoric of former Representative Tancredo who inspires, promotes, and speaks for the group; and (b) some of the discourse surrounding Tancredo's speaking engagement at UNC. We argue that a Nativist discourse emerges from these events and texts and evidences the operation of the hate stratagem.

As discussed in chapter three, the hate stratagem is characterized by attempts to construct a positive in-group identity, attempts to denigrate the out-group identity, attempts to inflict permanent harm on the out-group identity, and the rhetorical conquering of the out-group. (In our analysis of hate group discourse, we found that this last characteristic is observed in calls for violence or the celebration of real or potential violence.) We begin with a discussion of Nativism and Nativist hate speech in the mainstream media over the past few years.

Recent Nativist Discourse in the United States

We want to be clear about what Nativist discourse is and what it is not. It is discourse that has been used to construct immigrants and non-Westerners as different and unable or unwilling to assimilate to Western Civilization and American values. Nativist discourse is not oriented toward a rational engagement of American immigration policy or a rational guest worker program. Indeed, one could believe American immigration policies and problems lack coherence and are a detriment to America in multiple ways. One might even recognize growing research that implies that many undocumented Mexican workers do not truly desire American citizenship because they have been leaving the United States during poor economic conditions (Preston, 2009). Such positions need not vilify undocumented Mexican workers. Documented workers and undocumented workers go to where employment can be found because they want to protect their families and prepare the most profitable future for them (Cuardos, 2007). Nativist discourse, however, is focused on demonizing immigrants as un-American and positioning them as a threat to "real" Americans.

America has sustained a Nativist movement since its earliest days. Those who wanted America for Americans have sought to prevent the immigration of Catholics, Chinese, Italians, Irish, and, today, Mexicans and immigrants from other Latin American countries. Whether Nativist voices emanate from an organized hate group or from the "mainstream" of American society, the messages and the fears are the same: They see America as under attack and threatened by hordes of "non-whites" invading America, threatening our

Western traditions and values. As in years past, Hispanic immigrants are viewed as unwilling to assimilate into America by leaving their traditions and heritage (and, hence, their identity) at the U.S. border. Anti-immigrant rhetoric has reached a nearly fevered pitch over the past few years. Politicians, television and radio personalities, and Nativist activists, such as The Minutemen and the Republic of Texas, have played a steady drumbeat that has vilified and dehumanized undocumented workers, typically referred to as "illegal aliens" or "illegals." Such language not only highlights their legal (or lack thereof) status, but it positions them as outsiders and non-persons. This dehumanizing language also constructs persons in the United States without documentation as "criminals," an inaccuracy because undocumented entry to this country is a civil, not criminal, violation. As in the past, Nativists see illegal aliens coming to America for, ironically, two mutually exclusive purposes: (a) to exploit America's social welfare programs and benefits, and (b) to take jobs away from Americans (Perry, 2001).

Some Nativist rhetoric also attributes a conspiratorial motive of Mexican immigration to repopulate the Southwest and "re-take" land in the United States that had originally been a part of Mexico known as "Aztlán." Aztlán is comprised of Texas, New Mexico, Arizona, California, Nevada, and Colorado (Just Build the Fence Blog, 2007). Thus, Nativists see illegal immigration as a literal invasion of the United States. On November 18, 2009, Jim Quinn, of the syndicated radio show *The War Room with Quinn and Rose*, said in response to Mexico City's plan to distribute erectile dysfunction drugs to elderly men: "Viva Viagra. Well—after all, who's gonna father the next generation of illegals to come *swarming* across the border in their effort to re-conquer the Southwest?" (cited in SPLC Intelligence Report, 2009, p. 4; emphasis added). Quinn objectified and essentialized undocumented immigrants by calling them illegals as well as dehumanized them by equating them with a swarm of insects. If Quinn's listeners think of undocumented workers as insects, then it is only a short step for them to think of them as unworthy of human respect or as even deserving of violence, a bug to be squashed.

Accompanying this vitriol has been a steady rise from 2003 to 2007 in hate crimes targeting Latinos, a 40% increase over the four-year period (Potok, 2009; SPLC Intelligence Report, 2008). Given that F.B.I. statistics on hate crimes tend to be notoriously unreliable, and the fact that many undocumented workers typically avoid reporting hate crimes to authorities, this is likely a conservative estimate of the increase in hate crimes targeting undocumented Latinos. A few recent cases serve to personalize these statistics. In July 2008, in Suffolk County, New York, seven high school students

"went Beaner jumping" (as they put it) when they stabbed a 38-year-old Ec-
uadorian man, Marcelo Lucero (SPCL Intelligence Report, 2009). According
to the killers' friends, this was but one in a string of such "jumpings" the
seven had conducted. Lucero had lived in the United States for 16 years and
worked in a dry cleaning store.

Prior to Lucero's murder, the community had participated in hate-filled
debates over immigration law and Latino day laborers who had been moving
to the area since the early 1990s (SPCL Intelligence Report, 2009). Immediately following Lucero's death, County Executive Steve Levy would add to
the hateful rhetoric by claiming that if this murder had occurred in neighbor-
ing Nassau County, "It would be a one-day story." Following a pattern we
reference in the following chapters, Levy would quickly apologize for his
remark. Three weeks later, eight young men, shouting ethnic slurs, would assault two Latino men as they left a restaurant (SPCL Intelligence Report,
2009). Recently, a report by the Southern Poverty Law Center demonstrated
that this violence is a result of a climate of hate. Mark Potok is quoted in the
report:

> For 10 years, political leaders and anti-immigration activists in Suffolk County have
> demonized Latino immigrants and the police have appeared indifferent to their
> plight.... We should not be surprised that Latinos are regularly targeted for violence
> and harassment. (SPCL Report, 2009a, p. 5)

Four months earlier in Shenandoah, Pennsylvania, four male high school
students murdered Luis Ramirez, a Mexican immigrant, by beating him to
death. Two of the teenagers, Brandon Piekarsky and Derrick Donchak, were
charged with aggravated assault. Sixteen-year-old honor student and wide
receiver, Piekarsky, who allegedly initiated the attack, is reported to have
turned to Ramirez's friends and told them to "get the F--k out of Shenandoah, Penn., or be killed." (SPLC Intelligence Report, 2008, p. 7). Despite
this remark and the fact that teens had spray-painted racial graffiti on Ramirez's car, Shenandoah Police Chief and Town Manager claimed that the
crime was not racially motivated. As in the Suffolk County murders, the killing followed tensions produced between undocumented immigrants and
county legislation intended to punish employers and landlords from hiring or
renting to undocumented workers. After 12 potential jurors were dismissed
because they indicated that they could not deliver an impartial verdict in a
case involving a Latino immigrant (Hamill, 2009), an all-white jury convicted the two of simple assault in spite of the fact that prosecutors presented
evidence that Ramirez had been attacked by 6 white teenagers who shouted
racial epithets as they kicked him to death. In December 2009, however,

Piekarsky and Donchak were indicted on federal hate crimes charges and the Police Chief of Shenandoah and two of his officers were charged with obstruction of justice in their handling of the case:

> The federal indictment alleges that, among other acts, Police Chief Matthew Nestor, Lt. William Moyer and Officer Jason Hayes wrote false and misleading reports about Mr. Ramírez's death after hearing information that would point the finger at some of the teenagers. The indictment said that at the time of Mr. Ramírez's death, Officer Hayes was dating Mr. Piekarsky's mother, and Lieutenant Moyer's son was a freshman on the high school football team with all of those involved. Lieutenant Moyer was also charged with tampering with evidence, tampering with a witness and making a false statement to the F.B.I. (Hamill, 2009)

It would appear that hate of Mexicans was so institutionalized in Shenandoah that the teenagers allegedly felt little reason to restrain their violent impulses, and the justice system in Shenandoah was allegedly incapable of distributing justice.

As noted, the voices of several different groups of people co-mingle and contribute to an environment that encourages people to fear and hate undocumented workers, perhaps even Latino American citizens. These voices come from Nativist activists, many of whom belong to hate groups. Other voices come from mainstream sources, such as politicians and radio and television personalities (Perry, 2001). These voices are motivated by a range of potential factors. Politicians may "bash" immigrants in order to curry favor with voters. Radio and television personalities may appeal to audience prejudices and fears in order to achieve higher ratings and/or pander to an audience. Those audience members may be motivated to listen to people who tell them that their problems are due to undocumented workers who take their jobs, who depress their wages, and who contribute to economic conditions that make them more and more vulnerable to market circumstances. When economic conditions worsen, they see U.S. companies seeking greater profits by closing shops in the United States and moving them overseas where foreign, often dark-skinned, employees will work for much lower wages. It is within this frame that they see undocumented workers entering the United States to compete for a shrinking supply of jobs. Some politicians, activists, and radio and television personalities may see undocumented workers as a symptom of unsecured borders that represent a larger problem. They claim that if undocumented workers can enter the United States so easily, it is also possible for terrorists easily to enter the country to harm America.

The point is that immigration is a complicated issue and different voices emerge for a variety of reasons. How should we evaluate these different voices? We argue that it is important to distinguish these voices according to the degree to which they vilify undocumented workers as opposed to focusing on the legitimate issue of immigration. We do not suggest that this is an easy distinction to make. To the contrary, this is likely to be a difficult distinction to make, rendering this analysis all the more important. We examine some of these voices to highlight Nativist rhetoric that is more focused on bashing undocumented workers than on exploring solutions to U.S. immigration policy.

Lou Dobbs, of CNN, became a populist voice for the middle class in America. Presumed to be a "forgotten class" in American public life, Dobbs is more than willing to point out when politicians and policy work to erode middle-class lifestyle and values. He argues that the middle class in the United States has many enemies (corporate lobbyists, greedy executives, weak journalists, corrupt politicians), but illegal immigrants pose a unique threat to the middle class because they steal American jobs, which depresses wages, and pose a danger to American lives (Leonhardt, 2007). In 2005, Beirich and Potok of the Southern Poverty Law Center noted that for two years Dobbs had been preaching against the dangers of illegal immigration in a segment called "Broken Borders."

According to *New York Times* writer Leonhardt, Dobbs claimed in his April 20, 2005, show that "the *invasion* of illegal *aliens* is threatening the health of many Americans" (Leonhardt, 2007; emphasis added). A CNN reporter, Christine Romans, then observed that, according to Dr. Madeleine Cosman, there were 900 cases of leprosy in the United States in 40 years. However, over the past 3 years, there had been 7,000 cases of leprosy reported in the United States. Lou Dobbs response was, "Incredible." But CNN was incorrect. Because according to the National Hansen's Disease (i.e., Leprosy) Program, the official statistic is that there have been 7,000 cases in the past 30 years (not in the past 3). This is classic Nativist rhetoric. The United States should fear this "invasion" of "diseased aliens" bringing a historically feared illness that result in disfigurement and social isolation. The point of the argument is clear: When Americans see a brown body they should see filth and disease and be repulsed. They should see brown skin and think Leper colony.

Mr. Dobbs's reporting gained national attention in 2007 when Leslie Stahl of *60 Minutes* prepared a profile of him. She discovered Dobbs's 2005 report and questioned its accuracy. With the certitude of fundamentalism, Mr. Dobbs claimed: "Well, I can tell you this. If we reported it, it's a fact." (Leonhardt, 2007) Dobbs would repeat the argument when he defended himself against the *60 Minutes* profile and when he defended himself against charges of being wrong and unfair made against him by the Southern Poverty Law Center. Dobbs would also claim that fully one third of the people in U.S. prisons were illegal immigrants. This statistic has been demonstrated to be false (Leonhardt, 2007; Potok, 2007) and is closer to 6%.

Dobbs is not the only commentator to press a Nativist agenda. Indeed, many commentators press claims bashing undocumented workers that have been proven to be false. An example of this capitalized on the recent burst in the housing bubble that fueled an economic recession. The rumor: Undocumented immigrants held 5 million bad mortgages in the United States:

> On October 9, the conservative online news site *Drudge Report* included a link to a story on the website of conservative talk radio KFYI-AM in Phoenix that said HUD had reported that 5 million illegal immigrants held bad mortgages. That same day the *Phoenix Business Journal* posted an article stating that a HUD spokesman said there was "no basis" for the 5 million figure, and that the agency had no data reflecting the number of bad mortgages held by illegal immigrants. (Keller, 2009a, p. 25)

That evening, Roger Hedgecock would report the statistic as a hard fact on *Lou Dobbs Tonight*. Rush Limbaugh added to this falsehood when he claimed that "HUD was admitting 5 million illegal aliens were given mortgages…with fake Social Security numbers and so forth to go out and purchase homes that they didn't have to pay back" (cited in Keller, 2009a). This version of the falsehood would be repeated by Jim Quinn on *The War Room with Quinn & Rose* (Keller, 2009a).

Recent examples of Nativist discourse are being expressed through the power of the state. Long-term frustrations with the problems accompanying illegal immigration made Arizona state politicians and voters susceptible to "solutions" that appear to be doing more to divide Arizonans than to solve the problems of Arizona's porous border. Signed into law by the Governor, the law, SB 1070, requires immigrants to carry documents proving their citizenship and requires police officers to stop and check anyone "suspected" of being in the country illegally. The law also allowed for the disciplining of any police officers who failed to check and arrest a "suspicious" illegal immigrant (Eckholm, 2010).

Those opposed to the law, including many of the State's Attorney Generals, believed that the law would lead to racial profiling and lawsuits have been filed by human rights organizations and human rights activists (Archibold, 2010). Those supporting the bill are just as adamant that the bill would not lead to racial profiling. Opponents of the law have viewed it as legislative Nativism because the law does nothing to stop immigration at the border. Moreover, the law adds no new sanctions to the many Arizonan families and businesses that hire illegal immigrants. Put differently, the law sanctions brown people while ignoring white people who contribute to the problem by exploiting cheap illegal immigrant labor.

The law is dividing Arizonans from other Americans. A host of groups cancelled conventions in Arizona and consumers, including the city government of Los Angeles, began boycotting products made in Arizona (Duke, 2010). However, the law also has supporters outside Arizona. Eighteen other states are planning legislation based on the Arizona bill. At the time of this writing, United States courts have offered no legal opinion on the Arizona law.

Less than a month after this law was passed, Arizona passed additional legislation that would prohibit public schools from teaching courses that would teach Latino students to value their own heritage and culture (known as ethnic studies classes). These courses have been a part of the Tucson Public School curriculum for 14 years and are supported by a court-ordered desegregation budget (Santa Cruz, 2010). Those supporting this bill argue that the bill is needed to prevent teaching the "overthrow of the government" or that Latino students are an "oppressed" group (CNN Politics, 2010). Teachers in the Tucson school system are quick to note that their curriculum teaches neither of these points and they complain that no politician has visited their classes or contacted any teacher in the ethnic studies curriculum (Barr, 2010; Fernandez, 2010). The Anti-Defamation League studied the curriculum for more than a year, more time than the Superintendent and the legislature combined and concluded that the curriculum did none of the things the Arizona Legislature claimed and was a program that should be encouraged rather than discouraged (Fernandez, 2010).

New Mexico appears to be dealing with a larger proportion of Mexican American and illegal immigrants than Arizona while also understanding how to live in tolerance. New Mexico Governor Bill Richardson, however, is concerned that Arizona's actions may bode badly for New Mexico: "There is a decided positive in encouraging biculturalism and people working and living together instead of inciting tension. The worry I have about Arizona is it is going to spread. It arouses the nativist instinct in people" (Archibold, 2010).

Nativism Goes to College

This is the discursive world in which the protestors of April 14 viewed the Tancredo event. They saw Nativist rhetoric as a clear and present danger to the lives of both undocumented workers and Mexican-American citizens. This is important because many in the UNC community developed an image of those protestors from second hand reports and media stories that framed the protestors as obnoxious and rude children with no respect for freedom of speech or civil discourse. What were lost on many in the media, and in the community, were the reasons for their rude and disruptive behavior. Not a single story in the local media covered the purpose of Tancredo's speech because the speech never occurred. The protestors became the story. We attempt to provide a more complete and less simplistic view of the protest in the following pages.

Most in the UNC community saw the event as an opportunity to allow Tancredo to "show himself" to the community and to use that as a resource to oppose Nativism. Having taken a group of students to Tancredo's speech, the first author was present in the room when he was shouted down by protestors. We offer an account that is grounded in those first-hand observations, and then we discuss how the media and the university framed the event differently. Subsequently, we examine the Tancredo's actions and the rhetoric of the national organization of YWC. Our critique of YWC will focus on their national organization's Web Page and blog. Aside from bringing Tancredo to campus and being one of the targets of protestors' obscenities, the student organization of YWC did nothing to explicitly inject hate into the UNC community, during or following the protest.

Before we turn to YWC's Web Page and the protest of Tancredo's "No In-State Tuition for Illegals" speech at UNC, we look to some of his previous observations on Hispanics and undocumented workers. Few, if any, protestors or audience members came to that event with no knowledge of Tancredo's past positions on these issues. He is well-known for his shocking rhetoric and political advertisements that we discuss below. Regrettably, the local media reporting on the protest failed to consider these comments when they framed this story, choosing to portray him as a victim whose right to free speech was denied by intolerant protestors. His right to express his opinion on an important issue of the day was denied. But he is far from a victim with a history of civil discourse. Instead, he has a history of Nativist rhetoric in which he has constructed "illegal aliens" and Hispanics in demeaning and dehumanizing ways while portraying them as a threat to American democracy and Western Civilization. We discuss some examples of this rhetoric and illustrate how they evidence the characteristics of the hate stratagem.

Tom Tancredo and his Nativist rhetoric

On November 29, 2006, it was reported that Tancredo, while visiting Miami with other Republicans, referred to Miami as different from the rest of the country, and he blamed Hispanic immigration as the reason for the high crime rate in Miami: "You just pick it [Miami] up and take it and move it someplace.... You would never know you're in the United States of America. You would certainly say you're in a Third World country" (cited in Epstein, 2006; Kovacs, 2006). Apparently, Tancredo saw Hispanics living and working in Miami and observed a Third World country that was not a part of the United States, instead of as a place where different ethnicities live and work while influencing and enriching one another. This prompted then Governor Jeb Bush to say: "Miami is a wonderful city filled with diversity and heritage that we choose to celebrate, not insult." It is clear that Tancredo, and his team, want listeners to think of poverty and crime when they see Hispanic people who continue to celebrate their cultures. This is clearly an attempt to denigrate Hispanics and Hispanic cultures (the second characteristic of the hate stratagem).

On December 8, 2007, Tancredo went further to suggest that Hispanics who failed to reject their culture are a danger to American democracy and Western values. As we have discussed elsewhere in this text, this discursive tactic attempts to vilify and inflict permanent harm on the out-group (the third characteristic of the hate stratagem). When Univision (a Spanish language media station) hosted a Republican Presidential Primary debate, Tancredo elected to boycott the debate as a protest against any institution that would not force all citizens to speak and think in English. He would criticize the other candidates for participating in the debate:

> It is the law that to become a naturalized citizen of this country you must have knowledge and understanding of English, including a basic ability to read, write, and speak the language.... So what may I ask are our presidential candidates doing participating in a Spanish speaking debate? Pandering comes to mind.... America has been a melting pot of people from all over the world *but it can not survive as a nation* if our immigrants do not assimilate. A common language is essential to that goal. Bilingualism is a great asset for any individual but it has perilous consequences for a nation. As such, a Spanish debate has no place in a presidential campaign. (Terkel, 2007; emphasis added)

This "Spanish debate," of course, took place in English but was translated to Spanish for viewers of Univision. Tancredo treated this "Spanish" debate as a threat to American democracy. He would also make this claim more explicitly in a stop in Hereford, Arizona, at the ranch of the head of a group called American Border Patrol. He argued that the cost of illegal immigration is more than the cost of education:

> There's an issue that is so much broader than all that, so much more serious. It is the issue of our culture itself, and *whether we will survive*. (Merritt, 2007; emphasis added)

Tancredo went on to provide a concrete image of what that failure to protect our Western Civilization from immigrants of other cultures might look like when he described his 2004 trip to Beslan, Russia, shortly after Chechnya terrorists killed more than 300 people at an elementary school:

> I tell you this story for a reason. As I come down here through Sierra Vista toward the border, I am telling you that *there is nothing, absolutely nothing, that guarantees that the same kind of thing can't happen here in the United States*. And why could it happen? Because our borders are not defended. (Merritt, 2007; emphasis added)

Prior to this comment, Tancredo would release a Presidential campaign advertisement in which he equated Hispanic immigration with Hispanic gangs and crime, employing a menacing voice-over. The transcript was posted on Blog4President:

> Hi. I'm Tom Tancredo. I approved this ad because someone needs to say it. Mothers killed. Children executed. Vicious Central American gangs on U.S. soil. Pushing drugs. Raping kids. Destroying lives. Thanks to gutless politicians who refuse to defend our borders. One man dares to say what should be done. Secure our borders. Deport those who don't belong. Make sure they never come back. (Mike [Web log message], 2007)

In this 32-second ad, Tancredo employs pictures of bloody, lifeless bodies to correspond with each of the "consequences" mentioned in the ads (e.g., Mothers executed, raping kids). This ad clearly constructs immigrants as predators determined to thrive in America by preying on U.S. citizens (the third characteristic of the hate stratagem).

Employing suspicious logic, Tancredo ran another ad that linked immigration with terrorism:

> There are consequences to open borders beyond the 20 million aliens who have come to take our jobs. *Islamic terrorists now freely roam U.S. soil.* Jihadists who froth with hate here to do as they have in London, Spain, Russia. The price we pay for spineless politicians who refuse to defend our borders *against those who come to kill*. (Tancredo, 2006; emphasis added)

Thus far, the Islamic terrorists that have attacked the United States were in the United States legally, and there seems to be little evidence to support the assertion that Islamic terrorists "freely roam" U.S. soil. These two ads also add another set of enemies out to destroy America: U.S. politicians who are willing to sacrifice their own culture to waves of un-American immigrants because they are "gutless" and "spineless."

Tancredo has spoken at public events for YWC before. On February 25, 2009, he spoke at American University, again sponsored by YWC, where students from four Washington, D. C. area schools converged to protest his speech. With a large police presence, students were pressured to silent protest. According to Marissa Lang, editor of the University of Maryland's independent student newspaper, *The Diamondback:* "Tancredo's speech singled out both Latinos and Muslims as 'problem' cultures that are contributing to the fragmentation of American society." Tancredo specifically claimed:

> We are forcing children to participate in a world that promotes Muslim sensitivities.... We are losing the relevance of citizenship. Being an American used to mean something. We have every right to be proud of who we are. *And this is not something I think we can survive.* (SPLC [GALEO Web log posting] 2009; emphasis added)

Wherever he delivers remarks like these, Tancredo claims that he is not prejudiced but merely concerned for the survival of his country and his culture. This is a claim that is common on Web Pages maintained by hate groups and is another illustration of the third characteristic of the hate stratagem. For example, the Knights of the Ku Klux Klan claim not to hate African Americans and Jews but to "love their own race" (Waltman, 2003). As one student who heard his speech claimed, *"He said he's not being racist, but just look at the people he's railing against. What color are they?"* (SPLC [GALEO Web log posting], 2009; emphasis added). Later in April, Tancredo was not permitted to deliver a speech to Providence University because his views on immigration were unacceptable to the Roman Catholic administration of Providence, a clear bastion of Roman-Catholic liberalism with an anti-Western agenda (Baron, 2009).

Of course, there is also much to be learned about Tancredo and his motivations when he speaks in public in ways that are not highly scripted through a planned manuscript. Nativist rhetoric was bald, on record, and abundant during the nomination of Judge Sonia Sotomayor to Supreme Court Justice. His words about the first Latina Supreme Court Justice help us to understand his goals when speaking for Youth for Western Civilization.

Judge Sotomayor at the annual Judge Mario G. Olmos Law and Cultural Diversity Memorial Lecture at the University of California, Berkeley, commented: "I would hope that a wise Latina woman with the richness of her experiences would more often than not reach a better conclusion than a white male who hasn't lived that life." She claimed to be disagreeing with Sandra Day O'Connor and Ruth Bader Ginsburg that a wise old man and a wise old woman would reach similar conclusions in a court decision (Savage, 2009). Sotomayor would distance herself from this remark during her hearing. Tancredo decided to conclude from this sentence that Sotomayor is a racist, as he claimed on MSNBC's *The Ed Show:*

> I'm telling you she appears to be a racist. She said things that are racist in any other context. That's exactly how *we* would portray it and there's no one who would get on the Supreme Court saying a thing like that *except for a Hispanic woman.* (cited in Frick, 2009; emphasis added)

In the same sitting, Tancredo admitted that he "did not know anything about the cases she reviewed" because "he is not a lawyer." Sotomayor's comment may have been ill-conceived and inelegant, but it seems far from racist compared to the arc of Nativist rhetoric we have discussed thus far. Unfortunately, Tancredo would go further on May 28, 2009, and make claims that were demonstrably false.

On CNN's *Rick Sanchez Show,* Tancredo would claim that Judge Sotomayor belonged to a racist organization, the National Council of La Raza (NCLR), which is a "Latino KKK without the hoods or the nooses" (Kuznia, 2009). He then claimed that "the logo for La Raza is 'all for the race, nothing for the rest.'" The problem is that this is not the motto (or logo) of the NCLR (Kuznia, 2009). Instead, the group's motto is much less controversial: "Strengthening America by promoting the advancement of Latino families" (Crile, 2009). Moreover, NCLR is mainstream enough to qualify Cecilia Muñoz, Senior Vice President for NCLR's Office of Research, Advocacy, and Legislation, to be nominated to become the Director of Intergovernmental Affairs in the Obama administration (Binavedes, 2009; Latino Talk, 2009).

What about this controversial motto referenced by Tancredo? If it is not the motto of NCLR, from where did he remember it? According to Crile (2009), it is the motto of a separatist and nationalist student organization from the 1960s, Movimiento Estudiantil Chicano de Aztlán or, in English, "Chicano Student Movement of Aztlán." According to Wikipedia, the motto of this group is "Por La Raza todo, Fuera de La Raza nada," which translates to "For the Race, everything, outside the Race, nothing." Aztlán, of course, is the term intended to represent a conspiracy of radicalized Hispanics determined to retake the Southwestern United States for Mexico. It appears that Tancredo sees an organization that is intended to promote the advancement of Latino families—NCLR—and sees a radical separatist group from the

1960s. Intentionally or unintentionally, this is how Tancredo wants people to think about NCLR (and about a Latina nominee to the Supreme Court).

While protestors prevented Tancredo from completing his speech at the University of North Carolina, we have a clear understanding of his view of immigrants who refuse to leave their culture at our borders. He sees immigrants, legal or illegal, as a clear and present danger to individual American citizens, American democracy, and Western Civilization. The protestors at UNC viewed his speech as a danger to lives in their community. This concern seems warranted given the relationships we have discussed between the anti-immigrant vitriol and the hate-motivated murders we discussed earlier. We now turn to the protest that occurred on the UNC campus and on the YWC Web Page and blog.

Nativism and shame visit the University of North Carolina

Invited by UNC's student chapter of Youth for Western Civilization, Tom Tancredo was to speak April 14, 2009, against providing in-state tuition for undocumented workers/students. Since immigrants in the country without documentation face monumental obstacles to enroll in universities, it is difficult to imagine that this is a widespread problem. A flyer posted in various places on campus provided an image of Tancredo with the following caption: "No in-state tuition for Illegals! Come hear why." Following the caption was the time and place where the speech was to take place. Another flyer posted by opposition student groups advertised a demonstration advocating "No dialogue with hate." The demonstration was advertised to occur outside the building and room where the speech was to occur. In reality, the demonstration spilled into the room where the speech would be delivered. Audience members and protestors swelled the room far beyond the capacity of the room to accommodate them. The room is only approved for a capacity of 115, an interesting choice of a room to host a former Congressman and Presidential candidate. The demonstrators were composed of students and non-students from various groups. One group of demonstrators was intent on preventing Tancredo from speaking (no dialogue with hate). They shouted obscenities and held up signs denouncing YWC and Tancredo as racists. Supporters for Tancredo and YWC shouted, "Let him speak, you Communists." Eventually, the group was calmed enough for Tancredo to begin speaking. When two students held a banner in front of Tancredo, he pulled the banner down and became engaged in a "tug-of-war" with a young woman holding the banner. A photographer moved in to take a picture of the scene. Tancredo turned to the camera and dropped the banner after the photograph was taken. Cameramen for both groups filmed the angriest of the protestors as representatives of Tancredo walked the aisles engaging the angry protestors.

Students and members of the community shouted to the protestors to "let him speak." Two women walked to the front of the room. Junior Lizette Lopez, 22, vice president of the Carolina Hispanic Association, said: "We are the children of immigrants, and this concerns us. So we would at least like to hear what he has to say if you want to hear what we have to say" (Hartness, 2009) Tancredo left the building when a window was broken by someone from outside the building,. A cameraman from Americans for Legal Immigration PAC (ALIPAC) speaks into his microphone: "This is the United States! This is the United States where people can speak freely without being harassed.... Welcome to the United States...breaking out windows of people you don't like, does this sound familiar in history to anybody?" The reference to Kristallnacht was an explicit attempt to associate protestors with Nazi Fascism. That night, in Germany, 10,000 windows were broken, 91 Jews were killed, around 20,000 Jews were sent to concentration camps, 30,000 Jewish men were arrested, and nearly 300 synagogues were burned or completely destroyed (Gilbert, 2007; Schwab, 1990). There were numerous rapes and suicides (Schwab, 1990). It is both humorous and obscene to compare the two events. According to Wardle (2009) of Indyweek.com, Tancredo remarked after the event: "They're fascists.... These kids have been radicalized. That's what our institutions have created."

At the end of the video, the cameraman stood at the front steps of the building where he filmed more of the protests and remarked: "I just want to make sure that everybody knows that *the illegal aliens and their supporters* shut down this event by use of violence and destruction of property" (video posted on Youth for Western Civilization Web Page; emphasis added). It should be noted that there was no reason to believe that the Latinos, largely students, were not legal citizens of the United States. It appears that the cameraman saw Latinos and saw illegal aliens.

Notice that our description frames the scene as one in which a group of protestors were determined to prevent Tancredo from speaking. However, it also reveals an opposing side that understands the social capital to be gained from this confrontation, filming the scene and photographing student protestors, which will provide evidence for their claims that universities across America are liberal hotbeds where left-wing professors and administrators are brainwashing students, teaching them to devalue their own history and traditions (Youth for Western Civilization). So, the protestors' obscene and boorish behavior shamed the university, but it also worked against their own interests, making the evening more successful for Tancredo and the national

YWC than if he had been allowed to speak and answer questions from his audience.

The scene is framed differently in the media and discourse that followed the event (Hartness, 2009; Hughs, 2009; Thorp, personal communication, April 15, 2009). In that discourse, Tancredo and YWC are "constructed" as the noble victims who remained calm as their rights to free speech were violated. The student protestors were "constructed" as villains who did not represent UNC values. The university experienced shame as a result of the obscenity-laden talk and boorish behavior of student protestors. The University of North Carolina has a rich tradition, dating back to the 1960s, of fighting for free speech, especially for unpopular voices and ideas. The protestors' actions offended this tradition. This shame motivated UNC to purge the object of shame from the community (the students) through scapegoating (Williamson, 2002).

This shame was managed by distancing the university from the actions of the protestors. The Chancellor began this process through a university-wide email on April 15:

> We expect protests about controversial subjects at Carolina. That's part of our culture. But we also pride ourselves on being a place where all points of view can be expressed and heard. There's a way to protest that respects free speech and allows people with opposing views to be heard. Here that's often meant that groups protesting a speaker have displayed signs or banners, silently expressing their opinions while the speaker had his or her say. That didn't happen last night. (Thorp, personal communication, April 15, 2009)

The Chancellor also announced that Student Affairs would investigate and some students might have to face the honor court.

A day later, students with a representative from the local student chapter of YWC would gather in what has been known as the Free Speech Pit to reconfirm their commitment to free speech and civil discourse. Two days later, a young woman was arrested as she left a class and walked through campus for other students to observe. Both were powerful images employed by the university community to purge its shame. Interestingly, this is a common pattern of behavior found in communities that experience highly visible hate crimes. Williamson (2002) describes Burke's cycle of redemption in media coverage of what became known as the dragging trial of the hate murderers of James Byrd in Jasper, Texas. The murderers were perfected as White Supremacists and distinguished from the community that portrayed itself as "tolerant." In so doing, the town of Jasper could avoid "being a community where something like this could happen."

We claimed above that this kind of difficult analysis is important because it can paint a fuller understanding of the social actors and avoids that caricaturing of social actors that so often naturally follows a community's response to perceived hate-motivated activities. Below, we examine the discourse of the national YWC's Web Page and blog. We also examine the discourse of the speakers that YWC sends to university campuses on a regular basis to talk about why "illegals" should not receive in-state tuition.

Nativism and Youth for Western Civilization

Beginning at the top of their Homepage, YWC exhibits the first characteristic of the hate stratagem: They identify Western culture and Western identity as a valued and superior in-group that readers may identify with. The banner on the original (prior to mid-June of 2009) YWC Web Page proclaimed that they are "America's Right Wing Youth Movement." To the left of the banner is a disembodied arm swinging a hammer with a large head within a crest. To the right of the banner is a quote attributed to Tom Tancredo, "This is our culture—fight for it. This is our flag—pick it up. This is our country—take it back." These are the words of Nativists interested in constructing enemies and threats to our country, not people who want to pursue a rational conversation about immigration policy.

YWC proclaims their purpose:

> Youth for Western Civilization will educate, organize and train activists on campuses across the nation to create a culture that will promote the survival of Western Civilization and pride in Western heritage. This movement is focused on the support of Western history, identity, high culture, and pride and opposition to radical multiculturalism, political correctness, racial preferences, mass immigration, and socialism.

This is ambiguous and abstract language. Which Western identity? Are they referring to an African American identity? Is an African American identity part of their understanding of a Western identity? Is a Latino identity part of their understanding of an American identity? Which Western cultural institutions? There are many Western cultural institutions of which we should be proud. However, slavery and colonialism are institutions that also played key roles in the advancement of the West.

They continue:

> Initially, we would like to set up as many active campus chapters as possible that will host events such as speakers, debates, and protests. In the medium term, we want these groups to run for student governments, defend against left wing organizations and create new groups. We also want to change the social atmosphere of the

school, with YWC becoming the focus of social life at the school as well as political activism. In the long term, we want the majority of students to leave college more right wing than when they arrived. Eventually, we would like to start changing curriculum on campus to restore an emphasis on *real education* and classical learning, rather than *trendy multiculturalism*. (emphasis added)

It is clear that YWC is not simply attempting to bring figures to campus to speak about immigration. They view universities as homogenous "brainwashing" institutions controlled by left-wing ideologies. YWC provides more insight into their rationale in their "Join Us" section:

While we are grounded in the conservative tradition, conservatism is more suited to the defense of a traditionalist system in which *responsible elites* identify with and seek to preserve a people and its traditional liberties. The cultural, political, and especially *academic elites in this country hate the West and seek to destroy its identity and freedoms*. College education in this country is largely about left wing indoctrination, not actually grounding students in the liberal artis (sic). Youth for Western Civilization wants to create fundamental change on the university campus. For this reason, we use the term "right wing" and not just "conservative." (emphasis added)

By identifying universities as a dangerous threat to Western culture and Western identity, YWC has employed the third characteristic of the hate stratagem. In their own words, YWC does not mind elites running American universities. They simply want to be the elites controlling them. In their own words, YWC is pursuing a radical agenda against a group that they perceive to be just as radicalized. One predisposed to this view would see obscenity-shouting protestors (some of whom were students) calling the speaker a racist as evidence that university students have been brainwashed by liberal professors and administrators.

In the "Resources" section of the Web Page, potential student-members of YWC are told: "You will receive several guides from the Foundation on Individual Rights in Education containing valuable information on preventing discrimination against your group by *left-wing college administrators*" (emphasis added).

In June of 2009, YWC revised their Web Site and blog in order to tone down this confrontational rhetoric. However, there is still a hateful edge to some of their text. In their mission statement they explain why they care about Western Civilization: "*It is ours.* We have the self-evident right and duty to work for the survival of our own culture and civilization" (emphasis by YWC, *emphasis in original*). While we do not take exception to this claim, it should be noted that this is a tautology: Western culture is valuable because it is "ours." YWC continues:

> While this reason is sufficient in itself, Western Civilization has also given priceless gifts to the rest of mankind, including advances in medicine, the arts, and scientific exploration. *There is no reason to believe that the advances of modernity and the political freedoms we enjoy will endure with the extinction of the civilization that allowed them to exist.* Western Civilization is our civilization and in spite of the continual assault and hatred it endures from the radical left, we wish to revive the West, rather than see our civilization be sent to the graveyard of history. (emphasis added)

This is interesting language. First, it is clear that YWC truly believes that left-wing college professors and administrators are working to make Western Civilization extinct, including political freedoms and civil rights that have evolved from Western democracies. Second, this language is almost identical to the apocalyptic language of White Supremacists discussed in chapter four: "White people built this nation" and "White people have provided the world with civilization and culture the rest of the world would not have achieved without white people" (Daniels, 1997). Does this language mean YWC is a hate group or a racist organization? Not in and of itself. But it does give one pause. This message displays important characteristics of the hate stratagem: It glorifies the in-group (people who belong to Western Civilization) and it clearly specifies that this group is under attack (even threatened with extinction) by an evil enemy (left-wing college professors and administrators).

The attractiveness of the Web Page was improved and it now presents a more professional image. For example, much of the original rhetoric found in the Resources and Join Us sections has been removed entirely. Rather than explicitly vilifying professors and administration, they describe their purpose and mission in the following way:

> Youth for Western Civilization has stirred up debate on controversial issues like illegal immigration, multiculturalism and classical education that were thought to be driven off college campuses. *YWC stands alone in challenging the dogmatic left-wing orthodoxy of American higher education.* (emphasis added)

YWC's perception of higher education is stunning, but not because there are not remarkably liberal universities with liberal cultures that can sometimes appear dogmatic to many conservatives (and some liberals). What is stunning is their homogenous view of American higher education. The University of North Carolina *is* a very liberal campus, even though there may be some important differences among various colleges and schools on the campus. Moreover, YWC writes as if Baylor University, Bob Jones University, Patrick Henry College, and the University of North Carolina all share the same *liberal orthodoxy*, a liberal orthodoxy at the University of North Carolina that not only permits the presence of an admitted right-wing group but that rallied in support of YWC's right to free speech (and facilitated the visit of Bay Buchanan to speak about immigrants in October 2009). This denigration of university personnel and construction of a homogenous stereotype illustrate the operation of the second characteristic of the hate stratagem, the denigration of the out-group identity (professors and administrators in American higher education).

The banner of YWC's Web Page has replaced Tancredo's remarks about "taking back Western Civilization" with "Defending the West on Campus." They state that their "mission is to organize, educate and train activists dedicated to the revival of Western Civilization." Their rhetoric may be toned down but YWC still sees a threat to "citizenship" that is so profound that Western Civilization is in need of revival from right-wing college students. The silliness of this claim may be seen by a simple survey of classes on any campus devoted to the study of art, literature, and the various products and outcomes that stand as monuments to Western Civilization.

What are some of the ideas and images of Western Civilization that YWC adopts to illustrate the embodiment of Western Civilization values they support? The disembodied arm swinging a hammer is still present on the left the YWC's banner. Might this represent the building of culture and civilization of the West? No. In their FAQ section of their Web Page, they explain the meaning of this symbol:

> The logo represents Charles Martel, "the Hammer of the Franks." He defeated Muslim invaders at the Battle of Tours in 732 AD and prevented Western Civilization from being overrun.

It is interesting, and perhaps telling, that YWC selects a renowned warrior who defeated a marauding Muslim army to represent their organization, rather than democracy, a judicial system, art, or some other aspect of the "high culture" they wish to preserve. In this new version of their Web Page, they keep some of their rhetoric about what they oppose in their FAQ section:

> The governing ideology of Western universities is the pursuit of radical multiculturalism. It is used as a weapon to defeat any conservative, libertarian, classical liberal or even progressive, patriotic ideas. The *insane and extreme anti-Western bigotry on college campuses* must be directly confronted and defeated if any right-of-center group is to make any progress. *This also means that the people of the West need to stop apologizing for their own existence.* Youth for Western Civilization is unique in that we are openly confronting the forces that are leading to the deliberate destruction of our civilization. We are also distinguished in promoting an activist mindset among conservative and right-wing groups on campus. (emphasis added)

They tell readers what radical multiculturalism does (promotes insane anti-Western bigotry), however, YWC does not tell us what it is until later:

> In the words of conservative columnist Mark Steyn, multiculturalism is a cult of ignorance. The multiculturalism in practice on campuses today has nothing to do with actually learning about other cultures. Instead, it is about *learning politically correct slogans that are designed to denigrate Western heritage in general* and American heritage in particular. Multiculturalism is really about destroying and dispossessing the people and culture of the West, not about an appropriate education about other peoples. (emphasis added)

So, radical multiculturalism is ignorance and politically correct slogans. Again, readers are left looking for substantive meaning in YWC's attempt to define radical multiculturalism. The only thing that is clear in this text is that radical multiculturalism (whatever it is) is dangerous to Westerners (more evidence of the third characteristic of the hate stratagem, attempts to inflict permanent harm on the out-group identity by identifying that the out-group wants to destroy what we hold dear). Interestingly, in failing to provide anything but a pejorative definition of "radical multiculturalism," YWC engages in the very actions they accuse the "radical left" on campuses of engaging in—the production of empty slogans that would only have meaning for those steeped in right-wing ideology (Multiculturalism functions to destroy Western Civilization).

At the demonstration on April 14, 2009, UNC students marched and chanted "No racists in our town," and held up banners that read "No dialogue with hate." In the FAQ section, they address the question "Are you a racist/hate group?" Their response:

> *We realize that any patriotic group is going to be accused of this* regardless of what they do, so we don't take the accusation seriously. Youth for Western Civilization has no racial requirements for membership and we are not a racist group. Anyone who agrees with our values can join. (emphasis added)

They see charges of racism as part and parcel of the empty slogans employed by the left on college campuses, and this dismissive response is perfectly logical given the right-wing ideology they have claimed for themselves, an ideology that places them as subordinated and threatened by a left-wing hegemony seeking genocide against Western Civilization. The right is patriotic and supports Western Civilization. The left-wing ideology is unpatriotic and is out to destroy Western Civilization.

The last FAQ they pose is, "Who founded YWC?" This is a very important question for them:

Kevin DeAnna, a graduate student at American University, is the sole founder of
Youth for Western Civilization. He started the group after several years of working
full time in the conservative movement as a student organizer because he came to
realize that radical multiculturalism poses the greatest threat to real education and
the traditional values of Western Culture.

This is important to YWC because Marcus Epstein, an employee of Tom
Tancredo, was identified by the Southern Poverty Law Center as one of the
co-founders of the group (Houlthouse, 2009-b). In June of 2009, court
documents emerged that demonstrated that, two years ago, Marcus Epstein
became intoxicated in public in Washington, D.C. and walked the streets
loudly expressing racial slurs (Weigel, 2009a). When an African American
woman objected to his behavior, he called her by a slur (n-word). He then
struck her across the face. He was arrested by the police and charged with a
hate crime (Weigel, 2009a). This was plea bargained down to simple assault
(Weigel, 2009b). Weigel (2009b) noted DeAnna's observation of the event:

In college you have this culture of drinking all the time, and he kicked it cold," said
Kevin DeAnna, a friend of Epstein and the founder of Youth for Western Civilization, a student group founded in 2008 of which Tancredo is the honorary chairman.
"It's unfortunate that he's getting hit from this now, years after he stopped doing
this kind of thing."

Thus, YWC wants readers to understand that Kevin DeAnna is the only
founder of YWC. Otherwise, Epstein's actions might cause them to view
YWC's rhetoric as simply hateful and racist rather than confrontational and
right-wing. It might lead us to look at Tancredo's claim that Justice Sotomayor is a racist and that an organization devoted to helping Latino families is a Latino KKK "without the hoods" with suspicion to know that
Epstein was employed by Tancredo before and after his arrest, and that he
played an informal role in Tancredo's immigrant-focused Presidential campaign (Weigel, 2009b).

The problems with the kind of protest that took place at UNC are several.
The first problem is that it gives oxygen to the fire of fear and hatred that
speakers such as Tancredo and YWC need. Put simply, the protestors provided vivid visual "proof" for Tancredo's assertion that American universities are places where dissent from liberal views are not tolerated (Hughes,
2009). Second, this type of protest was a resource that Tancredo and YWC
used to raise money for their cause. According to Hartness (2009), the day
after the UNC protest Tancredo used news and video of the evening to raise
funds from right-wing individuals and groups for future speeches. Tancredo
claimed: "There is no freedom of speech on hundreds of university campuses

today for people who dare to dissent from the radical political agenda of the socialist left and the open borders agitators" (Hartness, 2009). Tancredo and other blogs even argued that UNC professors were orchestrating the actions of the protestors. The protest may have been satisfying for the protestors but it gave the Nativists the attention in the press that they desired and the resources they needed to further their message. Third, the protest became the story for the local media and the dangerous Nativist rhetoric was not critiqued and interrogated. Without the protest, the Tancredo speech would have received little attention and the memory of Tancredo's visit would have dimmed within a week. Because of the boorish and foolish tactics of the protestors, the Nativists were able to feel a sense of righteous indignation that would fuel their energies in ways that a silent protest would not. There are other reasons why this kind of protest should be discouraged in the long-term as a form of anti-hate discourse that will be discussed in chapter seven.

Conclusion

There is a sentiment that we would like to return to in order to more fully appreciate the Nativist rhetoric we have discussed, thus far:

> What you have to understand is that this massive immigration in this country is changing the face of this community, and it will transform America into something alien to the principles and values of the founding fathers of this country.... You will be eventually outnumbered and outvoted in your own land. (Cited in Cuadros, 2007)

This basic message was advanced numerous times by Tancredo and YWC. This time these words were not spoken by Tom Tancredo or written in YWC's blog. This statement was made by David Duke, former Grand Wizard of the Ku Klux Klan and former State Senator in Louisiana, at an anti-immigrant rally in the poultry-producing town of Siler City, North Carolina. We believe this is a telling comparison. There are those in America who veil their Nativism within the legitimate social problem of (un)controlled immigration. However, rather than propose solutions to the underlying problems driving illegal immigration, these rhetors use *immigration* to demonize and dehumanize *immigrants*. Illegal immigration is a far more complicated problem requiring a more nuanced analysis from our leaders.

For example, undocumented Mexicans came to Siler City because the poultry plant there advertised employment opportunities in the Southwestern United States and Mexico. In those poultry plants, specifically, white and African American residents refused to do the dangerous and health-threatening work; however, they wanted to consume the food produced there, creating a demand for the product and requiring that "someone" perform that work.

Globalization contributes to the demand for undocumented workers. Muscle jobs go to where the muscle is the least expensive in a global economy. Consequently, many manufacturing jobs are leaving the United States. Corporations can sell products in Mexico more cheaply than local farmers. This displaces local farmers, many of whom come to the United States for work. Moreover, Americans have become dependent on undocumented workers to do a range of tasks, from raising children to landscaping. The disappearance of undocumented workers would pose dire consequences for many American families and American businesses. These difficult problems with a labyrinth of causes and consequences make people susceptible to the simpletons and hate-mongers that are willing to tell their fellow citizens that all of this can be reduced to a group of people who wish to take things that are "rightfully yours," and who, ultimately, will destroy "your way of life." Calls to "simply enforce the law" are tragically simple and dangerous, as the hate crimes described earlier demonstrate.

Chapter 6

Nativism and the 2008
Presidential Election

The 2008 Presidential Election has been referred to as "historic" so many times that the power of that term has been lost. The child of mixed parentage, raised by his white mother and grandmother, who self-identifies with the African American community, was elected the 44th President of the United States. Perhaps even more surprising is that someone with a Muslim father and named Barack Hussein Obama could be elected President of the United States only seven years after the al-Qaeda terrorist attacks on the World Trade Center on September 11, 2001, and the subsequent hate crimes against people believed to be Arab. The end result of this election was a cause for celebration of the advances in tolerance made in this country. Unfortunately, this success came in spite of shameful attempts to defeat Obama by manipulating some Americans' hatred and fear of African Americans. Recently, the President's political opponents have attempted to defeat policy initiatives by relying on Nativist discourse to construct him as an un-American threat to the United States. In the last chapter, we illustrated how the hate stratagem operates through Nativist discourse through the media. We use the discourse in this election to illustrate another way that the hate stratagem operates in the mainstream of everyday American life.

Unlike other analyses in this book, we do not identify specific texts (e.g., particular interviews, debates, or memos) as the focus of this analysis. Our task is not so straightforward that our constructs of interest may be located in particular texts. When rhetors in the main of society attempt to manipulate the hatred of an audience in order to encourage them to reject another person or idea, they do so in ways that allow them to capitalize on the ambiguities of language and social context. Those who would invoke hate do not always make hate the cornerstone of a speech or the kernel of a message. Instead, those who rely on hateful appeals do so by dropping those appeals into a speech, blog, or memo that addresses a variety of issues. Eventually, these hateful appeals begin to cohere with other messages produced by a host of political rhetors. It is this larger system of messages that is most interesting to us. From our perspective, therefore, whether the comment(s) of any particular individual are racist is less important to us than the broader mural that we will try to paint through our analysis. Indeed, we will see that this mural conforms to our understanding of the hate stratagem, and that it is given weight and familiarity by the racial myths that are well-known parts of our culture. This broader system of appeals and ideas should be recognized for the hate and racism it invokes, and it will be another example of what Bonilla-Silva (2003), for example, argues is racism without racists.

We will be looking at a variety of sources where hateful appeals may be found or reported. This required us to monitor news sources from the primaries through the general election, looking for evidence of hate appeals in a variety of speeches and speech acts. The evidence of hate appeals certainly appeared in the substantive discussion of relevant political issues (e.g., homeland security). We were also surprised when the use of hate appeals seemed to emerge independent of substantive political messages. That is, many sources seemed to construct Obama as a cultural threat even in the absence of substantive political issues. So, we identified evidence of the elements of the hate stratagem from a variety of texts, talks, and symbols.

Our concern will clearly be with how Barack Obama's political opponents used hatred to gain political advantage. To be certain, Republicans used Obama's race and Clinton's gender to rally support during the Republican Primary and Convention. But the most meaningful examples of the hate stratagem will be found in those campaigns where Obama was a prominent actor. Consequently, we will focus on the Democratic Primary and the General Election. Finally, we examine recent protests and discourse that emerged in response to President Obama's policy initiatives. This discourse turns out to be a crucial portion of our analysis because it adds a layer of meaning that allows us to understand election rhetoric as fundamentally Nativist. It will be clear that Obama is not simply demeaned and portrayed as a man with dangerous ideas. He is portrayed as more than un-American, he is portrayed as not-of-America. He is a threat to our culture, our way of life, "our" America. This is a sentiment that was expressed in Town Hall meetings when protestors claimed to "want our country back."

The 2008 Democratic Primary

A good deal has been written about the fact that hate-mongers have changed the language they use to talk about the objects of their hatred (Perry, 2001). Cross burnings have become "illuminations." "Average Americans" and sometimes "real Americans" replace "white people" in their messages that might be shared with a broader audience. Such coded language has been seen in our politics for years. Richard Nixon won the South by what has become known as the "Southern strategy," the attempt to appeal to conservative Southern whites by advocating for "state's rights." On the campaign trail, this term was understood to be code for anti-segregation and anti-busing positions. This enabled the Republican Party to use race as a "wedge issue" for generations. In July of 2005, Ken Mehlman, the former Chairman of the Republican National Committee, apologized to the National Association for the Advancement of Colored People (NAACP), saying this strategy was wrong (Allen, 2005). Throughout the election, such coded language and ambiguous referents would be used to demean Obama and call the legitimacy of his identity into question (the second characteristic of the hate stratagem). Bob Kerrey, Clinton supporter and former Senator from Nebraska, commented on Obama:

> It's probably not something that appeals to him, but I like the fact that his name is Barack *Hussein* Obama, and that his father is a Muslim. There's a billion people on the planet that are Muslim, and I think that experience is a big deal.... I've watched the blogs try to say that you can't trust him because he spent time in a secular madrassa. I feel quite the opposite. (Herbert, 2008a; emphasis added)

This statement is structured to appear to be a compliment to Obama's experiences that might allow him to understand the perspectives of a wide range of Americans. It is not. The emphasis on his middle name, "Hussein," pairs him with Saddam Hussein, the former deposed leader of Iraq and actual enemy of the United States. The association with Saddam Hussein is an attempt to associate Obama with a threat to the United States (the third characteristic of the hate stratagem). The fact that Obama's experiences could be a "big deal" is not overtly positive. The fearful and the hateful mind could interpret these words as good reason to reject Obama. In fact, the reference to the time he spent in a secular madrassa is intended to "otherize" Obama, to make people believe that he is a Muslim and attracted to the religion of those who attacked the United States on 9-11 (the third characteristic of the hate stratagem). The fact that hate crimes had been growing against American Muslims since 9-11 suggests that this association would vilify Obama in the minds of many who harbored suspicions that all Muslims are enemies of the United States. Although Kerrey would later apologize for these comments, this is not likely to matter to those who would find them persuasive.

Former Senator Kerrey would not be the only source of a whispering campaign designed to encourage voters to believe that Obama was a secret Muslim (Kristof, 2008). Nicholas Kristof wrote: "When Hillary Clinton was

asked in an interview a week ago whether Mr. Obama is a Muslim, she denied it firmly—but then added, most unfortunately, 'as far as I know.'" Such
a qualifier allows Clinton to speak in support of Obama and against this
whispering campaign while leaving the door open for speculation among
voters who might see calling someone a Muslim as a slur. As we discuss
later, even during the general election, many white voters continued to believe that Obama could not be trusted because he was a Muslim, even an
Arab.

Clinton's tepid rejection of this whispering campaign (of Obama's secret
Muslim faith) would dovetail with another attempt to otherize Obama. This
time, former Vice-Presidential candidate and Clinton fundraiser Geraldine
Ferraro would tell the *Daily Breeze,* a local California newspaper, that "if
Obama was a white man, he would not be in this position. And if he was a
woman, he would not be in this position. He happens to be very lucky to be
who he is. And the country is caught up in the concept" (Parker, 2008;
Seelye & Bosman, 2008; Sinderbrand, 2008a). This remark drew on voters'
hatred and racism in at least two different ways. First, it implied that Americans have developed some fascination with African Americans that over-
whelms logic and reason, and that this fascination logically works in the
favor of African Americans and to the disadvantage of whites, especially
white women. Thus, Ferraro's logic promoted a positive white, female identity because the Hillary Clinton campaign had succeeded due to competence
and hard work (the first characteristic of the hate stratagem) while Obama
had succeeded by being the right race at the right time (the second characteristic of the hate stratagem). Second, Ferraro's claim would buttress a theme
that the Clinton campaign would emphasize throughout the primary: Obama
lacked the experience to be Commander in Chief (the only reason he is
"here" is because he is black). This statement appeared to have been made
with such a casual matter-of-factness that Ferraro appeared to expect it to go
unquestioned. When the Obama campaign complained that such racially divisive comments had no place in the campaign, Ferraro elaborated: "Any
time anybody does anything that in any way pulls this campaign down and
says, 'Let's address reality and the problems we're facing in this world,'
you're accused of being racist, so you have to shut up. Racism works in two
different directions. I really think they're attacking me because I'm white.
How's that?" (Conason, 2008; Seelye & Bosman, 2008).

These two quotes make it clear that Ferraro was drawing on the racially
and politically charged language from the 1990s. She was attempting to reduce Obama to a racial quota and to grant legitimacy to the concept of "reverse discrimination," a tired rationalization that hiring quotas threaten white

people. However, this would have resonance with older, white, working-class voters who had to deal with their perceived repercussions of Affirmative Action programs. This might be viewed as a shameful but brilliant attempt to enhance this important constituency's identification with Clinton. Conceptually, it is reminiscent of Jesse Helms's "Hands Commercial" that he ran against Harvey Gantt, an African American mayor of Charlotte, North Carolina, in 1990. The commercial showed a pair of white hands dolling out money to a second set of black hands. The voice-over on the ad stated:

> Harvey Gantt supports quotas. And you needed that job and you were the best qualified but they had to give that job to a minority and you were the best qualified. But they had to give it to a minority because of a racial quota. Is that really fair? Harvey Gantt thinks it is.... You'll vote on this issue next Thursday. For racial quotas: Harvey Gantt. Against racial quotas: Jesse Helms. (YouTube [2006], Jesse Helms "Hands" ad)

In 1990, this ad turned many frightened working white voters against Gantt, and Helms won a close race. If Ferraro was hoping to accomplish a similar outcome for the Clinton campaign, her comments and management of the press could not have been more usefully executed.

Was Ferraro a victim of reverse discrimination? Or was she a politician accustomed to manipulating people's hatred to her own political advantage? She made similar claims against another black politician in 1988, a story that was originally reported by Howard Kurtz in 1988 for *The Washington Post*:

> Placid of demeanor but pointed in his rhetoric, Jackson struck out repeatedly today against those who suggest his race has been an asset in the campaign. President Reagan suggested Tuesday that people don't ask Jackson tough questions because of his race. And former representative Geraldine A. Ferraro (D-N.Y.) said Wednesday that because of his "radical" views, "if Jesse Jackson were not black, he wouldn't be in the race.... Discussing the same point in Washington, Jackson said, "We campaigned across the South...without a single catcall or boo. It was not until we got north to New York that we began to hear this from Koch, President Reagan and then Mrs. Ferraro.... Some people are making hysteria while I'm making history." (Smith, 2008)

Senator Clinton told *USA Today* that she was the candidate favored by "hard-working Americans, white Americans" (Herbert, 2008b). Kiely and Lawrence (2008) quoted Mrs. Clinton:

> "I have a much broader base to build a winning coalition on," she said in an interview with *USA TODAY*. As evidence, Clinton cited an Associated Press article "that found how Sen. Obama's support among working, hard-working Americans, white

Americans, is weakening again, and how whites in both states who had not com-
pleted college were supporting me. There's a pattern emerging here."

These are racially divisive remarks, but their potential ambiguity gives the
candidate cover to deny that they are actually appealing to people's racial
views. The alternative view of these remarks is that the Clinton campaign
genuinely believed these comments were racially neutral.

Representative Rob Andrews, a Clinton Superdelegate, reported that a
high-ranking person in the Clinton campaign told him of a strategy to "win
Jewish votes by exploiting tensions between Jews and blacks" (Associated
Press News Release, 2008). This would result in attempts to denigrate
Obama's identity and construct him as a threat to Jews (the third characteristic of the hate stratagem). There is evidence that this strategy would be useful. Kantor (2008) reported in a *New York Times* article that Jews in Florida
believed Obama was (a) an Arab, (b) a Muslim, (c) backed by al-Qaeda, (d)
likely to fill his cabinet with followers of Louis Farrakhan, and (e) likely to
associate too closely with Iran because he associated too closely with Reverend Jeremiah Wright.

Oddly enough, a subsequent attempt to make white people fearful of
Obama came when his Christian minister, Jeremiah A. Wright, Jr., delivered
a controversial sermon that was leaked to news outlets and eventually made
its way to YouTube. Wright delivered sermons in which he claimed that
America was systemically racist and oppressive. The sound bites are vivid
and intended to make Wright appear to be an angry black man, whipping his
predominantly black parishioners into a wild frenzy. These sound bites
would be reported by the mainstream media but they would be used by opponents of Obama to associate him with this "dangerous black preacher"
who was using his church to preach hatred against America. The following
sound bites, taken from recordings made by his Trinity United Church of
Christ, and published by *The Chicago Tribune* in a staff report ("Rev.
Jeremiah Wright's words," 2008), were used by opponents of Barak Obama:

We've bombed Hiroshima, we've bombed Nagasaki, we've nuked far more than the
thousands in New York and the Pentagon and we never batted an eye.... We have
supported state terrorism against the Palestinians and black South Africans, and now
we are indignant. Because the stuff we have done overseas is now brought right
back into our own front yards. America's chickens are coming home to roost. (September 16, 2001)

In another sermon, Wright comments about America:

> The government gives them drugs, builds bigger prisons, passes a three-strikes law and then wants us to sing God Bless America? No, no, no, not God Bless America. Goddamn America. (July 2003)

In a third sermon:

> Hillary is married to Bill, and Bill has been good to us. No he ain't. Bill did us just like he did Monica Lewinsky. He was riding dirty. (January 12, 2008)

The Chicago Tribune (March 29, 2008) published excerpts from the larger sermons that would change the ways that many Americans would interpret these sound bites. The first two sound bites emerged from a sermon that was tied to scripture that Wright had clearly quoted. The first sermon dealt with the way in which violence begets violence and terrorism begets terrorism, hardly an unusual theme in a Christian sermon. The second sound bite is the climax of a sermon intended to encourage congregants to place their faith in an unchanging God (who is against slavery, segregation, etc.) rather than in earthly institutions, like a government, that might create the very institutions that many Christians would see as un-Christ-like. In the third sermon, Wright actually speaks positively about Bill Clinton's policies. In fact, the sentence following the last sentence of the sound bite is, "But he fixed it so that some of ya'll are now riding pretty." Most of us will have a negative visceral reaction to the comment, "Goddamn America." But there is a larger discursive context that might change the frame of these sound bites for many Americans. The more important issue is how these sound bites were used by Obama's opponents. However, any discussion of this issue should recognize this context.

We do not have evidence that the Clinton campaign explicitly manipulated this event to its own advantage. However, we have provided evidence that many primary voters used this event to draw erroneous but desired conclusions about Obama. When it became clear that Obama would be the nominee, the North Carolina Republican Party released an ad linking Obama to Reverend Wright. The North Carolina GOP then linked key North Carolina Democratic nominees to Obama. The Chairman introduced the ad thusly:

> I am here to unveil the North Carolina Republican Party's first ad of 2008 opposing Richard Moore and Beverly Perdue for Governor.... It is no secret that Barack Obama has also received scrutiny recently for his ties to controversial figures such as his former pastor Jeremiah Wright.... This ad presents a question of patriotism and judgment.

The ad went as below:

> Narrator: For twenty years, Barack Obama sat in his pew listening to his pastor. Jeremiah Wright: And then wants us to sing God Bless America. No, no, no. Not God Bless American. Goddamn America. Narrator: Now Bev Perdue and Richard Moore endorse Barack Obama. They should know better. He's just too extreme for North Carolina.

North Carolina GOP Chairwoman, Linda Daves, said about the ad: "The Democratic candidates also show poor judgment and a lack of leadership by endorsing Barack Obama, a man too liberal for North Carolina and linked to extremist figures throughout his political career." The ad was condemned by John McCain who told reporters:

> I have been committed to running a respectful campaign based upon an honest debate about the great issues confronting America today. I expect all state parties to do so as well. The television advertisement you are planning degrades our civics and distracts us from the very real differences we have with Democrats.... We do not need to engage in political tactics that only seek to divide the American people. (Luo, 2008)

The North Carolina GOP declined to pull the ad, even when some local stations declined to air the ad (Media Research Center, 2008). Based on McCain's response, many expected a different kind of general election. It was not to be.

How should we interpret these divisive and race-baiting remarks by Democrats and Republicans against the Obama campaign? Were they a random series of remarks made by individuals? Or were they a coordinated effort of the Clinton campaign intended to otherize Obama and make him appear different, un-American, and unpatriotic? There is much evidence to suggest that it was the latter.

A post mortem on the Clinton campaign, The Front-Runner's Fall, derived from memos among Clinton strategists and published in *The Atlantic*, illustrates a divided campaign. One camp in the campaign recommended a positive campaign and the other camp advocated a more negative campaign that would accuse various opponents of being unqualified and untrustworthy (Green, 2008). The strongest voice in this camp was Mark Penn, who argued that Clinton's natural base was women and lower- and middle-class voters. He recommended that, among other things, the candidate should establish herself as an in-group member by personal history and by emphasizing her sense of Americana and patriotism. In addition, Penn recommended that the campaign construct Obama as an "other" by attacking his "lack of American roots":

> All of these articles about his boyhood in Indonesia and his life in Hawaii are geared towards showing his background is diverse, multicultural and *putting that in a new light*. Save it for 2050. It also expresses a strong weakness for him—his roots to basic American values and culture are limited. *I cannot imagine America electing a President in a time of war who is not at his center fundamentally American in his thinking and values....* Let's explicitly own "American" in our programs, the speeches, and the values. He doesn't. (Green, 2008; emphasis added)

What goes unstated by Penn, because listeners will draw this conclusion on their own, is that the representative of American values is a white candidate. Moreover, the representative of un-American values self-identifies as an African American. In this context, an observation by Penn in a later memo sounds almost wistful: "Won't a single tape of…Wright going off on America with Obama sitting there be a game ender? Many people…believe under the surface that 20 years sitting there with Goddamn America would make him unelectable by itself" (Green, 2008).

When Penn's memos were made public, "Clinton people" claimed that she did not take his advice (Morris & McGann, 2008). Our analysis of the campaign discourse suggests otherwise. It is clear that the Clinton campaign employed key elements of the hate stratagem in order to otherize Obama in the minds of Americans, white Americans. However, this discourse will seem mild compared to attempts to otherize Obama in the general election.

The 2008 General Presidential Election

On February 18, 2008, Michelle Obama delivered remarks in Madison, Wisconsin, that would gain a lot of attention from extreme groups that would use the Internet to spread lies about both Obamas, especially during the general election a few months later:

> What we've learned over this year is that hope is making a comeback. It is making a comeback and let me tell you something for the first time in my adult lifetime I'm proud of my country, and not just because Barack has done well. But because I think people are hungry for change. And I think they are desperate to see people moving in that direction and just not feeling so alone in my frustration and disappointment. I've seen people who are hungry to be unified around this amazing time and issue. And it made me proud. And I feel privileged to be a part of even witnessing this and traveling around states all over this country and being reminded that there is more that unites us than divides us, that the struggles of a farmer in Iowa are no different than what's happening on the South Side of Chicago. The people are feeling the

same pains and wanting the same things for their families. (YouTube [Video file], 2008a)

Those looking for ways to vilify the Obamas focused on the remark: "and let me tell you something for the first time in my adult lifetime I'm proud of my country." These attacks would eventually float up to the mainstream media. On June 11, 2008, Fox news interviewed Michelle Malkin, a conservative commentator, about Michelle Obama's remark that "for the first time in my adult life I'm proud of my country." Ignoring all the remarks around this single sentence, the discussants focused on why someone who had benefited greatly from this country did not feel pride in their country and what could make a woman so "angry." In this story, the Fox "crawl line" read: "Michelle Malkin calls Michelle Obama's Bitter Half" and "Outraged Liberals: Stop Picking on Obama's Baby Momma" (Koppelman, 2008). So, Fox begins to construct Michelle Obama as an angry black woman and calls the future First Lady a whore (a Baby Momma is a colloquialism for an unmarried mother who is not in a relationship with the child's father). This is certainly an attempt to denigrate Obama's identity (the second characteristic of the hate stratagem).

On June 14, 2008, Cal Thomas would raise the issue in a discussion on his show on a panel whose topic was "Is Michelle Obama the Next Media Target":

> CAL THOMAS: In this campaign, we are being asked to accept three things simultaneously, the first woman with a credible chance of being president, the first African-American with the chance to being president and, whoever Michelle Obama is going to be styled, the angry black woman, first lady? This is an awful lot. . . . Look at the image of angry black women on television. Politically you have Maxine Waters of California, liberal Democrat. She's always angry every time she gets on television. Cynthia McKinney, another angry black woman. And who are the black women you see on the local news at night in cities all over the country. They're usually angry about something. They've had a son who has been shot in a drive-by shooting. They are angry at Bush. So you don't really have a profile of non-angry black women. (Scott, 2008)

So, the white discussants perpetuate the notion that Michelle Obama is an angry black woman, upset about the inequity she has seen from white America and waiting for the opportunity to unleash her anger from a position of power. Such a discussion is intended to portray Michelle Obama as constitutionally unqualified to be First Lady because of her race ("you don't have a profile of non-angry black women").

Shortly after the Democratic Convention, E. D. Hill would do a story on the "fist bump" that Michelle and Barack Obama shared after she introduced him at the Democratic Convention. Before introducing an expert on body language, Hill would imply that viewing this as a "terrorist fist-jab" was as reasonable an interpretation as any other (YouTube, 2008b). She would wonder "whatever happened to a handshake or a hug." Hill would subsequently apologize (YouTube, 2008c), saying she was merely reporting how this had been characterized in the media and did not mean to suggest that she, personally, would characterize the Obamas as terrorists. Perhaps, but an apology does not erase that implication. Even in the apology, Hill perpetuated the notion that Barack Obama was a terrorist because she claimed to merely be reporting how the "fist bump" was "characterized in the media." She failed to challenge the media characterization of the "terrorist fist bump," even though she personally would not characterize it thus.

This categorizing of Barack Obama as a terrorist would be extended by the McCain campaign. Beginning in early October, Sarah Palin began to tell largely Republican crowds: "This is not someone who sees America like you and I see America. This is someone who sees America, it seems, as being so imperfect, imperfect enough, that he's palling around with terrorists who would target their own country" (Garofoli, 2008). This was a reference to a rather superficial acquaintance that Obama had with William Ayers, presently a professor at the University of Illinois at Chicago, and a former member of The Weathermen, a radical left-wing organization of the 1960s that sought to end the war with Vietnam. FactCheck.org reported that the relationship between the two men amounted to overlapping political circles. The claim that the two men were "palling around" was disproven, but these claims would persist until the end of the election. This message served to create a positive in-group identity of patriotic American Republicans (the first characteristic of the hate stratagem) while associating Obama with people and ideas that were a threat (the third characteristic of the hate stratagem).

Beginning on October 16, 2008, the McCain campaign and the RNC funded an expensive set of robocalls across the United States. One of the robocalls suggested that Obama was not willing to protect Americans from terrorists:

> Barack Obama and his fellow Democrats aren't who you think they are. They say they want to keep us safe, but Barack Obama said the threat we face now from terrorism is nowhere near as dire as it was in the end of the Cold War. And congressional Democrats now want to give civil rights to terrorists. (Sargent, 2008a)

A follow-up robocall would perpetuate Palin's false claim that Barack Obama was a terrorist:

You need to know that Barack Obama has worked closely with domestic terrorist Bill Ayers, whose organization bombed the U.S. Capitol, the Pentagon, a judge's home, and killed Americans. And Democrats will enact an extreme leftist agenda if they take control of Washington. Barack Obama and his Democratic allies lack the judgment to lead our country. (Sargent, 2008b)

These claims were made repeatedly at Republican rallies and gatherings. In sum, these claims suggested that, at best, Obama was sympathetic with terrorists (the second characteristic of the hate stratagem) and, at worst, was himself a terrorist (the third characteristic of the hate stratagem). This point would be driven home on *Hannity's America* by Andy Martin who, according to the research firm Media Matters for America, has a long history of racist and anti-Semitic claims (Media Matters for America, 2008) when he claimed that "Obama's work as a community organizer was 'training for a radical overthrow of the government'" (Martin, 2008; Media Matters for America, 2008).

It is important to note that these claims would be all the more reasonable, for some, because of the foundation for this argument that had been advanced by Penn's Democratic strategy to construct Obama as an outsider without sufficient experience in American culture and *"who is not at his center fundamentally American in his thinking and values"* (Green, 2008; emphasis added).

Another attempt to portray Obama as a terrorist was undertaken by speakers at McCain rallies who would speak his middle name, Hussein, with disgust, implying that there is something vile in the name itself. Representative Steve King (R-Iowa) said: "Electing Obama, whose middle name is Hussein, would thrill radical Islamists" (Abdullah, 2008). This would be an ongoing theme at McCain rallies. It was effective enough among McCain supporters that by late October, days before the election, supporters in Florida and Pennsylvania would chant: "John McCain! Not Hussein!" (Bosman, 2008). In Florida, the individual starting the chant said: "I guess he was named after Saddam Hussein" (Bosman, 2008). Peter Wallsten (2008), in an article for *The Los Angeles Times,* noted that consistent with King's remarks, voters in Appalachia had developed similar beliefs about Obama. At a Democratic rally, one woman remarked: "Obama just doesn't seem like he's from America." Her Husband interjected that "Obama's middle name is Hussein, and we know what that means."

Palin also built on Penn's strategy by suggesting a corollary to the "terrorist" theme: Only the Republicans and their supporters are pro-America. On October 16, 2008, in Greensboro, North Carolina, Palin remarked:

We believe the best of America is not all in Washington, D.C. We believe that the best of America is in these small towns that we get to visit, and in these wonderful little pockets of what I call *the real America, being here with all of you hard working very patriotic, um, very, um pro-America areas of this nation.* This is where we find the kindness and the goodness and the courage of everyday Americans. Those who are running our factories and teaching our kids and growing our food and fighting our wars for us. Those who are protecting us in uniform. Those who are protecting the virtues of freedom. (e.g., Eilperin, 2008; Stein, 2008; emphasis added)

Functionally, this is an attempt to create a positive in-group identity with their supporters (the first characteristic of the hate stratagem). There is some ambiguity about what Palin might be trying to accomplish in this remark. It is clear that she believes that small towns of America are more patriotic than other areas of the United States *because that is what she said.* A spokesperson would say that this is not what she meant (Eilperin, 2008), that she merely meant to say that she was "highlighting the virtues of far-flung cities and towns across the nation." Unfortunately, that is not what Palin said, and it is not a reasonable interpretation of what she said. But this is not the first time that the McCain campaign, its surrogates, or other Republican politicians have referred to rural America as "real America" or "pro-America" (Rich, 2008). George Allen, a Virginia Senator, would turn to an Indian-American Democratic campaign worker filming his speech at a rally and call him macaca (a clear racial epithet) and say, "Welcome to America and the real Virginia." Allen was in southwestern Virginia, largely made up of white people in small towns. In an interview with MSNBC, Nancy Pfotenhauer, a McCain adviser, dismissed the northern Virginia suburbs that were being won by Obama and argued that the "real Virginia—the part of the state 'more Southern in nature'—will prove very responsive to the McCain message" (Rich, 2008).

These quotes all point to a shared Republican vision: There is a real, normal, and patriotic America that is largely white and rural, and there is another (an Other) America that is inauthentic, unpatriotic, urban, and more diverse (Fineman, 2008).

Palin would also try to link Obama to our old Cold War enemies for those older voters who might remember those old fears. To drive this point home further, on October 21, 2008, Palin would imply that Obama should be rejected by voters because he is a socialist: "I'm not going to call him a socialist, but as 'Joe the Plumber' has said, it looks like socialism to him" (CNN Election Center, 2008). However, Palin did call his tax policy "socialist." David Storck, Chairman of the Hillsborough County (Florida) Republican Party would be less careful when he forwarded an email to friends and colleagues:

The Threat: Here in Temple Terrace, FL. Our Republican HQ is one block away from our library, which is an early voting site. I see carloads of Black Obama supporters coming from the inner city to cast their votes for Obama. This is their chance to get a Black President and they seem to care little that he is at minimum, socialist, and probably Marxist in his core beliefs. After all, he is Black—no experience or accomplishments—but he is Black.... You and I understand the dangers the potential Obama presidency presents to *our way of life*. The suppression of free speech...increased dangers to our nation by terrorists...turning our tax system into a national welfare system. (Noon, 2008; emphasis added)

The McCain campaign was based on a vision of America as composed of Americans who are patriotic and pro-America (the first characteristic of the hate stratagem). Because the "other" America represents the antithesis of the good Americans, they can be vilified without shame or fear of the consequences that might befall them (the second and third characteristics of the hate stratagem).

Other Republicans would attempt to demean and otherize Barack Obama through code words that were not explicitly racial epithets but that were culturally significant and meaningful to speakers and auditors. To some degree, these code words render their attacks ambiguous for those outside their culture. These code words allow their users to express old hatred in more acceptable ways.

In early September of 2008, Representative Lynn Westmoreland (R-Georgia) volunteered to reporters that just from what she'd "seen of her [Michelle Obama] and Mr. Obama, Senator Obama, they're a member of an elitist class individual that thinks that they're *uppity*" (Abdullah, 2008; Weisman, 2008; emphasis added). When asked by the reporter, Westmoreland confirmed that he meant "uppity." Several newspapers recognized the racially tinged word as an attempt to activate racial concepts that are already part of the public consciousness. A spokesperson for Westmoreland would later say that he meant the *"Webster's* definition of uppity." Fair enough. But *Webster's* definition of uppity is not a synonym for elitist but is defined as "overstepping one's boundaries." Certainly, anyone from the South can recall when the term "uppity" was seldom used except as an adjective to a viler racial epithet (n-word) and was reported in hate the hate speech produced by Ben Klassen in the White Man's Bible (see chapter four).

Earlier in April, Republican Representative Geoff Davis of Kentucky referred to Obama as "boy." After observing his performance on a war simulation prepared for Congress, Davis said: *"That boy's* finger does not need to be on the button. He could not make a decision in that simulation that related to a nuclear threat to this country" (Abdullah, 2008). Diminutives, such as "boy," have long been employed as a way for racists and those with hateful minds to diminish the stature of the objects of their hatred (Roy, 2002). During slavery this term was used to infantilize male slaves, depicting them as incapable of living independently (or making important decisions), justifying their enslavement. Following what has become a recognizable pattern of "racial insult" followed by an "apology," Davis offered a written apology to Obama. Ray (2009) refers to this pattern as a speech act or speech ritual.

Were Westmoreland and Davis aware of their remark's racial implications? Perhaps this language was so ingrained in their culture, and in their minds, that they were merely speaking as their culture had taught them to speak. Were they *intentionally* altercasting Obama into a demeaned, inferior, and culturally understood role for their constituents (the second characteristic of the hate stratagem)? It does not matter. The altercasting took place, and those from their culture understood the racial implications of those words.

As we followed the 2008 Presidential Election in anticipation of writing this chapter, we believed that most of our analysis would focus on the veiled forms of hatred and coded language that make up a small portion of our analysis. We were surprised when Obama's competitors would produce messages that resonated so closely with the discourse produced by many in the organized hate movement. Sophomoric name-calling intended to otherize Obama seemed to be the path to victory for both the Hillary Clinton and McCain campaigns. Attempts to portray Obama as different, un-American, unpatriotic, a socialist, a radical, and a terrorist were evident whenever one was inclined to turn to newspapers or various species of television news.

There is some scant evidence that Obama volunteers may have contributed to this uncivil discourse in their attempts to persuade openly racist voters to support Obama. In a *New York Times* article, Jennifer Steinhauer (2008) reported that one Obama volunteer pursued the support of one such voter by claiming: "One thing you have to remember about Obama, he's half white and he was raised by his white mother. So his views are more white than black." Steinhauer reported that another Obama volunteer offered: "I'm canvassing for Obama. If this issue comes up (prejudice), even obliquely, I emphasize that Obama is from a multiracial background and that his father was an African intellectual, not an American from the inner city." Volunteers who used strategies like these were reverting to the language of white supremacy to seek support for Obama. We would suggest that they were not only reverting to the language of white supremacy, but that such talk reinforced, normalized, and sustained white hegemony. Obama is acceptable, after all, because he has characteristics and attributes that white people can see in them. As one college student told reporter Shaila Dewan (2008): "I don't have any problem with a black president.... I think it would be fine, because a lot of things people stereotype black people with, I don't think Obama has any of them." White Supremacists explain the success of people of mixed parentage as due to their "raiding of a White gene pool" (Rohter, 2008) Well-meaning people, like the Obama volunteers, are relying on this same claim in order to achieve their objectives.

How do well-meaning people, of all races, push for social change through forms of discourse that normalize and sustain white hegemony? We believe these brief examples begin to offer interesting insights into this question. It is also important to note that these volunteers were communicating with their neighbors in ways that many would recognize as sophisticated and listener-centered. That is, they were meeting the targets of their persuasion on common ground. They recognized their racist beliefs and explicitly adapted their persuasive appeals to those racist beliefs ("You have to remember, he was raised by his white mother"). We imagine that these volunteers were largely unaware of the influence of the ideology and hegemonic structures that shaped their own language.

How should we view the election of our first African American President? Does this represent a sea change in racial relations in the United States? This was a remarkable moment. Many people have lived lives that are book-ended by the viciousness of segregation-era race relations and the election of our first African American President. It is important to remember that advances in human rights have always taken circuitous and elliptical paths (Rhea, 1997). In part, this is so because advances in human rights have always occurred through struggle rather than through a gradual drift toward tolerance. We have seen post-election events that suggest that this progress is likely to remain elliptical.

Immediate Post-Election Hatred

Numerous newspapers and news outlets reported a plethora of hate-filled reactions to the election of Barack Obama. The night of the election, an African American youth in New York was attacked by several white men who beat him with baseball bats and shouted "Obama." Cross burnings, neighbors vandalizing the lawns and Obama signs of neighbors, racial epithets on homes and cars, children chanting "assassinate Obama" on school buses, and black figures hung from nooses were some of the things reported in many communities (France 24, 2008).

One Georgia native volunteered: "Our nation is ruined and has been for several decades, and the election of Obama is merely confirmation of the change. If you had real change, it would involve all the members of [Obama's] church being deported" (CBS News.com, 2008). There is the principal who told the mother of a student suspended for wearing an Obama shirt: "Whether you like it or not, we're in the South, and there are a lot of people who are not happy with this decision" (CBS News.com, 2008). In Standish, Maine, a store owner held a lottery to predict the day that Obama would be assassinated. Four students at North Carolina State University admitted to writing "Let's shoot that (n-word) in the head" on a tunnel dedicated to free speech (CBS News.com, 2008; Owens, 2008).

Keller (2009b) reports in the Intelligence Report of the Southern Poverty Law Center that (a) a black man wearing an Obama T-shirt in Shreveport was beaten so badly he required multiple surgeries as his attackers shouted, "f---- Obama" and "n--r President," (b) in Torrance, California, swastikas were painted on the cars of Obama supporters, (c) a poster of Obama with a bullet hole through his head was discovered in a Milwaukee police station, and (d) a black church was burned in Springfield, Massachusetts, only hours after the election was called for Obama. These instances and others like them demonstrate that the election of Obama certainly does not signal the end of hatred and racism in the United States.

Indeed, hate groups appear prepared to turn Obama's victory to their advantage. Thomas Robb, the Director of the Knights of the Ku Klux Klan, noted that the election of Obama is "an opportunity to mobilize whites" and "serves as an effective recruiting tool.... Every time the television shows an image of Obama, it will be a reminder that our people have lost power in this country" (Rohter, 2008). David Duke argued that an Obama victory would serve as a visual aid for the organized hate movement. Their efforts appear to be working. Recently, the number of hate groups in the United States has grown to 962, the largest number of hate groups in the history of this country (Holthouse, 2009b).

After the election, the Chairman of the RNC distributed, among other songs, a song entitled "Barack the Magic *Negro*" (sung to the tune of "Puff the Magic Dragon"; emphasis added). The thrust of the song is that Barack is magic because he is a black man who does not scare white people (Sinderbrand, 2008b). Note that the thrust of this message is consistent with the message of those Obama volunteers who reminded their racist neighbors that Barack was not so black because he was raised by a white mother and grandmother. This also dovetails with a message that Thomas Robb sent fellow Klan members: "I know that you have been hearing that Obama would be the first black president. However, you and I both know that is not true. Obama is only half black. Not only is he only half black—he was not raised in a black environment" (Rohter, 2008). Robb's point is that Obama is successful because his father managed to "raid the White gene pool." This tortured logic permits Robb to use Obama's success as evidence of the dangers of miscegenation preached by Robb and other leaders of organized hate groups, while simultaneously maintaining the myth of white supremacy.

The vitriol of the hatred and Nativist rhetoric has only increased since the 2008 election. In July of 2010, a game called Alien Attack appeared at a church carnival in Pennsylvania (Nunnally, 2010; Stauffer, 2010). The game depicted a crude figure of President Obama with alien antennae emerging from his head. In his pocket is a scroll with "health care" scribbled on the outside of the document. The President's image is wearing a belt buckle displaying the words "The Prez Sez." The President's image also had "bullseye" targets placed on his forehead and heart. Children and adults paid a few dollars to shoot foam bullets at the targets. "Winners" received stuffed animals. This carnival game converges with the computer games on Tom Metzger's Web Page, The Insurgent, that allows visitors to shoot undocumented Mexicans, gay men, and African Americans. We maintain that all of these games serve to radicalize and desensitize players inclined to see their "targets" as enemies. We see these games as a type of discourse that connects hatred in the virtual world of organized hate groups with the hatred in the actual world of "mainstream" society, a church carnival, no less.

In summary, the 2008 Presidential Election was an election filled with hateful discourse. Early in the Democratic Primary, the Hillary Clinton campaign mapped out plans for how Obama might be constructed as insufficiently American and too different from average Americans to be elected President or to be trusted should he win election (the second and third characteristics of the hate stratagem). The McCain campaign would begin where the Clinton campaign left off. They would go further and construct Obama as an anti-Christian Muslim, a friend of terrorists, and a Marxist. Obama volunteers would inadvertently reinforce the language of white supremacy by validating the racist beliefs of voters. Finally, post-election discourse would become more hateful and uncivil as hate crimes grew more intense. Children chanting "assassinate Obama," the image of a black figure in the crosshairs of a rifle presented with "let's kill this (n-word)," and the vandalizing of property where Obama signs were displayed are all attempts to take pleasure in the domination of the other (the fourth characteristic of the hate stratagem). The discourse surrounding this election painted a mural of the hate stratagem in action: Positive in-group identities were constructed for white political candidates; negative and demeaned identities were constructed for the black political candidate, and eventually portrayed Obama as a threat to white people. We even saw attempts to verbally dominate and take pleasure in the imagined killing of the black candidate.

Nativism Opposes a President: Birthers, Guns, and the Return of Militias

A strain of Nativism arose following the inauguration of Barack Obama known as the Birther Movement. The Birther Movement grew out of a conspiracy theory that posits that Obama is not qualified to be President of the United States for a range of reasons, all of which have been empirically debunked. The reasons included that (a) Obama was not qualified to be President because his father was not an American, (b) Obama was not born in the United States, (c) Obama's notarized birth certificate from Hawaii, where he was born, is falsified, (d) Obama was spirited into the United States by unknown actors with nefarious motives, (e) the fact that Hawaii state law prevents the release of the original birth certificate, thus fueling the conspiracy, and (f) Hawaii will not release the birth certificate because it is controlled by Democrats, even though it was Linda Lingle, Hawaii's Republican Governor, who refused to release the original birth certificate (Montopolli, 2009; Smith, 2009a).

This movement has literally claimed that President Obama is not-of-America. They have also constructed him as a threat to America. The Birther Movement has claimed that Obama and his policies will create a second Civil War in the United States. The latter claim was made by Alan Keyes who never questioned Obama's citizenship when he campaigned against him for the U.S. Senate out of Illinois (Pascoe, 2009). The naïve, angry, and uninformed who are unwilling to accept the results of the Presidential Election are fertile soil for the vile seeds of Nativism. During the summer of 2009, Birthers interrupted Town Hall meetings across America to pollute a national discussion on health care by screaming at Congressmen and Senators that they should explain why they are refusing to challenge Barack Obama's citizenship.

In spite of the fact that the Birthers have been embarrassed by numerous dismissed lawsuits challenging Obama's election, the movement has maintained a presence on the national scene, and mainstream politicians and commentators flirted with the possibility that there might be truth to their claims. According to David Weigel (2009c) of *The Washington Independent*, Kansas lawyer and Senate hopeful Kris Kobach told a joke at a political rally: "What do God and President Obama have in common? Neither of them have a birth certificate." When he tried to distance himself from the remark, he left open the possibility that the Obama presidency might be illegal: "Until a court says otherwise, I believe Barack Obama is a natural-born citizen." He could have said: "As far as I know...."

In February, Representative Posey of Florida introduced legislation that would require campaigns to provide their candidate's birth certificate, and he told a host of an Internet show that he had "discussed the possibility of Obama being removed from office over 'the eligibility issue' with 'high-ranking members of our Judiciary Committee'" (Weigel, 2009c). Weigel reports that as of July 15, nine fellow Republicans were backing the bill and a candidate for Governor of Oklahoma in 2010 claimed that he would support such a bill (Etheridge, 2009). A spokesman for Representative Dan Burton said such a bill would avoid this "hullaballoo." A poll released by the Daily Kos reports that 28% of Republicans believe that the President is not a legal U.S. citizen (Smith, 2009b). At a September 7, 2009, rally Representative Jean Schmidt of Ohio was confronted by a Birther who wanted her to investigate President Obama's legal status. Schmidt waited to calm the woman and then whispered into her ear: "I agree with you" (Thrush, 2009; Zapanta, 2009).

Lou Dobbs, famous for his Nativist rhetoric against "illegal aliens," commented: "I'm starting to think we have a document issue. You suppose he's un…no, I won't even use the word undocumented, it wouldn't be right" (Graham, 2009).

Were the Birthers a small but vocal group of Americans with a peculiar conspiracy theory to explain how an African American was elected to the Presidency, they should not represent a concern to our social and political fabric. However, it appears that elected members of Congress and mainstream television personalities provide support for their rants and not-so-veiled hatred, despite the public presence of a notarized copy of the President's birth certificate and the fact that courts have rejected all challenges to the President's legal status. Of course, those finding truth in this conspiracy theory will not be deterred by evidence. Why would these mainstream voices offer tacit acceptance of the Birther conspiracy theory? Are the politicians merely craven? Do they really believe the conspiracy themselves?

The Birthers are driven by a rage because they believe Obama to be an "illegal alien" who has taken control of the Federal Government, a likely puppet of a socialist New World Order. Ever-present at Birther rallies were vandalized images of Obama (a) that were made to look like Hitler, (b) that depicted a swastika embedded in his forehead, (c) that depicted the communist hammer and sickle embedded in his forehead, and (d) that were made to look like the terrorist Joker from the latest *Batman* movie. The logical inconsistency and mutual exclusivity between Fascism and Communism is not at issue. The point is that this vandalism of Obama's image becomes a way of symbolically defeating Obama (the fourth characteristic of the hate stratagem), in addition to otherizing and dehumanizing him (the third characteristic of the hate stratagem).

Another group of protestors began to rally against Obama. This time they brought guns. In New Hampshire, a man protested at an Obama rally with a gun strapped to his leg and held a sign with a Thomas Jefferson quotation: "The tree of liberty must be refreshed from time to time with the blood of tyrants and patriots" (Walsh, 2009). In an interview, this protestor claimed that health care reforms were taking us down the road to tyranny (Thompson, 2009). His name is William Kostic, an Arizonan recently moved to New Hampshire (Thompson, 2009; Walsh, 2009). Walsh (2009) reported on his involvement with several anti-government extremist groups and his identification with Randy Weaver, formerly a member of the Aryan Nations hate group, among his most admired individuals. The potential importance of this association is described below.

Another gun-toting (AR-15 semi-automatic assault rifle) protestor in Phoenix used similar language when he was interviewed by radio host Ernest Hancock. Hancock would comment: "We are up against a tyrannical government that will rob the next generation as long as they can get away with it" (CNNPolitics.com, 2009). Hancock later admitted that this interview was contrived and the protestor, whom he knew, was not a randomly selected protester. Hancock is an interesting actor in this staged performance because he was a friend and defender of two members of the Viper Militia when they were arrested in 1996 for plotting to bomb government buildings (Brooke, 1996; Elliott, 2009).

The Viper Militia was a close group of friends who were obsessed with bombs and guns. They frequently retreated into the desert to blow up rocks and fire assault rifles, preparing for their eventual struggle with the New World Order. After the Oklahoma City bombing, the F.B.I. was vigilant to such groups, and Viper activities caught their attention. The Vipers were arrested following an investigation. At the time of their arrest, police seized (a) 90 high-powered rifles, (b) hundreds of pounds of bomb-making compound, (c) nearly a ton of ammonium nitrate, (d) a truckload of ammunition, and (e) blasting caps, blasting chord, gas masks, bulletproof vests, and camouflage uniforms with the "Viper insignia" (Brooke, 1996). The Vipers had even scouted federal buildings for potential bomb attacks (Snow, 1999). The case appeared to be wrapped up when police found a video that contained instructions for the placement of bombs in the scouted targets (Brooke, 1996). Ten of the 12 Vipers would plead guilty to a host of charges. One Viper who went to trial was sentenced to over four years in prison. The final defendant had left the Vipers before their plans to bomb federal buildings ensued. He was found not guilty of one charge and the jury was hung on a second charge (Snow, 1999).

At the time of their arrest, Ernest Hancock claimed that the video produced by the Vipers was for "educational" purposes only. He did not seem to see that the purpose of the video was to educate themselves and others to terrorize the government. Why is Hancock's connection with the Vipers significant? Why is Kostic's connection to similar groups and his admiration of Aryan Nation affiliate, Randy Weaver, important? A special report from the Southern Poverty Law Center in August of 2009 reported that militia groups are, once again, on the rise: "Militia training events, huge numbers which are viewable on YouTube videos, are spreading. One federal agency estimates that 50 new militia training groups have sprung up in less than two years" (Keller, 2009c). Recently, the Southern Poverty Law Center Report identified two former organizers of a 1990's Michigan militia had surfaced in Alaska to spread the word that "something very evil this way comes" (SPLC, 2009-b). Today's militia rhetoric is as apocalyptic as the rhetoric of the 1990s. In Pensacola, Florida, a militia leader and retired F.B.I. agent tells militia members: "The federal government has set up 1,000 internment camps across the country and is storing 30,000 guillotines and a half-million caskets in Atlanta" (cited in Keller, 2009c, p. 32). In Lexington, Massachusetts, a leader of the militia group Oath Keepers tells followers: "We're in perilous times…perhaps more perilous than in 1775" (Keller, 2009c, p. 32). This kind of apocalyptic talk gave rise to Timothy McVeigh (and the Vipers) and other bloody militia attacks in the 1990s.

The Nativist discourse we discussed earlier is not unrelated to the rise in militia activities. According to Keller (2009c): "In fact, the anti-immigration movement is both fueling and helping to racialize the anti-government Patriot resurgence. More and more, members of the Nativist groups like the Minutemen are adopting core militia ideas and fears." (p. 37) Thus, Minutemen groups are beginning to see illegal immigration as a symptom of a broader problem (Holthouse, 2009c). As one Minuteman put it: "We're still concerned about the border intruders, but since this all started we've become aware of the fact that border intruders are *just pawns in the big game*" (Holthouse, 2009c, p. 44; emphasis added). So, who is the new enemy?

One Minuteman leader, Jeff Schwilke, claimed that the greater cause Minutemen would serve is to fight the "socialist" takeover of America:

Schwilke announced the formation of the Patriot Coalition, made up of 23 organizations including Minuteman factions, tax-protest groups, pro-gun rights groups, and two anti-immigration outfits listed as hate groups by the Southern Poverty Law Center. A subsequent press release described the common cause of the groups under the motto: Secure Borders, Constitution, and Rule of Law. (Holthouse, 2009c, p. 44)

So, it appears that a portion of this "Second Wave Militia" comes from a militia infiltration of Nativists, Birthers, and Tea Party devotees. This is interesting and suggests that militia groups have learned from their past when Christian Identity groups infiltrated militias in the 1980s and 1990s and used militias as their foot soldiers (Perry, 2001).

Conclusion

In chapter two we described how the hate movement was evolving and changing through the integration of the different cultures of hate. We may be witnessing another morphing of the hate movement. Nativists and hate-mongers may be in the process of camouflaging themselves with tax protestors, Birthers, and anti-immigration protestors. We have seen people in these movements raise substantive objections to many of Obama's policies. We have also seen Obama attacked with racial and xenophobic slurs. This makes these groups all the more inviting for the hate-monger because they may express all manner of hateful ideas and rage, while claiming to be talking about substantive issues. For example, one may claim to be speaking against illegal immigration even as one attacks a non-American or non-Western culture as inferior.

We see how hate-mongers may camouflage their hate by embedding themselves among Tea Party/tax protestors and protestors of "big government" health care reform. Former President Jimmy Carter called for more civil discourse in discussions of these political issues and suggested that many people who opposed Obama were animated by racism (Franke-Ruta, 2009). *New York Times* columnist David Brooks disagreed and argued that this was merely anti-government populists who were rejecting the elitism of Obama because he observed white anti-health care/anti-Obama protestors having lunch with African American protestors from another rally (Brooks, 2009). Carter and Brooks can both be correct, of course. A portion of those opposing Obama policies may be populist/anti-government protestors and some of them may still be motivated by, and expressing, hate. In other words, the hate-mongers are camouflaging themselves among those populists observed by David Brooks. This allows them to employ hateful Nativist rhetoric, calling Obama an illegal alien, un-American, Hitler, a terrorist Joker, a Communist, a Fascist, etc. We have illustrated how this kind of discourse has produced violence in the recent past. When we hear white people claim that they are fearful for what America is becoming and that they "want their America back," we are inclined to expect more violence.

Chapter 7

Anti-Hate Narratives

The United States is unlike most of its Western cousins in terms of the laws that regulate, or do not regulate, hate speech. U.S. courts have held fast to Oliver Wendell Holmes's logic that "The best test of truth is the power of the thought to get itself accepted in the competition of the market.... I think that we should be eternally vigilant against attempts to check the expression of opinions that we loathe and believe to be fraught with death" (cited in Liptak, 2008). As we have illustrated numerous times, hate speech is often fraught with violence and death. Liptak (2008) provides examples of the countries, many of them Western countries, which treat hate speech differently than the United States:

> Canada, England, France, Germany, the Netherlands, South Africa, Australia and India all have laws or have signed international conventions banning hate speech. Israel and France forbid the sale of Nazi items like swastikas and flags. It is a crime to deny the Holocaust in Canada, Germany and France.

In the United States, the courts have treated Klan and neo-Nazi rallies as constitutionally protected speech. The labyrinth of racist novels, Internet Web Pages, podcasts, White Power music, and online newspapers and newsletters discussed in this text are forms of constitutionally protected speech.

This U.S. perspective on hate speech makes anti-hate discourse, and the principles discussed in this chapter, all the more important. Hate speech probably should be constitutionally protected in order to safeguard the First Amendment. Most Americans are probably uncomfortable with the government determining what speech is legal and what speech is illegal. Arguably, Holmes's notion of a "market place of ideas" assumed responses to offensive speech would be met with opposing speech and that "the people" would regulate the ideas that become a part of public discourse.

While hate speech should be protected, we should not lose sight of the fact that it is a deadly form of speech that poses dangers to individuals and to liberal democracies. In chapter three, we quoted Tsesis (2002) who described hate speech as providing a puppet show in which old prejudices and hatred

are portrayed to indoctrinate new generations into ideologies of racial, ethnic, and religious superiority. Liberal democracies are also grounded in a belief in the importance and dignity of the individual. For liberal democracies
to thrive, all individuals must be willing and able to participate in that democracy, people and their speech and actions are the lifeblood of democracies. As Alinsky (1971) notes: "Anything that opposes people because of
race, religion, creed, or economic status is the antithesis of the fundamental
dignity of the individual" (p. 122). Tsesis (2002) makes the same point differently when he argues that hate speech treats people as expendable resources for the pursuit of a specific political interest.

By posing a threat to the dignity of the individual, hate speech poses a
threat to the social fabric of democracies. As we have made clear, people
pursue a variety of social and political goals through the vilification of other
identities. Thus, hate speech sows conflict between groups and diminishes
social stabilities on which democracies depend.

Hate speech also poses a threat to personal liberties that define democracies. Hate speech is used to cultivate fear of the Other. In so doing, hate
speech victimizes the in-group of the producer of hate speech through fear. It
is fear that often leads people in democracies to sacrifice their own personal
liberties in order to seek safety from the "dangerous" Other. Recently, many
Americans were willing to sacrifice an unknown degree of privacy to allow
the government to protect the homeland. As we suggest in chapter seven,
Americans, white Americans, have experienced decades of politicians telling
them who and what they should fear for the small and shortsighted purpose
of winning elections. Now, white Americans are seeing their first African
American President, their first African American Attorney General, and their
first Latina Supreme Court Justice. This comes at a time when America will
not have a statistical majority by the year 2042 (Chideya, 2008).

Finally, hate speech poses a threat to many of our constitutional ideals,
such as the equality of individuals. Hate speech, through its vilification of the
Other, demeans and dehumanizes the Other. In this way, the in-group learns
to think of itself as superior to the out-group—physically, spiritually, and
morally superior. This may eventually justify all manner of sins. In the
American colonies, slave traders viewed themselves as doing the work of
God (Tsesis, 2002). Such rationales were only logical once the African
slaves had been dehumanized through hate speech.

So, an anti-hate discourse is important because it may serve to protect a
relatively vulnerable out-group. However, an anti-hate discourse may also
protect larger communities and democracies that are threatened by hate
speech. Clearly, hate speech may not always pose an immanent threat to spe-

cific persons. However, hate speech is always destructive and dangerous to communities within which it is practiced (Waltman & Haas, 2007).

Purpose

The purpose of this work is to identify an ideology of tolerance espoused by the Southern Poverty Law Center's Teaching Tolerance program, and that will serve as a rationale for a desirable anti-hate discourse. The Teaching Tolerance program was selected for analysis in this research for several reasons. First, it is clear to most that this is a program that attempts to respond to the ideology of hate by creating and espousing an alternative set of beliefs that envision more humane communities. Second, this program represents one of the most well-known and influential anti-hate programs in the United States. Teaching Tolerance is distributed, without cost, to educators and schools throughout the country. Third, this program is probably the most comprehensive anti-hate program in the country; its materials were created to address hatred among children at K-12 grade levels, on university campuses, and in adult working and social environments. Fourth, program materials are distributed in a variety of forms (e.g., physical texts, documentaries, and a Web Site, Teaching Tolerance).

Conceiving an Anti-Hate Discourse

A desirable anti-hate rhetoric must do more than stand in opposition to hatred; it must also strive to achieve that which we might take to be the antithesis of hate speech. We argue that one way of understanding the antithesis of hate speech is to understand what is destroyed by hate speech.

As we have argued, hate speech is discourse that is directed at the politicization of social differences. It creates a social environment where identity-mania (Meyer, 2001) thrives, where nothing matters but the confirmation of one's own identity. In this environment, the advancement of any other identity is seen as a threat to one's own identity. To accomplish identity-mania, the hate-monger employs linguistic stratagems that have proven effective across time and culture, such as (a) the creation of identification with an in-group, (b) the creation of moralized differences with a specified out-group, (c) the vilification of the out-group identity, and (d) the expression of the desire to dominate or do actual violence to the other (Waltman, 2003; R. K. Whillock, 1995). This "hate stratagem" creates enemies, an ideology of hate, and a symbolic code that justifies ethnoviolence against the enemy (Waltman, 2003; Waltman & Davis, 2004, 2005). Anti-hate rhetoric, therefore, should encourage a view of social identities that depoliticizes social differences and attempts to create moments that encourage groups to see the possibility of a collective life that values and respects difference. What discursive concept(s) would be useful for encouraging this view of collective life? Researchers in Communication Studies and allied disciplines have argued for some time that the storytelling, or "narrative," construct offers insights into human reasoning and persuasion, and into the ways that people construct their understanding of their social world (e.g., Bonilla-Silva, 2003; Bormann, 1972; Doxtader, 2003; La Rossa, 1995; Sternberg, 1995; Walker & Dickson, 2004). Doxtader (2003) explored reconciliation as a rhetorical concept and offers insight into the importance of narrative to the reconciliation pursued by the Truth and Reconciliation Commission of South Africa:

> Reconciliation beckons story-telling. To be more accurate, it is frequently thought that reconciliation involves hermeneutic dialogue that aims for the restoration of the capacity to narrate. Confronted with the need to deal with the past, facing questions about the meaning of history and its capacity to shape the future, reconciliation seems to begin with expressions of experience. (p. 280)

Doxtader is referring to narratives detailing the experiences of oppression, domination, and subjugation created by the evil of Apartheid, including the relatively minor harms Apartheid visited upon those who benefited from that system. These narratives played a central role in the creation of a set of "facts" that would shape a dialogue that might make reconciliation possible. Similarly, we believe that narratives play an important role in the creation of an anti-hate discourse. In the following pages, we define and describe the narrative construct and the social outcomes and functions of stories.

Narrative Defined

A narrative is a discourse structure that relates people, events, and objects together through a plot device. Through a plot, social actors are characterized (identified, if you will), allied with one another (e.g., Jews and African Americans), or positioned in opposition to another group (e.g., Aryans). Through a plot, a set of events is related, made coherent, and rendered understandable (Hart, 1997). Clearly, social actors seldom have a neutral quality relative to one another. That is, they play complementary roles (e.g., heroes and villains). Within the racist Aryan imagination, one can identify a number of plots or storylines (Bonilla-Silva 2003). For example, Jews may be understood to be a villainous counterpart to the heroic Aryan and the living embodiment of the Zionist-Occupied Government plot or the Jewish International Conspiracy plot. African Americans may be positioned as a threat to Aryans through a Black Predator plot (Waltman & Davis, 2004, 2005).

The Potential Influence of Narratives

We argue that the de-politicization of social differences and the healing of community wounds may be accomplished discursively through strategic forms of storytelling and narration. Narratives may have a powerful impact on social memory due to the way they construct desired identities and promote desired forms of behavior (Winslade & Monk, 1999, pp. 67–70). The power of storytelling is recognized by scholars and activists who have used stories to promote the positive reconstruction of identities in therapeutic contexts (Bowen, 1997), in educational contexts (Compton, 1997; Winslade & Monk, 1999), in children with disabilities (Lawton & Edwards, 1997), and in abused children (Leisten, 1997).

Researchers have found that storytelling in the classroom may be used effectively to uncover and change social injustices and to promote inclusiveness in children's play (Paley, 1992; Rosenberg, McKeon, & Dinero, 1999; Sapon-Shevin, Dobbelaire, Corrigan, Goodman, & Martin, 1998a; Sapon-Shevin et al., 1998b). Interpersonal communication scholars are describing the various ways that people use stories to make sense of their relationships (La Rossa, 1995; Sternberg, 1995; Walker & Dickson, 2004; Wood, 2000, 2001).

In summary, there is a good deal of evidence that narratives can be useful for the recuperation of social identities that have been rejected, vilified, or dehumanized. We believe that a desirable anti-hate discourse responds to various forms of hate speech through the narrative format. This initial investigation explores this assumption and explores the kinds of stories told by the Teaching Tolerance program.

Procedures

Our analysis of the anti-hate discourse produced by the Teaching Tolerance program began with a critique of Teaching Tolerance. We analyzed Teaching Tolerance to identify and more thoroughly understand the narratives used to oppose hate and promote a more tolerant society. This is a Web Site maintained by the Southern Poverty Law Center, and it is a program devoted to fighting hatred and teaching tolerance in a variety of communities that serve both children and adults. A Web Site that has received awards for activism, education, and public service, Teaching Tolerance provides (a) current news about groups and individuals committed to working for tolerance, (b) guidebooks that help adult and young activists respond to hatred in their communities, and (c) resources for teachers and parents and games for young children that teach the values of tolerance and diversity. Teaching Tolerance should be understood as a complicated master text that draws together a number of smaller texts published by the Teaching Tolerance program in one locale in cyberspace (e.g., *10 Ways to Fight Hate; Responding to Hate in Communities; Responding to Hate at School*). Additionally, our analysis is also based on two documentaries produced by Teaching Tolerance: (a) *Starting Small: Teaching Tolerance in Preschool and the Early Grades* (including a handbook by the same title that provides additional narration and background on the activists, teachers, and schools that are highlighted in the documentary), and (b) *A Place at the Table* (a documentary that features high school-aged students representing different groups and who tell the stories of their family's experiences in their struggle to become fully participating U.S. citizens following immigration or enslavement). While the *Starting Small* documentary is intended to provide teachers with activities and resources that are useful for teaching children respect for social differences, it is also a persuasive text that instructs adults on the proper attitudes, beliefs, and actions for one who wishes to live a life in opposition to hate and in support of tolerance and inclusion. *A Place at the Table* creates a common ground among various identities through narratives that illustrate each person's (family's) struggle to realize the American dream.

The "text" for the present research is usefully understood as a diffuse text (e.g., Brummett, 1994; Williamson, 2002). A diffuse text is a collection of signs working for the same or related rhetorical influence (Brummett, 1994). Brummett (1994) writes: "A diffuse text will sometimes not be recognized as a text by those experiencing it, and at other times will be recognized by them as a very complex experience" (p. 64). The elements of our diffuse text constitute a collection of signs that do work toward the same rhetorical influence: the promotion of tolerance and an appreciation for diversity in community. When we quote or reference material from Teaching Tolerance, we identify the specific subsection of the Web Page by citing the title of that subsection where the material can be found (e.g., *10 Ways to Fight Hate*). The *Starting Small* documentary and manual describe the anti-hate programs in seven communities: (a) the Peace Education Foundation in Miami, Florida, (b) the Happy Medium school in Seattle, Washington, (c) the Cabrillo College Children's Center in Aptos, California, (d) Maria Mitchell Elementary in Denver, Colorado, (e) Elmwood Elementary in Shawnee, Ohio, (e) Edgewood Elementary in New Haven, Connecticut, and (f) State Pre-K Demonstration Center in Chicago, Illinois. When we quote or reference the *Starting Small* manual, we cite the project directors and their co-authors

(Bullard, Carnes, Hofer, Polk, & Sheets, 1997) and identify the program under discussion. When referencing or quoting from *A Place at the Table*, we simply identify the documentary by name.[2]

To identify the narratives in our text, the researchers followed procedures conceptually similar to open and axial coding procedures employed in the grounded theory approach to coding qualitative data (see Lindlof & Taylor, 2002; Strauss, 1987; Strauss & Corbin, 1990).

Open Coding Procedures

The first author and another coder read Teaching Tolerance separately and made note of the narratives. A broad taxonomy of narratives was initially constructed from this procedure. Similar phrases, sentences, and images were coded as representing the same narrative. After reading Teaching Tolerance completely, the researchers perused the text to ensure their own satisfaction with the consistency of their individual categorizations. The first author continued open coding procedures by engaging in a similar critique of *Starting Small* (both the documentary and the companion manual) and *A Place at the Table.*

Axial Coding Procedures

Next, the first author engaged in axial coding procedures (Strauss & Corbin, 1990), or procedures that resulted in a constant comparative analysis that involved concurrent refining of the narratives. During this data collection phase, narratives that occurred infrequently were folded into a larger category of narrative or dropped from the analysis. Narratives remained in the final taxonomy due to the recurrence of words (i.e., different words that expressed the same idea or meaning), repetition (i.e., key words or phrases repeated verbatim), or forcefulness (i.e., an idea or image represented as vivid or intense by underlining, punctuation, or other artistic elements). The first author engaged in axial coding until no additional myths could be identified. This analysis found three super-categories of narratives: (a) Personal Responsibility, (b) Individual Action, and (c) Community Building. The spe-

---

[2] It should be noted that this Web Page was changed after this chapter was written. However, the preponderance of texts produced by Teaching Tolerance and the SPLC are still represented in the new structure. There is still much to be learned from our analysis and that is reported in the following pages. Because we frequently reference the original texts (e.g., *Starting Small* and *10 Ways to Fight Hate*) readers should not be distracted by changes in the Teaching Tolerance Web Page.

cific findings of this research, and the narrative subcategories, are presented below.

This close reading and critique of Teaching Tolerance materials provides useful insights into the ways that stories contribute to an ideology of tolerance.

Analysis

Teaching Tolerance was structured similar to a news publication with feature stories and a right-hand navigation toolbar that could be accessed on every page of the site. This navigation bar contained three categories of information: *Tolerance Watch*, *Do Something*, and *Dig Deeper*. One of the most prevalent themes presented on the Web Site is its commitment to an extremely broad definition of hate and bias. The home page included articles that link to issues of prejudice concerning race, ethnicity, sexual orientation, economic status, disability, and gender. This is an intellectual choice as well as a mission statement and political position. It reflects an understanding that most haters do not specialize when selecting the objects of their hatred. Indeed, the hate ideology we described earlier is composed of a set of interrelated anti-Semitic, homophobic, and racist beliefs (Perry, 2001). Consequently, one may not strive for tolerance by picking and choosing those groups and issues one will respect. Each article on Teaching Tolerance highlighted one of these types of prejudice. These articles provided narratives from people who are experiencing prejudice in their own lives, many of whom are actively taking part in combating the hate around them. In the About Us section, the following definition and discussion of Tolerance was offered:

> Tolerance is respect, acceptance and appreciation of the rich diversity of our world's cultures, our forms of expression and ways of being human. Tolerance is harmony in difference. We view tolerance as a way of thinking and feeling—but most importantly, of acting—that gives us peace in our individuality, respect for those unlike us, the wisdom to discern humane values and the courage to act upon them.

The themes that prevailed throughout the site are echoed here: a commitment to peace, respect, wisdom, and action. Teaching Tolerance also established the main mission of the Web Site not as one that opposes hate, *but as one that embraces tolerance*. The content of this Web Site did not seek to create an in-group in diametric opposition to hate-based groups. Instead, the substance of this site attempted to build community, through unity in diversity, committed to "anti-bias activism" (About Us). This Web Site rhetorically constructed an ideology of tolerance while also providing explicit instructions and materials constructed to counter hate speech on a concrete level involving both individual and community action. This ideology of tolerance is found in personal responsibility, concrete actions, and community building narratives.

Personal Responsibility Narratives

Themes of personal responsibility were not only present in the news and human interest stories on the site, but they were also extended directly to the readers. Regardless of the article or subject matter, the Web Site almost always offered ways for readers to examine their own biases and to learn more about those who may be different from themselves. This implies, therefore, that tolerance is not achieved but pursued. Part of this pursuit is vigilance to the causes and threat of hate (Tolerance Requires Vigilance narrative). Consequently, Teaching Tolerance did not assume that readers were free of bias, but instead, it assumed that readers are open to examining the biases they may have as a means to countering them through education and reflection. In the Dig Deeper section, readers could access a variety of articles that helped them to examine their own biases. Again, by digging deeper, readers may learn what is required to remain vigilant to their own personal intolerance.

After reading "Easy Targets: Arab Americans Fight Bias," an article about the still pervasive workplace discrimination that Arab Americans face in the post 9-11 world, the reader could choose to follow the links provided to three topically similar articles. In the article, "EEOC, Arab Americans Press Enforcement of Anti-Discrimination Law," the reader could learn more about the response of the Equal Employment Opportunity Commission (EEOC) to the discrimination against Arab Americans in the workplace following the September 11th attacks. The article ended with the EEOC's plea that employers "follow the law rather than turning reflexively to the stereotype of national origin or religion as a basis for employment decisions." Again this article illustrated the need to remain vigilant, and it detailed how social circumstances may lead one to act in an intolerant manner (Tolerance Requires Vigilance).

Following the dedication of the Civil Rights Memorial on October 24, 2005, a number of quotes from individuals who witnessed the dedication supported the Tolerance Requires Vigilance narrative:

> I think people have gotten really confused about what our priorities should be and I think that they've gotten focused on what I call an 'occupation with the unimportant'.... So they watch the sports, and watch the Internet and listen to songs that aren't about strength, pride and justice, but about just the opposite.... I think many of us have separated from that, not wanting to remember the pain and the anguish.

Similarly, another witness noted:

> Some of the people want to forget about the sit-in at the Woolworth counter in
> Greensboro, but I've always believed that if you forget about something then you
> have to relive it…I think today was wonderful and uplifting.

These quotes echo the position taken by Teaching Tolerance, which urged people to pursue a perspective that encourages critical reflection on the way they live their lives and on the implicit values reflected in their behavior (occupation with the unimportant or refusing to forget history).

In *Starting Small,* classroom teachers are encouraged to be vigilant by being careful to structure classroom environments that respect all racial and ethnic groups by (a) developing lesson plans and using resources that reflect both cultural diversity and human commonality, (b) watching for stereotypical images in classroom decorations, lessons, books, and music, (c) supporting children's curiosity about racial and ethnic differences to help them understand diversity and see differences as natural and special, (d) providing opportunities for cross-racial and cross-gender interactions, and (e) affirming children's home cultures through classroom resources and "sharing" of family traditions (Bullard et al., 1997, p. 103). Moreover, classroom teachers learn that vigilance encompasses not only awareness of how they structure their environment, but also reflection on their own personal behavior. Teachers are encouraged to assume accountability for personal and school practices that promote discrimination. For example, teachers are instructed to (a) examine and reflect on their "own patterns of response toward children and adults of different races, ethnic groups, social classes, religions, etc.," (b) discuss with staff members any biased actions or comments directed at young children or adults by staff, (c) evaluate school policies and procedures for prejudicial elements, and (d) seek in-service diversity training for staff and parents. (Bullard et al., 1997, p. 104) Of course, teachers learn that they must not only practice vigilance, but that they must teach students to engage abstract concepts such as power, control, personal rights, and personal needs (Bullard et al., 1997, p. 108). These principles and practices are highlighted in the example of the Illinois State Pre-K Demonstration Center, which "has been committed to celebrating diversity, eliminating bias and nurturing relationships based on mutual respect":

> Demo Center teachers make self-scrutiny a part of the daily routine, regularly taking
> stock of their classrooms and their thought processes for signs of stereotyping…they
> continuously monitor…the emotional climate of the school. They set aside one
> lunch period each week for focused discussion of classroom concerns…they take
> part in anti-bias workshops around the city. (Bullard et al., 1997, p. 172)

In the Speak Up section on Teaching Tolerance, an African American woman shared her personal challenge to confront her own biases while raising her teenage niece. The niece joined her school basketball team and came home and said: "Auntie, there are 12 girls on the team, and 6 are lesbians." The woman went on to share:

> I thought I wasn't homophobic, but, boy, I had to sleep on that one. I was thinking, you know, they're going to recruit her. And here I thought I was cool. It used to be my fear—and I hate to say this, but it's true—it used to be my fear that she would come home with a white man. Now I'm asking myself, "Would I be more upset if she came home with a white man or a black woman?"

This is followed by advice: Talk to family members about your bias and get their feedback, say aloud what it is about yourself that you want to work on and commit to learn more, and set a date that you will sit down and take stock of what you have learned.

A second narrative of personal responsibility is the You're Not Alone narrative. This narrative was illustrated, once again, in a quote from a visitor who witnessed the Civil Rights Memorial Dedication Ceremony on October 24, 2005:

> It will always be a close-run struggle between those who will stand for justice and those who will try to divide us. But I submit to you that standing here, five minutes away from where George Wallace declared that men and women could not be equal, there is a new ground rising. There is a new Alabama in sight. There is a new country in sight. But only if we keep believing in each other, in the power of right.

This narrative also emerged as readers were instructed in ways they can take individual action in their communities:

> The good news is.... All over the country people are fighting hate, standing up to promote tolerance and inclusion. More often than not, when hate flares up, good people rise up against it—often in greater numbers and with stronger voices.

Additionally, "Tolerance Watch: A Backlash Continues Against American Arabs and Muslims" provided not only a catalogue of instances of discrimination against Arab Americans, but it also provided more informational links such as "Who are the Arab Americans?", "What is Islam?", and "100 Questions and Answers About Arab Americans." Part of the Web Site's message of tolerance was a commitment to the idea that through education and by combating ignorance we can successfully create tolerance (Tolerance Requires Learning narrative). These three links provided readers with a chance to educate themselves about the Arab American community. By providing information about a wide variety of cultures and lifestyles, Teaching Tolerance provided ways for readers to confront their own biases and gain valuable information that will help them to be more tolerant.

A third choice after the "Easy Targets: Arab Americans Fight Bias" article was a more direct link to "Who are the Arab Americans?" This link took readers a step further and proposed an activity that is designed to be done in a classroom, but that could be adapted to any situation, that fosters discussion about what it means to be Arab American, from where Arab Americans emigrate, and many additional questions that address and correct many of the perceptions of Arab Americans that are based on biased or incorrect information. The Tolerance Requires Learning narrative was also evident in the Dig Deeper section of the Web Site where readers were encouraged to explore The Power of Language, a text that organizes a set of activities that helps the reader to deconstruct biased language that objectifies men, women, gay people, and a variety of ethnic groups.

In North Miami's Peace Education Program, children learn to be tolerant and value differences by talking about some of the bad examples that adults set for them through violent and anti-social ways of handling inter-group conflict. They also learn about how problems can be solved peacefully instead of through violence (Bullard et al., 1997, p. 149).

The principle that tolerance requires learning is also illustrated through Cabrillo Colleges' Child Development Center where early childhood education is pursued through a comprehensive anti-bias curriculum (Bullard et al., 1997). Julie Olsen Edwards, the founding Director of the Cabrillo program, noted that one of the big differences between an equity program and a diversity program is education that pursues the long-range goal of helping children to find the courage to take a stand against bias. She described four steps to an early childhood equity program:

> (a) helping children develop a sense of pride in and a language to describe their own heritage, (b) exploring differences of all kinds, (c) building on children's notions of fairness to create a sense of justice and the capacity to recognize bias, and (d) helping children find ways to confront and eliminate biases they encounter. (Bullard et al., 1997, pp. 34, 35, 36)

All of the articles linked from Teaching Tolerance provided opportunities to dig deeper. After reading the article, "Coming Out Day: A Letter to the Past," the story about a gay man confronting a homophobic gym teacher from his past not as retaliation, but as a form of healing, readers could "Dig Deeper" and find more personal narratives by following the links to "Finding My Stride," "The Real Face of the Teacher," and "Ready or Not: A Coming

Out Story." These articles portrayed homosexuals not as a stereotyped "others," but as individuals from all walks of life. In the "Ready or Not" article, the gay man's bravery in coming out prompted this response:

> You know...maybe I am a little prejudiced. When you said that you were gay it really bothered me. I am very religious. So maybe it is good that you were here speaking because it's opened a new door for me to look into. Thank you.

This also suggested another narrative. It offers reconciliation as an ideal when both parties to conflict are willing to look beyond differences to imagine a new way of being in the world (Tolerance Embraces Reconciliation narrative).

Elmwood Elementary in Shawnee, Ohio, for example, adopted a school-wide program devoted to teaching respect for social differences, to appreciate diversity, and to respect opinions different from their own. Of course, the school realizes that children will not always respect diversity and opinions different from their own. They take such moments as opportunities for learning and reconciliation. A tangible practice is described in *Starting Small*: "Near the principal's office is a Peace Wall, each paper brick represents a conflict between students that has been resolved. The wall grows as children add drawings to illustrate their mastery of the peace process" (Bullard et al., 1997, p. 68).

The Personal Responsibility narratives underscore the need for personal reflection and an acceptance and investigation into the biases we all hold. The articles found in the Dig Deeper section are all possible catalysts for individuals to experience personally rewarding moments through a dedication to tolerance. The more people examine the lives of those who are different from themselves, the greater the chances that they will discover opportunities to identify personal prejudices, and thus create the possibility of becoming more tolerant.

The Personal Responsibility narratives are important for reasons other than personal vigilance and moral development. An ideology of tolerance also requires individual action, and personal responsibility will serve as a catalyst for personal action.

Action Narratives

One action narrative is the Speak Up narrative. A host of narratives describe people's action, or lack of action, in a range of scenarios taken from actual, everyday, casual conversation. The thrust of the Speak Up narrative is that the easiest way for us to respond to intolerance is to immediately address the issue when others carelessly use biased and dehumanizing language in front of us:

> Your brother routinely makes anti-Semitic comments. Your neighbor uses the N-word in casual conversation. Your co-worker ribs you about your Italian surname, asking if you're in the mafia. Your classmate insults something by saying, "That's so gay." And you stand there, in silence, thinking, "What can I say in response to that?" Or you laugh along, uncomfortably. Or, frustrated or angry, you walk away without saying anything, thinking later, "I should have said *something*."

Instances of the Speak Up narrative emphasize the personally rewarding feelings that people felt for speaking up and the frustrations people felt when they did not speak up. This also reinforces the role of education in the ideology of tolerance. Namely, people often do not speak up because they are not sure what to say in such encounters.

Olsen Edwards emphasized the need to teach children to speak out about intolerance and differences early: "When we don't give them a language to talk about differences because we're so scared of it, it becomes something that children feel is forbidden and dangerous" (Bullard et al., 1997, p. 35). She continued: "Following a conversation with (or about) a large lady on the bus a parent might say, 'you know, some people look at people with big bodies and think just because you're big, I'm not going to like you…isn't that awful?" (Bullard et al., 1997, p. 37). She felt that such comments that focus on a child's sense of fairness can help children pick up on notions of injustice. In a description of activities entitled "Facing Prejudice," Edwards notes that simply by speaking up when children make thoughtless remarks about those who are different, teachers can prevent the formation of long-term stereotypes and entrenched biases because children have not yet learned the ideology of prejudice (Bullard et al., 1997, p. 103).

A second narrative that emerges is the Powerful Individual narrative. The individual is presented as a powerful tool to respond to hate-mongers through a variety of forms of individual, political action. In *10 Ways to Fight Hate,* the reader is admonished:

> You can spread tolerance through church bulletins, door-to-door fliers, Web Sites, local cable TV bulletin boards, letters to the editor and print advertisements. Hate shrivels under strong light. Beneath their neo-Nazi exteriors, hate purveyors are…surprisingly subject to public pressure and ostracism.

Individuals are also encouraged to push powerful others, such as legislators, to support, for example, hate crime legislation.

The *Starting Small* program encourages teachers to teach children to recognize heroic qualities in ordinary people in their lives (e.g., a grandmother who walks a 5-year-old to kindergarten every day or an uncle who coaches a football team). This teaches children to recognize these qualities in other people, which, in turn, will help them to see this potential in themselves (Bullard et al., 1997, pp. 106, 107). Thus, a focus on everyday heroes (such as nurses and bridge builders) may help young children to see themselves as powerful enough to stand up for tolerance.

The Peace Education Foundation is particularly focused on teaching children to view themselves as powerful individuals. Lourdes Ballesteros-Barron, Director of the Peace Education Foundation says their goal is to talk about peace in, and outside, the classroom:

> I encourage them to think about the future and tell them that they will be responsible in the future for what will happen. I let them know that even though they're five, when they grow up, they can be anything they want. But if they don't learn to talk about problems now, they won't be able to solve their problems when they grow up. (Bullard et al., 1997, p. 149)

In Ballesteros-Barron's classroom, children are taught to be powerful by practicing the skills that will make them influential:

> Story time is followed by brainstorming sessions in which students create solutions for the story character's conflicts. During dramatic play periods, Lourdes helps children practice skills of respectful communication by re-creating typical classroom clashes such as line-breaking or crayon grabbling. Whenever a real problem arises, the students involved move to the "Peace Table," where they work a putting the classroom philosophy into action. (Bullard et al., 1997, p. 142)

Farmer, a teacher at the Demonstration Center, encourages teachers to view themselves as powerful. She believes that early childhood teachers have "a unique opportunity to 'immunize' children against stereotypes before they take hold on young minds" (Bullard et al., 1997, p. 182).

Also applicable to the Powerful Individual narrative is Teaching Tolerance's flyer entitled "101 Tools for Tolerance." The flyer is a list of specific actions that individuals may take at home, work, school, and with themselves to make meaningful progress toward more humane communities (e.g., frequent minority-owned businesses and get to know the proprietors; participate in a blood drive; identify issues that reach across racial, ethnic, and other divisions, and forge alliances for tackling them, start a monthly "diversity roundtable" to discuss critical issues facing your community; invite someone of a different background to join your family for a meal or holiday; give a multicultural doll, toy, or game as a gift). Such concrete actions can be a very useful way to deal with a problem that can feel large and overwhelming to many people.

A third narrative that emerges is the Peaceful Action narrative. Individuals are encouraged to fight hate by exercising free speech rather than through protest or counter-protests that may be attention-getting but that detract from the message that hate is a threat to liberal democracies:

> Hate must be exposed and denounced. Help news organizations achieve balance and depth. Do not debate hate-group members in conflict-driven forums. Instead, speak up in ways that draw attention away from hate, toward unity.

Readers are encouraged to create constructive alternatives to confrontations with hate groups because physical confrontations serve the purposes of hate groups and burden law enforcement:

> Ann Arbor...was stung by a rally in which 300 police failed to protect the Klan from a chanting crowd that threw rocks and sticks, hurting seven policemen and destroying property. The Klan members were able to stand on the First Amendment, surrounded by what one of their leaders called "animal behavior." A 25-minute march by the Aryan Nations through 15 blocks of Coeur d'Alene, Idaho, cost the state, county and city more than $125,000 for public safety. Mayor Steve Judy described this as money spent to protect free speech. "But we could have taken the money and done a lot for human rights with it."

Of course, the quotes about the Peace Education Foundation, while illustrating that people are capable of becoming powerful individuals through peaceful action, also indicate the value of peaceful conflict resolution strategies (the Peace Table and the Peace Wall).

Community Building Narratives

Personal Responsibility and Individual Action narratives are not merely ends in themselves. These narratives also contribute to the building of community. The goal of Teaching Tolerance is to build a particular kind of community, a multicultural community. Within a multicultural community, a variety of identities and families are accepted (the Multicultural Community narrative). In a reflection called Family Diversity, Bullard, et al. (1997), write:

> Myths and stereotypes about the "ideal" family can influence teacher expectations and attitudes regarding the ability to learn and behave.... By acknowledging and celebrating a wide spectrum of families in the curriculum, early childhood educators can discourage prejudgment and reinforce the vital link between home and school. (p. 23)

Moreover, in a multicultural community, a variety of cultural values are accepted and respected:

> The challenge for teachers is simultaneously to help children recognize and appreciate religious diversity and to avoid promoting a particular religion. Some teachers meet these goals by allowing children to "share" religious traditions in the larger context of "what we do in my family." Sensitivity to these issues will ensure that every child's religious beliefs and practices—or lack thereof—receive equal respect and accommodation. (Bullard et al., 1997, p. 25)

For example, Cabrillo College's Child Development Center in Aptos, California, is described as a place where diversity isn't just talked about but where it's demonstrated daily:

> Admission to the program is tailored to reflect, as closely as possible, the racial, cultural, religious and economic diversity of the community. Each baby doll in the house-play area is a different shade from pink to brown. Little boys are encouraged to cook and dance...and school visitors are likely to be a woman or member of an ethnic minority or someone in a wheelchair. (Bullard et al., 1997, p. 31)

At Cabrillo a class might investigate the various ways that people around the world eat or sleep or celebrate birthdays (Bullard et al., 1997, p. 35). In an application entitled Discovering Diversity, Bullard et al. (1997), write:

> Teachers in any society can prepare students for a pluralistic society by helping them discern and value the multiple dimensions of diversity.... Appreciation for diversity at hand can be used to cultivate a commitment to equity and justice in the wider society. (p. 81)

In the *Starting Small* documentary, we see this appreciation for diversity being illustrated in a concrete way. A teacher at Happy Medium uses People Paint to illustrate that people are not representatives of the awkward way we sometimes talk about race. The paint is placed on a child's skin and colors are blended until the paint "disappears." This teaches the child their "color." Some white children learn they are a blend of melon and terra cotta; other white children learn that their skin color is paler. This teaches children to see the diversity in their own "race," and it makes it easier for them to appreciate diversity overall.

Also in the *Starting Small* documentary, we observe a teacher who introduces her students to a friend who sits in a wheelchair. The children are allowed to touch and examine the chair. As the chair becomes more familiar, we can see the children relax and begin to interact more freely with the friend. As with the People Paint demonstration, familiarity with difference enhances appreciation for difference.

A Place at the Table provides a visual portrayal of a multicultural community. High school-aged students who have written stories about their family's experiences in the United States have come together to share their stories. The students represent a range of social identities (e.g., a girl whose family emigrated from Ireland, an African American young man whose family was brought from Africa and sold into slavery, a Jewish boy whose grandparents were victims of the Holocaust, an African American lesbian). The documentary illustrates how all of these individuals (and their families) are united by the common ground of their efforts to belong to the United States. At one point or another, almost every student describes their family's belief in the American dream. Moreover, the story that each student tells about their family is compelling and renders their identity an American identity.

A multicultural community is a special kind of community that requires specific resources. The creation of a diverse community where identities and cultural values of all kinds receive mutual respect requires the contributions of enlightened individuals who seek what is just (what is best for the community) and not necessarily what is good (for the individual). One multicultural educator argues that a multicultural community, in this case a multicultural classroom community, requires responsible citizens (Responsible Citizen narrative):

> Classroom activities...and visits from local heroes are two approaches to the same goal—for children to start to see themselves as responsible citizens, even at three, four, five and six years old...to...begin asking not "What can I get?" but "What is my contribution?" (Bullard et al., 1997, p. 96)

Moreover, teachers encouraging a pluralistic community must teach children to reach beyond the boundaries of their own group:

> ...stimulating children to reach out to other people even through the barriers of disability and language differences and unfamiliar backgrounds. Diversity on paper...can be studied and appreciated, but it doesn't demand the personal commitment of actually talking and listening to someone who is different. (Bullard et al., 1997, p. 112)

In the Make Every Victim Count portion of Teaching Tolerance, readers were told of the inaccuracies and limitations of hate crime statistics. Readers are encouraged to look beyond abstract statistics that distract readers from the individual targeted for hate crime and ethnoviolence (Responsible Citizen narrative). To illustrate, readers are told the story of Sasezley Richardson:

> A 19-year-old black teenager shot dead as he strolled back from a mall in Elkhart, Ind., with diapers for a friend's baby. Police called it a hate crime from the start. But today, Sasezley Richardson isn't even a statistic. If you pick up a copy of the FBI's "Hate Crime Statistics: 1999" report, you won't find anything representing the death of this young man, shot dead on Nov. 17, 1999. And Richardson wasn't the only forgotten victim.

After this narrative, readers are encouraged to contribute to more humane communities by acting to encourage hate crime training for police, hate crime reporting for every police department, and hate crime policies for every police department. Readers are told that they will help to fix the system.

The notion of responsible citizenship is reflected in Happy Medium's belief that individual rights are always tied to responsibilities to the community. The right to learn is complemented with the responsibility to teach. The right to have things is complemented with the responsibility to share with others. The right to play brings the responsibility to play fairly and follow rules that benefit others (Bullard et al., 1997, p. 14). A pluralistic society is understood to add richness to the community (Bullard et al., 1997, p. 82). The Peace Education Foundation teaches that "we are all one family under one sky" and "together everyone achieves more" (Bullard et al., 1997, p. 143).

Teaching Tolerance modeled this enlightened community participation by sharing stories reported by readers who write to describe the bias of their parents. They wrote to the Speak Up section (Parental Attitudes) to ask how to respond to the prejudicial comments of their parents. For example, "My mother uses racial and ethnic terminology—the Mexican checkout clerk, the Black saleslady—in casual stories in which race and ethnicity are not factors. Of course, if the person is white, she never bothers to mention it." The editor's response justified speaking up to the parent by indicating that such action is part of being a mature, adult child (a Responsible Citizen) and it offered a range of responses, such as simply repeating the comments without the offensive language or appealing to moral principles espoused by the parent when the child was growing up (e.g., "That does not sound like a very respectful way to treat someone").

This illustrates that "maturity" is an enabling attribute that permits enlightened citizenship in a pluralistic society. Another important attribute that permits enlightened citizenship is "empathy." Empathy is an attribute that most of the peace activists described in *Starting Small* mention as essential to building multicultural communities (Empathic Citizen narrative). In the *Starting Small* documentary, Bullard, et al. (1997) note: "The inner experience of empathy... is the lifeblood of multiculturalism" (p. 90). Linda Alston, a Kindergarten teacher at a public Montessori school and interviewed for *Starting Small*, stated: "It's not enough just to say, 'Here are some facts about Native Americans or about African Americans.' We have to create something that comes from the heart, to find our commonalities." She explains: "When I ask 'How would you feel if...?'—then we have a moment where they can really reflect and notice in their bodies how they are actually feeling" (p. 90). Olsen Edwards of the Cabrillo Center notes what happens when one child tells another not to make a racially derogatory remark around a mutual friend because it will hurt the friend's feelings:

> [It] embodies a whole chain of cognitive and emotional connections: First came some concrete information about Native Americans, which the child then linked to the life of her friend. From the friendship arose her recognition of the stereotypes real consequences and, from there, the impulse to respond. (Bullard et al., 1997, p. 33)

Learning empathy also involves learning to talk about feelings. One teacher uses this through the Peace Table (described earlier) where children talk to one another about their conflicts and how they feel about the conflict/problem (Bullard et al., 1997, p. 152).

So, while the ability to feel empathy is an individual quality, Teaching Tolerance focuses on empathy as something that one pursues to build the kind of multicultural community envisioned by peace activists. At Happy Medium school in Seattle, the belief is that this empathy is achieved through communication and understanding. A proverb at Happy Medium is: "Let's talk. Let's all talk. What we don't talk about hurts us all" (Bullard et al., 1997, p. 13).

The growth of pluralistic communities based on mutual respect for social differences is grounded in more than enlightened citizens' maturity, empathy, and communication. The pluralistic community is also grounded in concrete action. Specifically, pluralism is ensured when all social identities and families are confirmed. At Happy Medium, children are encouraged to notice and appreciate their own physical attributes and those of others; the school encourages cross-cultural interactions between students; and lessons and class materials that honor the contributions, values, and heritages of diverse groups of people are used (Bullard et al., 1997, pp. 20, 21). At Cabrillo, little boys are encouraged to cook and dance and little girls may play "Mommy" to a doll that represents a different race (Bullard et al., 1997, p. 31).

Teaching Tolerance offered suggestions for how all identities may be confirmed in a community. They offer models of how individuals and communities have supported victims of hate crimes (Support Victims, *10 Ways to Fight Hate*):

> As white supremacists marched in Coeur d'Alene, Idaho, a number of families invited black and Latino neighbors to dinner. "Just as a way of saying, 'You are welcome,'" said one host. In Montgomery, Ala., after hate mail and nails were thrown at black families in a formerly all-white neighborhood, a woman left a rose and a card, telling them, "You are not alone." At Gonzaga University in Spokane, Wash., administrators moved final exams for harassed black students to a safer location. When vandals spray-painted racial slurs, swastikas and references to the Ku Klux Klan on the driveway and home of a resident in a small Florida town near Tampa, neighbors showed up with a pressure-washer and paint to remove and cover up the hateful graffiti.

Teaching Tolerance also recommended that people Unite (from *10 Ways to Fight Hate*) by Declaring a "Hate Free Zone" with a poster contest and a unity pledge, going door-to-door in a neighborhood targeted by a hate group, offering support and inviting participation in a rally, candlelight vigil, or other public event.

By making explicit efforts to support groups and individuals marginalized through oppression and intimidation, peace activists can demonstrate that theirs is a community where all kinds of identities are valued. Identities also can be valued by supporting different forms of families. One reader who contributed to Speak Up Against Excluding Families wrote:

> My wife and I both went, and the teacher leaned toward us and whispered, "I can always tell the children in my class who have two parents at home." She meant it as something nice to us, but my son's best friend happens to be being raised—and raised well—by a single mom. It made me wonder how the teacher treated my son's friend in class.

Teaching Tolerance provided a number of tangible things that adults may do to ensure that families are not excluded in their school:

> Lobby to have library resources and classroom curricula that include positive examples of non-traditional families, including grandparents as parents, single-parent households, adoptive families, foster families and families with gay or lesbian parents. Discuss the issue with the school principal or a guidance counselor, and ask for staff training on issues of family diversity…ask your school to have a "family night" instead of a "parent's night," and avoid judgmental terms like "broken home."

The pluralistic community being advocated by Teaching Tolerance is the core element in the fight against hate because a tolerant community is one where hate is less likely to take hold. As noted in *10 Ways to Fight Hate*:

> The best cure for hate is a tolerant, united community. As Chris Boucher of Yukon, Penn., put it after residents there opposed a local meeting of the Ku Klux Klan, "A united coalition is like Teflon. Hate can't stick there." Hate exists "because the ground in the area is receptive for it," says Steven Johns Boehme, leader of the Michigan Ecumenical Forum. "If you drop the seeds of prejudice in soil that is not receptive, they won't take root."

This is no longer a society that permits white individuals to proclaim themselves racists or White Supremacists without sanction. The inappropriateness of these attitudes is so clear that people are inclined to deny their racist motivations, even when their racism is apparent to others. Indeed, some of the individuals quoted and situations discussed throughout this text suggest that many people fail to see even blatant acts of racism or hate-motivated crimes. Despite reported shouting of racial epithets and the scrawling of racially charged graffiti on the scene of a hate killing, a Shenandoah Sheriff failed to report the killing as a hate crime. Politicians see the denigration of non-white immigrants as commentary about the "problem" of assimilation and not hate speech.

Perhaps these denials are merely bald-faced rationalizations. They may also be a symptom of a different kind of racism and hatred that is not blatant; a form of racism that is institutionalized and systemic. This kind of racist discourse has the potential to be seen as ambiguous. That is, this kind of racist discourse and action may be subject to multiple interpretations, permitting individuals or groups to deny the racism underlying their words and actions (Fiske & Taylor, 2008). This has also been studied under a number of monikers: (a) Elite Racism (e.g., van Dijk, 1991, 1995), (b) Everyday Racism (e.g., M. Jaeger, Cleve, & S. Jaeger, 1998; Reisigl & Wodak, 2001; Wetherell & Potter, 1992), (c) Color-Blind Racism (Bonilla-Silva, 2003, 2006), and (d) Whiteness Studies (e.g., Dyer, 1997; Wise, 2008). While there are important theoretical distinctions between these projects, they share a common set of assumptions that are important for our discussion of anti-hate discourse.

First, current forms of Everyday Racism exist in language in specific forms and contexts (that is, in action). In some disciplines, this has led to a fairly anti-cognitivist approach to the study of racism, if cognitivism is understood in terms of an American approach to social cognition dedicated to the study of structures in human memory (e.g., schemas, stereotypes, attitudes). Instead, attitudes and stereotypes are assumed to exist in language and discursive practices (Billig, 1995; Reisigl & Wodak, 2001).

Second, Everyday Racism is studied in a variety of social structures that perpetuate the power of dominant identities (such as a white identity in the United States). For example, the authors mentioned above have studied the Everyday Racism expressed in (a) newspapers and other media, (b) textbooks, (c) politics, (d) corporate texts, (e) academic discourse, and (f) everyday conversations (to name a few).

Third, Everyday Racism assumes that such discourse "otherizes softly" (Bonilla-Silva, 2003). In other words, Everyday Racism encourages us to think of the Other in demeaned and dehumanized terms in a way that often escapes our conscious awareness. This is often because stereotypes and prejudices are activated through collective cultural symbols that can go uninterrogated by naïve social actors.

While most of this work has focused on the harms of Everyday Racism on minority identities, much of this work holds that Everyday Racism wreaks enormous damage on the majority (in the United States, white) identity. Bonilla-Silva argues that racism confines white people to "white prisons," the result of voluntary racial segregation (Bonilla-Silva, 2003; Bonilla-Silva, Embrick, Ketchem, & Saenz, 2004). A consequence of this segregation is a distorted and inaccurate view of the world that comes from whiteness being defined as the norm (Bonilla-Silva, 2003; Wise, 2008). This norm confers a privilege that makes it less necessary for white people to understand the perspective of others (Jhally, 2008; Wise, 2008). Privilege allows white people to take comfort in their segregated white spaces but fail to see the dangers that being overly privileged poses for them. Wise (2008) observed that a resounding question among white people following the terrorist attack on the World Trade Center was: "Why do they hate us?" He argues that such a question would only be asked by people so privileged that they could not understand the anger produced by American corporate and political hegemony, a cultivated stupidity (Wise, 2008).

Wise also argues that privilege is dangerous because it creates a mentality of entitlement. When the overly privileged's expectations are frustrated, they often lack the internal resources to cope with problems that make their world seem out of control. To support this claim, Wise (2008) notes that young people who go on shooting sprees, attacking family and classmates, are typically white and male (Jhally, 2008). To continue with a specific example of a spree killing, a member of the SWAT team responding to the April 1999 rampage at Columbine High School in Colorado reported that they were held back after preparing to storm the high school because "if they stormed the building and in the process killed anyone, those [wealthy white] people would sue them blind" (Wise, 2008, p. 133). This is certainly a concrete instance in which privilege may have caused injury or death for the children of Columbine.

There are actions that may be taken to oppose Everyday Racism. To some extent, Teaching Tolerance's admonition to be vigilant to the racism and hatred in one's own life and to promote communities of tolerance is a useful point at which to contemplate opposition to Everyday Racism. Particular, individual responses to racism will not bring an end to such a systemic form of racism; however, individual responses can call attention to the unearned privileges whiteness confers on white people (Bonilla-Silva, 2003; Wise, 2008).

So, a first step in responding to Everyday Racism is to learn to recognize instances of this form of oppression. Forms of Everyday Racism are powerful and pernicious precisely because white people have learned not to recognize the unearned advantages that they draw upon daily (McIntosh, 1988; Wise, 2008) and often actively participate in the maintenance of their own ignorance (Bonilla-Silva, 2006). There are many ways white people may actively, if not consciously, participate in the maintenance and hiding of these structures. The process by which a community perfects hate killers into scapegoats through trials, media reports, and community activities permits the community to avoid examining the very racism in their community that produced the hate criminal and the hate crime (Williamson, 2002).

Bonilla-Silva (2006) examined the narratives shared among white people to rationalize (a) their unearned advantages, (b) the under-privileging of people of color, and (c) the maintenance of the ideology of Color-Blind Racism. For example, white people deny the need for programs such as Affirmative Action through "The Past Is the Past" narrative. In its various forms, this narrative claims that racism is a thing of the past and is a problem that was solved. According to this narrative, continuing to talk about the issue of race is divisive and keeps negative feelings alive between the races.

White people also deny any responsibility for racism through the "I Never Owned Slaves" narrative. This narrative is used to deny the over-privileging of white people by claiming that the disadvantaging of people of color was primarily about slavery rather than systems of oppression that continue to operate today. This narrative is also used to avoid personal responsibility for their unearned advantages because present-day whites can't be held responsible for what their ancestors did and, consequently, they have no obligation to work for justice.

A third narrative that sustains Color-Blind Racism is the "If Other Ethnic Groups Have Succeeded, How Come Blacks Have Not?" This narrative points to Jews, Italians, Irish, etc., to point out that America is a place where other groups have succeeded. The point of this narrative is to blame under-privileged black people for their under-privileged status.

A fourth narrative identified by Bonilla-Silva is the "I Did Not Get a Job, Promotion, or Was Not Admitted to College Because of a Minority." This narrative is used by whites to scapegoat minorities for their failures.

Bonilla-Silva argues that these narratives, and others, serve as symbolic expressions of white dominance. Because they reflect a collective rationale among whites that is accepted as a truism, these stories are not subject to interrogation and inspection. Consequently, the stories will not be refuted by facts and statistics:

> In the eyes of most Whites, for instance, evidence of racial disparity in income, wealth, education, and other relevant matters becomes evidence that there is something wrong with minorities themselves; evidence of minorities' overrepresentation in the criminal justice system or on death row is interpreted as evidence of their overrepresentation in criminal activity; evidence of black and Latino underperformance in standardized tests is a confirmation that there is something wrong (maybe even genetically wrong) with them. (Bonilla-Silva, 2006, p. 179)

As these stories illustrate, forms of Everyday Racism may be systemic and hidden but they require the collaboration of white people in their everyday interactions. Therefore, the elimination of these forms of racism requires white people to oppose them. There is another reason the eradication of racism requires the active opposition of white people. Throughout U.S. history, white people, as a group, have failed to see discrimination as a problem and are inclined to see people of color who attempt to point out racism, including Everyday Racism, as speaking from self-interest or as troublemakers (Wise, 2008). While white people who speak out against Everyday Racism may be accused of being "bleeding hearts" or as dupes of "radical multiculturalism," we are still crucial voices as the beneficiaries of this system.

There are a number of factors that may help white people to comprehend and respond to Everyday Racism. First, as evident in this discussion, scholars and activists are documenting the forms and maintenance of Everyday Racism. The more this becomes a part of our public discourse, the more white people (as a group) may gradually become more aware of forms of Everyday Racism. Second, even if we have learned not to notice forms of Everyday Racism, we may also learn to see it. McIntosh (1988) pulled the veil of Everyday Racism from her own eyes by thinking and writing about the benefits that whiteness affords her that people of color do not receive. This is a model that others may follow in order to comprehend some of the ways they are overly privileged.

We attempt to add to this discussion by examining ways of speaking against the soft hatred of Everyday Racism. Once people are able to recognize Everyday Racism, they may begin to take steps to avoid the ideology of Color-Blind Racism (Bonilla-Silva, 2003) and other forms of Everyday Racism. Wise (2008) argues that one powerful form of resistance against Everyday Racism is to refuse to accept the benefits of unearned privilege. Don't accept admission to a university that was gained through the efforts of a friend, unless people of color also have access to your friend's efforts. Commit to accepting employment from organizations that have recruited a diverse workforce. Send your children to schools that seek a diverse student population, one that reflects the racial makeup of the community. If you have input into a hiring decision, explicitly bring discussion back to candidates who would add diversity to your work environment. Ensure that people of color, and those with other marginalized identities, have mentors that help them to feel "at home" in the work environment and are not alienated from the organization.

Wise (2008) argues that another way to avoid collaboration with Everyday Racism is to raise anti-racist children. This is a process that must begin early. Babies at six months of age are able to distinguish adults on the basis of racial categories (Bronson & Merryman, 2009) and children two to three years old will start to exhibit a preference for other children of their own race (Stern-LaRosa & Bettmann, 2000). It is important that children be exposed to a racially diverse environment, especially because whites tend to self-segregate into white enclaves (Bonilla-Silva et al., 2004). Having friends of a different race or ethnicity is not sufficient to raise anti-racist children, but it is a good beginning. Teach children to be critical consumers of media that perpetuate racism. As children grow, expose them to movies that portray whiteness as beautiful and good and other racial categories as less beautiful and desirable. Wise suggests making it a game to pick out images and strategies through which the movie makers send these messages explicitly and implicitly. There is a plethora of children's movies that make for useful teaching aids. Another benefit of such "games" is that parents also will be teaching their children to be more critical consumers of the media more generally.

Truthfully, society is complicated enough, with interlocking systems of oppression (white privilege, male privilege, and heterosexism) that make collaboration with Everyday Racism difficult to avoid entirely (McIntosh, 1988; Wise, 2008). Consequently, those wishing to live an anti-racist lifestyle may find it useful to join others who wish to do the same. The group may help one another to identify instances of Everyday Racism as they encounter it, and to discuss ways to confront white privilege. One such anti-racist group in Durham, North Carolina, developed a calendar with photographs of 12 white people who lived in significant opposition to racism and hatred. This calendar served a very practical purpose because white people often lack models of white people who opposed racism and offered alternative ways of being white. Indeed, the "invisibility" of these examples is a product of Everyday Racism. This calendar provided pictures of white anti-racists, with brief stories, that allowed white people to reflect on and to draw inspiration from their lives.

Conclusion

The Teaching Tolerance program promoted an ideology of tolerance through narratives that coalesce around the three major themes of personal responsibility, individual action, and community building. These themes organize a rich typology of stories that influence readers to oppose hatred by seeking peace, promoting communities that value and accept social differences, and encouraging reconciliation where intolerance has alienated individuals from their community.

The narratives organized around the first two themes, personal responsibility (Tolerance Requires Vigilance, You Are Not Alone, Tolerance Requires Learning, and Tolerance Embraces Reconciliation) and individual action (Speak Up, Powerful Individual, and Take Peaceful Action), make the individual the primary focus of the narratives. Most of these narratives treat these individual perceptions, knowledge, and actions as ends in themselves. For example, individuals should remain vigilant to hate because vigilance helps people to monitor hate in their community or in them. These narratives provide the image of the individual who wishes to live a tolerant lifestyle. Such a lifestyle requires commitment, social awareness, and sensitivity to social positions that one may or may not understand through direct experience. In the Teaching Tolerance program, we encounter narratives indicating that tolerance requires learning. Even when we have learned about the lives of those who are different, we encounter narratives that reiterate the vigilance required to be aware of the ways that language may marginalize some social groups. This is coupled with narratives that assure potential audience members that they can be influential (Powerful Individual). We also encounter narratives that tell us that living a tolerant lifestyle requires a commitment to peace. We learn that there may be a certain degree of satisfaction from direct counter-demonstrations against hate groups or that shouting insults at the hate-monger may be a temporary balm to our frayed and offended sensibili-ties. But, in the end, responding in kind to hate does not persuade anyone to be more tolerant and consumes needed community resources (Peaceful Ac-tion).

This concern for community is reflected in the third set of narratives fo-cused on the building of a pluralistic community that respects and values so-cial differences. It is important for individuals to live a tolerant lifestyle. But it is a tolerant, pluralistic community that, in the words of one peace activist, is like Teflon to those who would hope to stir up hate. The construction of such a community is an attempt to move away from identity politics and vio-lence in order to reinvent collective life. The reinvention of collective life re-quires that previously dehumanized identities be humanized. This may be done through the use of narratives that restore images and identities that may be embraced by other groups (such as affirming all identities and families). One concrete example of this is found in the narrative of Sasezley Richard-son whose story in Teaching Tolerance serves as a remembrance to those killed by hate.

The ideology of tolerance integrates the constructs of individual respon-sibility and individual action with the construct of community building. Teaching Tolerance teaches that individuals must be responsible for con-structing a tolerant community. Individuals are encouraged to be responsible to the community and to look beyond their own individual interests and to seek what is good for the community. To look beyond their own interests, individuals are encouraged to develop their empathic abilities in order to be sensitive to the perspectives and cultural values of those who are different from themselves. This is encouraged for all identities in the pluralistic com-munity because a genuinely tolerant community will be negotiated through mutual adaptation rather than the assimilation of one identity. Empathic citi-zenship is crucial to the negotiation of a tolerant society because empathy should enhance identification with those who are different and should dimin-ish the motivation to stereotype and essentialize those who are different.

The notion that a pluralistic and tolerant community is the result of nego-tiation and mutual adaptation of social identities makes the accomplishment of such a community a daunting task. Some have argued (Meyer, 2001) that our society is caught up in a state of identity-mania, a social condition in which social differences are so politicized that individuals see the advance-ment of any other identity as a threat to their own identity. This drama is played out in the Nativist discourse discussed in chapters five and six. This kind of environment makes the accomplishment of tolerant communities es-pecially difficult. However, this simply makes our quest for a more humane society all the more important. We are sympathetic with an observation made by Stuart Hall:

> I am convinced that no intellectual worth his or her salt and no university that wants to hold up its head in the face of the 21st century can afford to turn dispassionate eyes away from the problem [to] understand what keeps making the lives we live and the societies we live in, profoundly and deeply anti-humane. (Hall, 1992, p. 18)

Anti-hate activists should turn a critical eye on their own discourse, not to elevate this group over that group but to ensure that our language will really constitute the kinds of communities we say we envision.

Chapter 8

Conclusion

We reflect on some of the implications of our research in this conclusion. It has been noted that hatred is stabilized in the discourse that is used to express it and pass it from one generation to the next (Tsesis, 2002). That is, hatred comes alive in our language. Many who study racism and hatred through discourse reject the cognitivist orientation to racism that may be found in research from the social cognition field. Mindful of this sentiment, we still believe there is much to be gleaned from social cognition research that informs this work. Specifically, we find social cognition research to be useful for demonstrating that hatred is not an unusual state of mind, existing only in the minds of professional hate-mongers.

If hatred lives in language, the seeds of hatred exist in human cognition. Human cognitive processes shape the way we understand and respond to others. The key to understanding how cognitive processes can lead to hate speech may be traced to the way we store information about others. The human mind requires a storage system that allows for efficient access to information that is stored in memory. This process is similar to the way that a computer directory works. We store information in categories that capture common characteristics and unique features about people or objects. For example, features such as gender, attire, and education level may be associated with the category of nurse. Moreover, the categorization process in each individual is tied to the cultural beliefs, the social norms, and the values of that individual (Tajfel & Forgas, 2000).

For years, researchers have understood that simply categorizing people into different groups leads us to (a) perceive an out-group as less variable than the in-group (e.g., Park & Rothbart, 1982; Quattrone & Jones, 1980; Wilder, 1979), (b) form less complex conceptualizations of the out-group than the in-group (e.g., Linville, 1982; Linville & Jones, 1980), (c) favor the in-group over the out-group (e.g., Brewer, 1979; Gerard & Hoyt, 1974; Wilder, 1981), and (d) evaluate the out-group more extremely than the in-group (e.g., Linville & Jones, 1980).

More recent research in this area suggests that categories are often used in combination, and that combinations of categories constitute stereotypes. That is, categories such as race, occupation, or gender, when used in combination, make up stereotypic knowledge that influences how we judge others and determine how we will relate to them (Lepore & Brown, 1997). These group member stereotypes can be viewed as the cognitive component of prejudice, and that prejudice springs from normal cognitive processes involved in categorization. Thus, all people have the potential to form impressions and make judgments of others based on positive or negative stereotypes linked to the others' category memberships (race, sexual orientation, religious orientation, etc.).

While they have the potential to bring about stereotypes, categories serve a number of important functions for people (Markman & Ross, 2003). One of these functions is communication. Simply put, the messages that a person produces are reflective of the categories that he or she possesses. Hate speech could not be produced unless stereotypic knowledge was available to an individual and the individual used that knowledge as the basis for judging others. The cognitive effect of communicating to accentuate differences is that categories become increasingly pure and make the task of information storage and retrieval easier (Graumann & Wintermantel, 1989). The benefits of economizing on cognitive functioning in this regard are immediately apparent. If someone is understood as a stereotype, the perceiver readily knows what he or she is dealing with and has clear expectations for what members of this category say or do (i.e., gays will be gays, Jews will be Jews, women will be women, etc.).

When stereotypes come into play, do all individuals categorize information about others in their social world in similar ways? The answer to this question appears to be no. Lepore and Brown (1997) and Markman and Ross (2003) suggest that when a member of a category (e.g., white, African American, Asian, etc.) is encountered not all of the characteristics are activated in memory because some of the characteristics are more strongly coupled because of their frequent association (e.g., nurse and female, engineer and male). The combination of categories that appear to be considered by the individual is the stereotypic features believed to be true of the category (i.e., to many people nurses *are* female). Strongly connected characteristics that are triggered most frequently vary systematically with factors such as level of prejudice. For highly prejudiced people, triggering a category associated with a stereotype results in negative evaluation of the other party.

It would follow that a highly prejudiced individual would be motivated to correctly categorize others so as to facilitate in-group/out-group categorization. Building on social identity theory, Blascovich, Wyer, Swart, and Kibler (1997) tested this notion by exploring whether racially prejudiced individuals were more motivated to make accurate racial categorizations than non-prejudiced individuals. Study participants were presented with images of racially ambiguous targets and asked to categorize them as black or as white. Racially prejudiced individuals not only took longer to categorize the racially ambiguous targets but also uttered a significantly greater number of nonverbal vocalizations suggesting response hesitation. Taken together, these results suggest prejudiced individuals are more motivated and devote more cognitive resources to the task of accurately categorizing the social group membership of others than non-prejudiced individuals.

Can the automatic triggering of stereotypes be controlled? Can we achieve control over racist, sexist thinking and eliminate all such tendencies? These questions are particularly problematic because stereotypic knowledge is by its very nature available to all members of a culture. Interestingly, some evidence suggests stereotype activation can be overcome by both intention and learning (Blair, Ma, & Lenton, 2001; Legault, Green-Demers, & Eadie, 2009; Sassenberg & Moskowitz, 2004). For example, people embracing altruistic goals toward a specific group suppress automatic stereotype activation (Moskowitz, Gollwitzer, Wasel, & Schaal, 1999; Moskowitz, Salomon, & Taylor, 2000). Interestingly, it also appears that people can be trained to suppress stereotypic images by reflecting on examples that run counter to the stereotype (Blair et al., 2001). In a study designed to explore suppression of automatic stereotype activation, Sassenberg and Moskowitz (2004) reported that negative associations may be suppressed by priming creativity in people. That is, inducing a creative mindset in a person may suppress stereotypes from coming to mind at all. This method of suppressing stereotypes does not erase the stereotype from a person's mind; rather, individuals thinking creatively about others are simply less likely to invoke stereotypes. More recently, Legault, et al. (2009) observed that high levels of self-determined prejudice regulation may also suppress automatic stereotype activation. Thus, it does appear that each of us has the potential to counter stereotypic thinking. This notion is reinforced by Akarami, Ekehammar, and Araya (2006) who note that perceivers low in prejudice tend to engage in intentional suppression of activated stereotypes resulting from their controlled processing of information. For their counterparts high in prejudice, they simply do not seek to suppress stereotypical thinking. This research suggests that the vigilance and self-monitoring suggested in the last chapter should be an effective strategy for responding to hatred in our everyday experiences.

When stereotypes are triggered, the way we make use of that stereotypic knowledge has been linked to cognitive processes involving judgmental heuristics. Judgmental heuristics refer to general "rules of thumb" that can be applied across a broad range of situations (Bless, Fielder, & Strack, 2004). For example, a commonly used rule of thumb in judging others is that you cannot trust a person who will not look you in the eye. People make use of many different kinds of simplifying judgment rules that are shared by many (such as in the previous example) or reflect individualized rules that are shaped to fit their personal social environment. The nature of how judgment heuristics are initiated is a matter of some debate. De Neys, Vartanian, and Goel (2008) report that one school of thought holds that people are mere heuristic thinkers and are not aware that triggered stereotypes might be inappropriate. A second school of thought is that people do recognize the conflict between normative thinking and stereotypic knowledge but simply fail to suppress stereotypical thinking. The results of the investigation by these authors indicate that people *do* detect their biases when engaged in making judgments about others. This does not mean that people are irrational and lack the cognitive ability to more fully reflect on others in their environment. For many, the temptation to use simple decision-making rules may be too difficult to overcome even though they know that stereotypic judgments of others are not warranted and that seeds of hate may be germinating.

However, if we think about hatred only as an element of social cognition or only as an emotion, we may fail to see the communicative practices responsible for the production and maintenance of hatred. This project illustrates the profound importance of everyday language in the construction, reconstruction, and perpetuation of hate. It is through language that truly terrible narratives and cultural myths are expressed, are shared for strategic purposes, and are passed from one generation to the next. It is through discourse that group members may express and perform the ideology of hate that is an important feature of the collective memory of the group. It is through language that valued identities are expressed and hated identities are demeaned. It is through discourse that people learn to negotiate the phases of the hate stratagem that make hate crime and ethnoviolence logical responses to hate. Indeed, hate speech becomes the tool we use to construct the enemy before that enemy is killed (Keen, 1986). It should be horribly clear at the end of this text that hatred comes alive in the language we use to influence one another and participate in group life.

However, an appreciation for the role that language and discourse play in the production of hate allows us insights into the ways that dangerously similar out-groups may be otherized so thoroughly that the hatred appears illogical to outsiders. Many in the West needed to educate themselves about the differences between Shiite and Sunni Muslims because, as outsiders, they only see Muslims. Perhaps many Muslims fail to distinguish between Catholics and Protestants and see only a homogenous Christian out-group. Perhaps it is surprising for many white people to think that they might be understood by many racially conscious Aryans to be race-traitors, actually non-white, and sheep to be conquered (Gardell, 2003). In part, this is because the essence of the sleeping white man is close enough to the essence of the racist Aryan that the factors that distinguish them must be made even more explicit, and this is done through the language that is used to represent them.

We have examined the operation of the hate stratagem in three very different contexts: (a) in several different texts employed by a variety of hate-mongers in the organized hate movement (see chapter four), (b) in the Nativist discourse of those committed to vilifying undocumented immigrants, largely Latino and Latina immigrants (see chapter six), (c) in the political discourse surrounding the 2008 Presidential Election, and (d) in the political discourse of Birthers, anti-immigration(ant) reformers, and re-emerging militia members following the election of Barack Obama (see chapter six). The language and discourse of all these groups is unified by the presence of the hate stratagem. This suggests that hate is animating the discourse of all these groups, and we believe that their discourse should be treated as hate speech.

Without a doubt, there are those who would take exception with this claim. To them we would say that it is possible to talk about the issue of undocumented immigration without (a) constructing an American, or Western, identity as more valuable than other identities (or even equating those identities with white identities), (b) equating Mexican immigrants with disease and contamination of the essence of the American identity, (c) constructing immigrants as a dangerous threat to the existence of America, and finally, (d) rhetorically conquering Mexican immigrants by celebrating their suffering. Put simply, we can talk about immigration without vilifying the immigrant. Perhaps people in the Shenandoah Valley, for example, fear that undocumented immigrants are taking jobs that they would be willing to do. We have discussed politicians and media pundits who gain votes and listeners from their Nativist rhetoric and exploitation of the immigration issue, those who trade in hate. These individuals could discuss globalization and the role of the North American Free Trade Agreement (NAFTA) in the displacement of Mexican farmers who, subsequently, enter the United States, without documentation, to find jobs to feed their families. Unfortunately, these are complicated issues that require thoughtful critique of social and political policies.

Our discussion of discourse surrounding the 2008 Presidential Election illustrates the operation of the hate stratagem. We provided extensive examples of both Republican and Democratic opponents of Barack Obama who attempted to manipulate the hatred of voters in order to defeat Barack Obama. We learned that Barack Obama (a) was insufficiently American, (b) was a Muslim, (c) was a terrorist, (d) was a socialist, (e) was a fascist, (f) would give aid and comfort to our enemies, and (g) was unwilling to keep America safe. Those who shouted, wrote, or shared these stories interpersonally through formal and informal gatherings might not like to think of themselves as hate-mongers, but they are trading in hate. They are using people's fear of a foreign-sounding name, like Barack Hussein Obama, to win an election or to oppose policies with which they disagree. They are trading in hate.

But Barack Obama's opponents were not the only ones to trade in hate during the 2008 Presidential Election. We cited evidence of Obama volunteers who furthered the language of white supremacy by reminding their neighbors that Obama was raised by his white mother and grandparents, and they concluded that he was really like them. Such comments, made in the service of the election of Barack Obama, served to make him palatable to some white voters by maintaining the normalcy of whiteness (and consequently maintaining the non-normalcy, the deviance, of non-white identities).

Are there larger lessons to be gleaned from some of the things we have discussed? Hazlitt (2005) suggested that we attempted to turn from hate when we left the bonds of tribalism for the comparative advantages of civilization. The operation of the hate stratagem across the different forms of discourse may suggest that we have not fully left the bonds of tribalism. Our discussion of anti-hate discourse suggests that one cost of living in more tolerant, humane communities is ongoing vigilance to the hatred and tribalism that seems to be our impulse. Our discussion of the role of perception in this chapter provides more evidence that the categorization process is the initial cognitive process that seems to cause us to be preoccupied with the group essences that drive our creation of in-groups and out-groups. The good news is that this impulse can be attenuated by our vigilance. Put simply, we can learn to reject the cultural stereotypes and prejudices and perceive our way through our tribal impulses. Our analysis of the narratives employed by the Teaching Tolerance program of the Southern Poverty Law Center suggests an array of stories that may be used to shape our responses to hate and guide the discourse we produce to re-humanize identities that have been demeaned and dehumanized through hate speech.

When people are bombarded by hate discourse, they may not always recognize it as such. Our public discourse has coarsened to the point that someone might hear a politician demean Mexican immigrants or describe Miami as a "third-world" city or "worse than Baghdad" and fail to recognize his use of hate. Worse yet, we may hear and see hateful messages targeting Mexicans working in this country illegally and assume that their legal status makes them less deserving of our sympathy or of even our protection. One of the benefits of subtle stereotypes and Everyday Racism is that we may hide these socially unacceptable ideas from other people and from ourselves (Bargh, 1999; Bonilla-Silva, 2003; Wise, 2008). This ability to conceal hatred in other ideas (e.g., "I'm not against immigrants, I'm for Western civilization; we don't promote hate, we promote love for our own people") makes it difficult to recognize our own hatred and even more difficult to address the problem.

In many ways, hate is a topic we are uncomfortable addressing (Bonilla-Silva, 2003). Perhaps this is because there is little effort made to deal with it directly. Hate crime and ethnoviolence is probably not something that most people experience on a daily basis. The F.B.I. relies on local law enforcement to report hate crimes to the F.B.I. The problem is that communities don't want to be known as places where hate crimes occur (Williamson, 2002). So, the present system of tracking and reporting hate crime is less than systematic. We have cited instances in which witnesses to hate killings have reported the shouting of racist slurs during the commission of a killing, and yet the police still failed to identify the killing as a hate crime. Consequently, many hate crimes are not likely to be widely reported to the general public. The forms of hatred animated by Everyday Racism and Color-Blind Racism may be difficult to observe precisely because those forms of racism are intended to be ambiguous and difficult to notice as more overt racism.

Perhaps the general public is not the only audience that might fail to recognize the hate that lives in the language hate-mongers use to influence others. By and large, the uses of hate speech have not been addressed in our textbooks and our curricula in a systematic way. We believe that we have made it clear that hate is employed as a form of social influence throughout our everyday interactions. We encounter it from pundits on television shows, in the political campaigns we follow, and in our discussions of important social and political issues of the day (such as immigration reform and health reform). However, we do not see this issue being addressed in texts and the curricula of departments in Communication Studies. Failing to incorporate the study of hatred into our classes is to ignore an important dimension of how people communicate and attempt to influence others. Hatred should be studied as a form of proof in Persuasion classes, and it should be written about in the Persuasion texts we write for those classes.

We discussed Eduardo Bonilla-Silva's work on the narratives shared by white people on a regular basis to promote what he called Color-Blind Racism. Narratives are studied in interpersonal communication classes across our discipline, and given that so many of the stories described by the Teaching Tolerance program involve stories about how to respond to the racism and hatred of a family member, it would seem that the issue of hatred would be an important topic in almost any interpersonal communication class. Moreover, a standard topic in introduction to interpersonal communication classes is the role of perception in interpersonal communication. Perception is certainly central to the essentializing that gives rise to in-groups and out-groups necessary for the discursive production of hate. Moreover, discussions of the discursive production of hate would enliven and add depth to the discussion of stereotypes that are a part of all introductory interpersonal communication texts. Social difference is often discussed as a group dynamic in many organizational communication texts/classes. It would seem that the politicization of social difference that gives rise to hatred would be an important part of organizational life for which students should be prepared.

The important concepts that we have discussed throughout this text are the hate stratagem, myth, narratives, and heuristic appeals. These concepts may operate distinctively as tools that rhetors may use to manipulate hatred to encourage violence. Alternatively, they may work in concert as Waltman (2003) suggested when he described the KKK's use of the hate stratagem and heuristics to recruit children into the Youth Corps of the Knights of the Ku Klux Klan. Both the hate stratagem and the use of heuristics encouraged the children to engage in superficial information processing because the hate stratagem is conceived of as a "trick" (Whillock, 1995) and the value of heuristics is that they take the persuadee's attention away from the substance of an argument. We described myth as a master narrative that reflects commonly held beliefs shared by a group or community. Many of the myths we discussed in previous chapters reflect common cultural stereotypes, images of the Other that reflect simplified understandings of the category member. These myths and stereotypes allow the perceiver to reduce the burden of thinking by falling back on categories that treat all members of the category in homogenous and overly simplified terms. Thus, the hate stratagem, myth, and the encouragement of heuristically driven judgments manipulate a perceiver's hate by encouraging oversimplified and superficial thinking.

It is not unusual for writers of texts in a series such as *Language in Action* to address the state of theory development in an area of study or around a particular problem area, such as "hate speech." Questions are posed, such as: (a) Do we have adequate theoretical tools to expand research in this area?

(b) Do we need a special "micro" theory of hate speech? and (c) What kinds of research projects are needed in the United States and internationally? We address questions like these as we take some time to peer into the future.

We see Communication Studies and allied disciplines as being rich with constructs that will yield an interesting and multi-dimensional view of hatred and hate speech. We did not "invent" new constructs with which to view hate speech; rather, our analysis and critique of hate speech is informed by other researchers who have worked with some of these constructs in the past, some of which were tied explicitly to hate speech and some that were not (e.g., Balthrop, 1984; Bonilla-Silva, 2003; Burke, 1995; Cialdini, 2001; Waltman, 2003; Waltman & Davis, 2004; R. K. Whillock, 1995). We are confident that rhetoricians, discourse analysts, and social scientists of various strips will continue to find a wealth of constructs that will help them to understand the features of hate speech of interest to them. We have seen hatred theorized in this way in the discipline of Sociology (Perry, 2001).

We are reticent to recommend the a priori development of any kind of theory related to the study of hate or hate speech. First, we believe the most useful theory of hate speech emerges from researchers' examinations of specific texts and questions, unique to the problems they wish to explore. We are confident that others who find our work useful or thought-provoking may take our theoretical tools and adapt them to their own purposes. Second, a priori theories of hate speech would possess a priori definitions of hate speech. We think this is a potentially dangerous circumstance that could work against those of us who wish to critique and challenge hate speech. Hatred and hate speech are fluid and complicated ideas that may be manifested in a variety of forms, within and across cultures. We are doubtful that any single definition may capture all expressions of hatred and may turn the gaze of researchers away from important phenomena. The ideas of Institutionalized Racism and Everyday Racism are useful examples that illustrate our concerns. These are not constructs that are universally recognized by all academics as a "real" form of racism because they do not fit a common-sense view of racism as something that only involves explicit and overt expressions of prejudice. Should future research suggest that an a priori theory of hate speech would be useful, we are confident that such theory would emerge organically from the research and research questions of specific projects.

What directions might hate speech take in the future? We believe that politicians and pundits will only continue to accelerate their use of appeals to the hatred of Americans. Literally, at the time these sentences are being constructed, people who have made vile and threatening calls to Senators and Congresspersons due to their support of health care legislation are being arrested. Our politicians have been called racial and sexual epithets as they walked to their offices. This has come after various groups have appealed to American's hate to oppose health care reform. We believe this will continue to be fertile ground for hate speech research.

We expect that the problem of international terrorism and the manipulation of hatred are interlocking problems. Americans are only recently gaining a glimpse into the ways that radical elements of Islam are recruiting potential terrorists. Like their Christian Identity and racist Neo-Pagan counterparts in the United States, Islamic terrorists are able to identify and discursively entice those looking for meaning and significance in their lives to kill their enemies. We believe that it is not controversial to claim that politicians have appealed to our fear in order to gain support for laws that limit the rights of ordinary Americans. Have they also employed (or are they employing) a hate stratagem in order to gain support for those policies and laws? This, too, may be an important and profitable problem that may be addressed by communication scholars. Both of these problems would lead to the study of hatred, internationally. This could lead to a variety of questions. Is the hate stratagem a concept that is used by radical Islamists in ways similar to hate-mongers in the United States? How do Islamic terrorists use U.S. military "victories" to encourage Iraqi and Afghan citizens to hate the United States? Those images become powerful weapons in their war against America.

Hatred is a part of our lives. Communication departments across the country are committed to helping their students to live richer and more meaningful lives by understanding how communication functions in a variety of different contexts: the media they encounter, the persuasive contexts they are exposed to, the interpersonal and family relationships they develop. Hatred is produced through communication in all of these contexts and, consequently, the manipulation of hatred should become a feature of future textbooks and courses.

Appendix A

Myths from *The Turner Diaries* (Waltman & Davis, 2005)

Myths of Racist Aryan

Moral Aryan Myth: The Moral Aryan Myth is a narrative that enunciates the values and personal behavior that constitute moral conduct for the racially conscious white person. One of the most notable elements of Aryan morality is the compassion one should show other Aryans, particularly Aryan women.

Vigilant Aryan Myth: A vigilant Aryan acts in ways that are consistent with his or her racial beliefs. This involves strict adherence to an ideology of hate that guides and shapes one's behaviors and interpretations of daily events.

Dispassionate Aryan Myth: This myth teaches that the proper racist is calm in all circumstances. This dispassionate state is most valuable when the racist Aryan is engaged in violence or preparing for violence.

Martyr Hero Myth: The Martyr Hero Myth exemplifies morality, vigilance, and dispassion by making the ultimate sacrifice for one's race, martyrdom. This involves the complete subordination of individual identity to racial identity that is rewarded with a kind of eternal life when one is remembered by other Aryans after an honorable death.

Myths of the Other

Black Predator Myth: This myth constructs black people, particularly black men, as an ongoing threat to white people. Blacks are understood to be robbers, murderers, and rapists. Blacks are constructed as taking pleasure in the harming of white people.

Black Savage Myth: The Black Savage Myth is used to construct the African American identity as inferior and subhuman. This is accomplished through frequent use of animalistic metaphors (e.g., swarming hordes, cannibals).

Jewish Vampire Myth: The Jewish Vampire Myth is grounded in the belief that the Jewish race has never produced its own culture depicting Jews as both living off other cultures and "sucking" them dry of their resources. This process of cultural conquest is said to be so gradual and subtle that only a "racially aware" white person can recognize it.

Repulsive Jew Myth: The Repulsive Jew Myth impersonalizes and distances the Jew from the reader. Jewish women are described as fat and grotesque looking. This is also evident in constructions of Jews as animal-like and living solely for the sake of gratifying their senses. Jewish is assumed to be equivalent to ugly.

Jewish Pornographer Myth: The Jewish Pornographer Myth seeks to link the corruption of wholesome whites (through race-mixing and other liberal agendas) to the Jew. The notion of Jewish pornography has a less literal reference to the government (through laws such as the legalization of same sex civil unions) and the media (e.g. through movies and television shows that encourage race-mixing).

Zionist-Occupied Government Myth: The Zionist-Occupied Government, or ZOG, Myth can be viewed as an extension of the Jewish Vampire Myth. Racists view ZOG as both the manifestation of Jewish conspiracy within the personnel of the government *and* the government's promotion of "Israel-dominated policy."

Sleeping White Man Myth: This myth explains white people's complicity in their oppression by ZOG. Their lack of racial consciousness prevents them from identifying with Aryan culture, and participating in an Aryan collective memory. Sleeping white men are appropriately viewed as an Other. In part, the white man is sleeping because he is weakened and made comfortable by the creature comforts of Capitalism. White men are sleeping due to brainwashing and materialism. The Sleeping White Man Myth is ultimately used to justify the racial holy war.

Racial Holy War Myth: The Racial Holy War, or RAHOWA, Myth is seen as the sole remedy to the "diseases" described above (predator Jews and savage black people). Ethnoterrorism and an eventual racial holy war are necessary solutions because ZOG and the Jewish-controlled media have made Aryans second-class citizens, reversing the natural superiority won by Aryans.

Appendix B

Myths Constructed in *Hunter*

Aryan Myths

Moral Aryan Myth—See Appendix A

Vigilant Aryan Myth—See Appendix A

Dispassionate Aryan Myth—See Appendix A

Terrorist's Burden Myth: The Terrorist's Burden Myth depicts the dilemma that racially aware Aryans face concerning ethnoviolence: the unavoidable sacrifice of some innocents (racially conscious Aryans) to ultimately save the Aryan race.

Female Aryan Ideal Myth: In general, the Female Aryan Ideal Myth perpetuates a gendered narrative of Aryan woman as pure and innocent. Readers learn the Female Aryan Ideal Myth as the main character glorifies the physical attributes of Aryan women. Women are revered for their ability to produce white children. Thus, Aryan women are key to the survival of the Aryan race. Women are also revered when they support men and avoid Feminist beliefs.

Pleasure of Murder Myth: The Pleasure of Murder Myth advanced in *Hunter* celebrates the delight an Aryan should take in the commission of ethnoviolence. *Hunter* teaches readers the pride Aryans should take in a job well-done. Thus, Aryan pleasure is realized by committing ethnoviolence against the enemies of the Aryan race.

Independent Aryan Myth: The Independent Aryan Myth teaches readers the ideal stratagem for ethnoviolence: Lone Wolfism. The Independent Aryan Myth blends identity and societal myths to explain, on the one hand, specific characteristics a Lone Wolf should cultivate. Independent Aryans (a) develop a technical background, (b) are educated, (c) trust one's own conscience, (d) are stealthy, (e) are private, and (f) are versatile. These are all qualities that facilitate Lone Wolf violence.

Sleeping White Man Myth—See Appendix A

African American Myths

    Black Savage Myth—See Appendix A

    Black Predator Myth—See Appendix A

Jewish Myths

    Repulsive Jew Myth—See Appendix A

    Jewish Vampire Myth—See Appendix A

    Zionist-Occupied Government Myth—See Appendix A

    Jewish-Controlled Media Myth—See Appendix A

    Jewish Pornographer Myth—See Appendix A

    Treacherous/Violent Jew Myth: This myth portrays Jews as fundamentally and pathologically treacherous and violent in their desire to defeat and destroy Aryans.

References

Abdullah, H. (2008, September 4). Georgia lawmaker describes Obama, wife as "uppity." *Azcentral.com.* Retrieved from http://www.azcentral.com/news/election/election08/articles/2008/09/04/20080904campaign0904slur.html

Akrami, N., Ekehammar, B., & Araya, T. (2006). Category and stereotype activation revisited. *Scandinavian Journal of Psychology, 47,* 513–522.

Alinsky, S. D. (1971). *Rules for radicals: A pragmatic primer for realistic radicals.* New York: Vintage.

Allen, M. (2005, July 14). RNC chief to say it was "wrong" to exploit racial conflict for votes. *The Washington Post.* Retrieved from http://www.washingtonpost.com/wp-dyn/content/article/2005/07/13/AR2005071302342.html

Anti-Defamation League-a. Retrieved from http://www.adl.org/learn/ext_us/wcotc.asp

Anti-Defamation League-b. Retrieved from http://www.adl.org/hate_symbols/acronyms.asp

Anti-Defamation League-c. Retrieved from http://www.adl.org/curtis/default.asp

Archibold,R.C. (2010, May11). Side by side but divided over immigration. *The New York Times.* Retrieved from http://www.nytimes.com/2010/05/12/us/12newmexico.html?th&emc=th

Associated Press News Release. (2008, June 6). Clinton camp accused of dividing Jews, Blacks. Congressman: High ranking person in camp used racial line of argument. *MSNBC.com.* Retrieved from http://www.msnbc.msn.com/id/25002392/ns/politics-decision_08/"

Balthrop, V. W. (1984). Culture, myth, and ideology as public argument: An interpretation of the ascent and demise of "Southern culture." *Communication Monographs, 51,* 339–352.

Bargh, J. A. (1999). The cognitive monster: The case against the controllability of automatic stereotype effects. In S. Chaiken & Y. Trope (Eds.), *Dual process theories in social psychology* (pp. 361–382). New York: Guilford.

Baron, J. (2009, April 30). Amid protesters, Tancredo blasts illegal immigration. *Pawtucket Times.* Retrieved from http://www.pawtuckettimes.com/content/view/79519/27/

Barr, A. (2010, May28). Arizona bans ethnic studies. Politico.com. Retrieved from http://www.politico.com/news/stories/0510/37131.html.

Barthes, R. (1972). *Mythologies* (Annette Lavers, Trans.). New York: Hill and Wang.

Beirich, H., & Potok, M. (2005, Winter). Broken Record: Lou Dobbs' daily 'Broken Borders' CNN segment has focused on immigration for years. But there's one issue Dobbs just won't take on. (Intelligence Report No. 120). Retrived from the Southern Poverty Law Center's website http://www.splcenter.org/getinformed/intelligence-report/browse-all-ssues/2005/winter/broken-record

Berger, P. L., & Luckman, T. (1966). *The social construction of reality: A treatise in the sociology of knowledge.* New York: Anchor Books/Doubleday.

Bernstein, R. J. (1978). *The restructuring of social and political theory.* University Park, PA: University of Pennsylvania Press.

Billig, M. (1995). Rhetorical psychology, ideological thinking, and imagining nationhood. In H. Johnston & B. Klandermans (Eds.), *Social movements and culture.* Minneapolis, MN: University of Minnesota Press.

Billig, M. (2001). Humour and hatred: The racist jokes of the Ku Klux Klan. *Discourse & Society, 12,* 267–289.

Binavedes, T. (2009, August 13). White house officials brief HACU interns. *Hispanic Association of Colleges and Universities.* Retrieved from http://www.hacu.net/hacu/NewsBot.asp?MODE=VIEW&ID=681&SnID =2

Blair, I. V., Ma, J. E., & Lenton, A. P. (2001). Imaging stereotypes away: The moderation of implicit stereotypes through mental imagery. *Journal of Personality and Social Psychology, 70,* 1142–1163.

Blascovich, J., Wyer, N. A., Swart, L. A., & Kibler, J. L. (1997). Racism and racial categorization. *Journal of Personality and Social Psychology, 72,* 1364–1372.

Blee, K. M. (2002). *Inside organized racism: Women in the hate movement.* Berkley, CA: University of California Press.

Bless, H., Fielder, K., & Strack, F. (2004). *Social cognition: How individuals construct social reality.* New York: Psychology Press.

Bonilla-Silva, E. (2003). *Racism without racists: Color-blind racism and the persistence of racial inequality in the United States.* Lanham, MD: Rowman & Littlefield.

Bonilla-Silva, E. (2006). *Racism without racists: Color-blind racism and the persistence of racial inequality in the United States* (2nd ed.). Lanham, MD: Rowman & Littlefield.

Bonilla-Silva, E., Embrick, D. G., Ketchum, P. R., & Saenz, R. (2004). Where is the love? Why Whites have limited interactions with Blacks. *The Journal of Intergroup Relations, 31*, 24–38.

Bormann, E. (1972). Fantasy and rhetorical vision: The rhetorical criticism of reality. *Quarterly Journal of Speech, 58*, 396–407.

Bosman, J. (2008, November 1). "Hussein" chant at Palin rally. *The New York Times.* Retrieved from http://thecaucus.blogs.nytimes .com/2008/11/01/hussein-chant-at-palin-rally/

Bowen, B. (1997). Stories in the context of family therapy. In K. N. Dwivedi (Ed.), *The therapeutic use of stories* (pp. 171–184). London: Routledge.

Brewer, M. B. (1979). In-group bias in the minimal intergroup situation: A cognitive-motivational analysis. *Psychological Bulletin, 86*, 307–324.

Bronson, P., & Merryman, A. (2009, September 14). See baby discriminate: Kids as young as 6 months judge others based on color. What's a parent to do? *Newsweek.* Retrieved from http://www.newsweek. com/id/214989/page/1

Brooke, J. (1996, July 5). Volatile mix in Viper Militia: Hatred plus a love for guns. *The New York Times.* Retrieved from http://www.nytimes.com/ 1996/07/05/us/volatile-mix-in-viper-militia-hatred-plus-a-love-for-guns.html

Brooks, D. (2009, September 17). No, it's not about race. *The New York Times.* Retrieved from http://www.nytimes.com/2009/09/18/opinion /18brooks.html?_r=3&em

Brummett, B. (1994). *Rhetoric in popular culture.* New York: St. Martin's.

Bullard, S., Carnes, J., Hofer, M., Polk, N., & Sheets, R. H. (1997). *Starting small: Teaching tolerance in preschool and the early grades.* Montgomery, AL: Southern Poverty Law Center.

Burke, K. (1995). The rhetoric of Hitler's "battle." In C. R. Burgchardt (Ed.), *Readings in rhetorical criticism* (2nd ed., pp. 208–223). State College, PA: Strata.

CBS News. (2008, November 15). Post-racial USA? Not so fast. Obama's election spurs widespread vitriol: Children chant "Assassinate Obama." *CBS News.com.* Retrieved from http://www.cbsnews.com/stories/2008 /11/15/national/main4607062.shtml

Chideya, F. (2008, October 12). The countdown: Day 23: "Majority-minority" America. News and Views NPR.org Retrieved from http://www.npr.org/blogs/newsandviews/2008/10/the_countown_day_23 _tiptoes.html

Chirot, D., & McCauley, C. (2006). *Why not kill them all? The logic and prevention of mass political murder*. Princeton, NJ: Princeton University Press.

Cialdini, R. B. (2001). *Influence: Science and practice* (4th ed.). Boston: Allyn & Bacon.

Clark, M. (2010, January 9). Report shows that hate crimes a lingering fear for Collier, Lee minorities. Retrieved from http://www.naplesnews. com/news/2010/jan/09/report-shows-hate-crimes-lingering-fear-collier-le/

CNN Election Center. (2008, October 22). Palin discusses potential plans for America. *CNN.com*. Retrieved from http://www.cnn.com/2008/ POLITICS/10/21/palin.sitroom/

CNN Politics. (2010, May 13). Arizona limits ethnic studies in public schools. Retrieved from http://www.cnn.com/2010/POLITICS/ 05/12/arizona.ethnic.studies/index.html.

CNN Politics. (2009, August 18). Interview with gun-toting protester at Obama rally was staged. *CNN.com*. Retrieved from http://www.cnn.com/2009/POLITICS/08/18/obama.protest.rifle/

Compton, S. (1997). Stories used therapeutically with children in educational settings. In K. N. Dwivedi (Ed.), *The therapeutic use of stories* (pp. 157–170). New York: Routledge.

Conason, J. (2008, March 14). Geraldine Ferraro still needs to apologize. *Salon.com*. Retrieved from http://www.salon.com/opinion/conason/2008/ 03/14/ferraro_clinton/print.html

Crile, S. (2009, May 28) Tancredo claims Sotomayor in "Latino KKK." *The Huffington Post*. Retrieved from http://www.huffingtonpost.com/2009 /05/28/tancredo-claims-sotomayor_n_208831.html

Crothers, L. (2003). *Rage on the right: The American militia movement from Ruby Ridge to homeland security*. Lanham, MD: Rowman & Littlefield.

Cuardos, P. (2007). *A home on the field: How one championship soccer team inspires hope for the revival of small town America*. New York: Harper.

Daniels, J. (1997). *White lies: Race, class, gender, and sexuality in White Supremacist discourse*. New York: Routledge.

Davis, M. J. (2005). Learning by myth: The ideal Aryan in *Hunter*. Master's thesis, University of North Carolina at Chapel Hill.

De Neys, W., Vartanian, O., & Goel, V. (2008). Smarter than we think: When our brains detect that we are biased. *Psychological Science, 19*, 483–489.

Dewan, S. (2008, October 14). In generation seen as colorblind, black is yet a factor. *The New York Times*. Retrieved from http://www.nytimes.com/2008/10/15/us/politics/15youth.html

Doty, W. G. (1986). *Mythography: The study of myths and rituals*. Tuscaloosa, AL: University of Alabama Press.

Doxtader, E. (2003). Reconciliation—A rhetorical concept/ion. *Quarterly Journal of Speech, 89*, 267–292.

Duke, A. (2010, May 12). Los Angeles passes Arizona boycott over immigration law. CNN.com Blogs. Retrieved from http://news.blogs.cnn.com/2010/05/12/los-angeles-passes-arizona-boycott-over-immigration-law

Dyer, R. (1997). *White*. New York: Routledge.

Eckholm, E. (2010, June 12). A race for Governor of Arizona, with a lap in New York. *The New York Times*. Retrieved from http://www.nytimes.com/2010/06/13/us/politics/13immig.html?ref=us

Eilperin, J. (2008, October 17). Palin's "pro-America areas" remark: Extended version. *The Washington Post*. Retrieved from http://voices.washingtonpost.com/44/2008/10/17/palin_clarifies_her_pro-americ.html

Elliot, J. (2009, August 19). Heavily-armed '90s militia, linked to anti-Obama activist, resisted "New World Order." *Talking Points Memo*. Retrieved from http://tpmmuckraker.talkingpointsmemo.com/2009/08/heavily_armed_militia_defended_by_activist_resisted_new_world_order.php

Ellul, J. (1965). *Propoganda: The formation of men's attitudes* (Konrad Kellen and Jean Lerner, Trans.). New York: Vintage Books (Random House).

Epstein, M. (2006, December 13). Tom Tancredo vs. third world Miami: "Capital of Latin America." *VDARE*. Retrieved from http://www.vdare.com/epstein/061213_tancredo.htm

Etheridge, E. (2009, July 22). "Birther" boom. *The New York Times*. Retrieved from http://opinionator.blogs.nytimes.com/2009/07/22/birther-boom/

Ezekiel, R. S. (1995). *The racist mind: Portraits of American neo-Nazis and Klansmen*. New York: Viking.

Federal Bureau of Investigation. (2009, August 23). *Hate Crime*. Retrieved from http://www.fbi.gov/hq/cid/civilrights/hate.htm

Fernandez, V. (2010, May 28). Arizona's ban on ethnic studies worries more than Latinos. *La Prensa San Diego*. Retrieved from http://laprensa-sandiego.org/stories/arizona%E2%80%99s-ban-on-ethnic-studies-worries-more-than-latinos/

Fineman, H. (2008, August 13). Can a patriotic pitch save McCain's campaign? McCain has been styling himself as a man who puts "country first." *MSNBC.com*. Retrieved from http://www.msnbc.msn.com /id/26180568/

Fiske, S. T., & Taylor, S. E. (2008). *Social cognition: From brains to culture*. New York: McGraw-Hill.

France 24 (2008, November 19). Racist attacks surge after Obama's victory. *France24*. Retrieved from http://www.france24.com/en/20081119-usa-barack-obama-racist-attacks-surge-after-victory-race

Franke-Ruta, G. (2009, September 15). Carter cites "racism inclination" in animosity toward Obama. *The Washington Post*. Retrieved from http://voices.washingtonpost.com/44/2009/09/15/carter_cites_racism_inc linatio.html

Frick, A. (2009, May 27). Tancredo: Sotomayor "appears to be a racist." *Think Progress*. Retrieved from http://thinkprogress.org/2009 /05/27/tancredo-sotomayor-racist/

Gabriel, J. (1998). *Whitewash: Racialized politics and the media*. London and New York: Routledge.

Gardell, M. (2003). *Gods of the blood: The pagan revival and white separatism*. Durham, NC and London: Duke University Press.

Garofoli, J. (2008, October 9). Veiled racism seen in new attacks on Obama. *SFGate.com*. Retrieved from http://www.sfgate.com/cgi-bin/article. cgi?f=/c/a/2008/10/09/MNB313DUTE.DTL

Gerard, H. B., & Hoyt, M. F. (1974). Distinctiveness of social categorization and attitude toward ingroup members. *Journal of Personality and Social Psychology, 29*, 836-842.

Gilbert, M. (2007). *Kristallnacht: Prelude to destruction*. London: Harper Collins.

Graham, N. (2009, July 22). Lou Dobbs speculates if Obama is undocumented [Audio file]. *The Huffington Post*. Retrieved from http://www. huffingtonpost.com/2009/07/21/lou-dobbs-speculates-if-o_n_242430.html

Graumann, C. F., & Wintermantel, M. (1989). Discriminatory speech acts: A functional approach. In D. Bar-Tal, C. F. Graumann, A. W. Kruglanski, & W. Stroebe (Eds.), *Stereotyping and prejudice: Changing conceptions* (pp. 184–204). New York: Springer-Verlag.

Green, J. (2008, September). The front-runner's fall. *The Atlantic*. Retrieved from http://www.theatlantic.com/doc/200809/hillary-clinton-campaign

Guttentag, W., & DiPersio, V. (Writers and Directors). (2003). Hate.com: Extremists on the Internet [Television series episode]. In J. Anderson (Producer), *America undercover*. New York: Home Box Office.

Hall, S. (1992). Race, culture, and communications: Looking backward and forward at cultural studies. *Rethinking Marxism 5*:10–18.

Hamill, S. D. (2009, December 15). Federal charges are filed in the killing of immigrant. *The New York Times.* Retrieved from http://www.nytimes.com/2009/12/16/us/16hate.html?_r=2&ref=us

Hamm, M. S. (1993). *American Skinheads: The criminology and control of hate crime*. Westport, CT: Praeger.

Hart, R. P. (1997). *Modern rhetorical criticism* (2nd ed.). Boston: Allyn & Bacon.

Hartness, E. (2009, April 15). UNC officials denounce raucous student protest. *WRAL.com.* Retrieved from http://www.wral.com/news/local/story/4954946/

Hazlitt, W. (2005). *On the pleasure of hating*. New York: The Penguin Group.

Heaney, S. (2000). *Beowulf* (S. Heaney, Trans.). New York: W. W. Norton.

Herbert, B. (2008a, January 26). Questions for the Clintons. *The New York Times.* http://www.nytimes.com/2008/01/26/opinion/26herbert.html

Herbert, B. (2008b, May 10). Seeds of destruction. *The New York Times.* Retrieved from http://www.nytimes.com/2008/05/10/opinion/10herbert.html

Herek, G. M., Cogan, J. C., & Gillis, J. R. (2003). Victim experiences in hate crimes based on sexual orientation. In B. Perry (Ed.), *Hate and bias crime: A reader* (pp. 243–260). New York: Routledge.

Holthouse, D. (2009a, Spring). The year in hate, 2008: Number of hate groups tops 900 (Intelligence Report No. 133, pp. 48–50). Retrieved from the Southern Poverty Law Center website: http://www.splcenter.org/get-informed/intelligence-report/browse-all-issues/2009/spring/the-year-in-hate

Holthouse, D. (2009b, February 26). "Right Wing Youth" group debuts at CPAC [Web log posting]. *Hatewatch.* Retrieved from http://www.splcenter.org/blog/2009/02/26/white-nationalist-linked-right-wing-youth-group-debuts-at-cpac/

Holthouse, D. (2009c, Fall). *Nativists to patriots: Nativist vigilantes adopt "patriot" movement ideas* (Intelligence Report No. 135, pp. 42–44). Retrieved from the Southern Poverty Law Center website: http://www.splcenter.org/get-informed/intelligence-report/browse-all-issues/2009/fall/nativists-to-patriots

Hughes, L. (2009, April 16). University reacts to protestors: May bring students to Honor Court. *The Daily Tar Heel*. Retrieved from http://issuu .com/dailytarheel/docs/april16

Iganski, P. (2003). Hate crimes hurt more. In B. Perry (Ed.), *Hate and bias crime: A reader* (pp. 243–260). New York: Routledge.

Insurgent. Retrieved from http://www.resist.com/ on January 10, 2010.

Internet Modern History Sourcebook. (1997). *Benito Mussolini: What is fascism, 1932*. Retrieved from http://www.fordham.edu/halsall/mod/ mussolini-fascism.html

Jaeger, M., Cleve, G., Ruth, I., & Jaeger, S. (1998) cited in Reisigl, M., & Wodak, R. (2001) *Discourse and discrimination: Rhetorics of racism and antisemitism*. New York: Routledge.

Jhally, S. (Producer & Editor). (2008). *Tim Wise on white privilege: Racism, white denial, and the costs of inequality* [DVD]. Northampton, MA: The Media Education Foundation.

Johnson, A. G. (1997). *Privilege, power, and difference*. Boston: McGraw-Hill.

Just Build the Fence Blog. (2007, June 14). Aztlán rising: The illegal subversion of America [Web log message]. Retrieved from http://justbuildthefence.blogspot.com/2007/06/aztlan-arising-700000-march-in-los.html

Kahneman, D., & Tversky, A. (1972). Subjective probability: A judgment of representativeness. *Cognitive Psychology*, *3*, 430–454.

Kantor, J. (2008, May 22). As Obama heads to Florida, many of its Jews have doubts. *The New York Times*. Retrieved from http://www.nytimes. com/2008/05/22/us/politics/22jewish.html?pagewanted=all

Keen, S. (1986). *Faces of the enemy: Reflections of the hostile imagination: The psychology of enmity*. San Francisco: Harper & Row.

Keller, L. (2009a, Spring). *Minority meltdown: Immigrants blamed for mortgage crisis* (Intelligence Report No. 133, pp. 24–27). Retrieved from the Southern Poverty Law Center website: http://www.splcenter.org/get-informed/intelligence-report/browse-all-issues/2009/spring/minority-meltdown

Keller, L. (2009b, Spring). *White heat: Racist backlash greets new U.S. president* (Intelligence Report, No. 133, p. 36). Retrieved from the Southern Poverty Law Center website: http://www.splcenter.org/get-informed/intelligence-report/browse-all-issues/2009/spring/white-heat

Keller, L. (2009c, Fall). The second wave: Evidence grows of far-right militia resurgence (Intelligence Report No. 135, pp. 32–39). Retrieved from the Southern Poverty Law Center website: http://www.splcenter.org/get-informed/intelligence-report/browse-all-issues/2009/fall/the-second-wave

Kessler, J. (1999). *Poisoning the web: Hatred online. An ADL Report on Internet bigotry, extremism and violence* New York: Anti-Defamation League.

Kiely, K., & Lawrence, J. (2008, May 8). Clinton makes case for wide appeal. *USA Today.com*. Retrieved from http://www.usatoday.com/news/politics/election2008/2008-05-07-clintoninterview_N.htm

Klassen, B. (1973). The white man's bible. Retrieved from http://www.resist.com

Koppelman, A. (2008, June 11). Fox News calls Michelle Obama "Obama's baby mama." *Salon.com*. Retrieved from http://www.salon.com/politics/war_room/2008/06/11/fox_obama/

Kovacs, J. (2006, November 19). Bush doesn't think America should be an actual place: Tancredo says president believes nation should be merely "idea" without borders. *World Net Daily*. Retrieved from http://www.wnd.com/index.php?fa=PAGE.printable&pageId=38951

Kristof, N. D. (2008, March 9). Obama and the bigots. *The New York Times*. Retrieved from http://www.nytimes.com/2008/03/09/opinion/09kristof.html

Kuznia, R. (2009, May 29). Tancredo calls Sotomayor "racist"; compares La Raza to KKK. *Hispanic Business.com*. Retrieved from http://www.hispanicbusiness.com/news/2009/5/29/tancredo_calls_sotomayor_racist_compares_la.htm

Langer, E. (1990). The American neo-Nazi movement today. *The Nation, 25*, 82–108.

La Rossa, R. (1995). Stories and relationships. *Journal of Social and Personal Relationships, 12*, 553–558.

Latino-Talk. (2009, March 10). Cecilia Munoz for director of intergovernmental affairs. *Latino-Talk.com*. Retrieved from http://latino-talk.com/politics/director-of-intergovernmental-affairs/263

Lawton, S., & Edwards, S. (1997). The use of stories to help children who have been abused. In K. N. Dwivedi (Ed.), *The therapeutic use of stories* (pp. 185–197). New York: Routledge.

Legault, L., Green-Demers, I., & Eadie, A. L. (2009). When internalization leads to automatization: The role of self-determination in automatic stereotype suppression and implicit prejudice regulation. *Motivation and Emotion, 33*, 10–24.

Leisten, R. (1997). Stories for children with learning disabilities. In K. N. Dwivedi (Ed.), *The therapeutic use of stories* (pp. 198–210). New York: Routledge.

Leonhardt, D. (2007, May 30). Truth, fiction and Lou Dobbs. *The New York Times*. Retrieved from http://www.nytimes.com/2007/05/30/business /30leonhardt.html?_r=2&pagewanted=1

Lepore, L., & Brown, R. (1997). Category and stereotype activation: Is prejudice inevitable? *Journal of Personality and Social Psychology, 72,* 275–287.

Levin, J., & McDevitt, J. (2002). *Hate crimes revisited: America's war on those who are different.* Boulder, CO: Westview.

Lindlof, T. R., & Taylor, B. C. (2002). *Qualitative communication research methods* (2nd ed.). Thousand Oaks, CA: Sage.

Linville, P. W. (1982). The complexity-extremity effect and age-based stereotyping. *Journal of Personality and Social Psychology, 42,* 193–211.

Linville, P. W., & Jones, E. E. (1980). Polarized appraisals of outgroup members. *Journal of Personality and Social Psychology, 38,* 689–703.

Liptak, A. (2008, June 12). Unlike others, U.S. defends freedom to offend in speech. *The New York Times.* Retrieved from http://www.nytimes.com/ 2008/06/12/us/12hate.html?pagewanted=1&ei=5070&en=c2f1656cced6 6e63&ex=1213934400&emc=eta1

Lone Wolf Survivalist. Retrieved from http://www.lonewolfsurvivalist.com.

Luo, M. (2008, April 23). N.C. Republicans preview Wright-Obama ad. *The New York Times.* Retrieved from http://thecaucus.blogs.nytimes .com/2008/04/23/nc-republicans-preview-wright-obama-ad/

MacDonald, A. (1989). *Hunter.* Hillsboro, WV: National Vanguard.

MacDonald, A. (1996). *The Turner diaries* (2nd ed.). New York: Barricade.

Marinetti, F. T. (1909). The Futurist manifesto. Retrieved from http://www.cscs.umich.edu/~crshalizi/T4PM/futurist-manifesto.html

Markman, A. B., & Ross, B. H. (2003). Category use and category learning. *Psychological Bulletin, 129,* 592–613.

Markovitz, J. (2004). *Legacies of lynching: Racial violence and memory.* Minneapolis, MN: University of Minnesota Press.

Maroney, T. A. (1998). The struggle against hate crime: Movement at a crossroads. *New York University Law Review, 73,* 564–620.

Martin, A. (2008, October 6). "Hannity's America" examines the job Barack Obama says qualifies him for the nation's highest office. *Fox News.com.* Retrieved from http://www.foxnews.com/search-results/m/21112719/ community-organizer-years.htm

McIntosh, P. (1988). White privilege: Unpacking the invisible knapsack. Ex-cerpted from *White privilege and male privilege: A personal account of coming to see correspondences through work in Women's Studies.* Re-printed from the Winter 1990 issue of *Independent School.*

Media Matter for America. (2008, October 7). On Fox News, Hannity hosted Andy Martin—who has called judge a "crooked, slimy Jew," accused African-Americans in public office of corruption—in Obama smear-fest. *Media Matters.org.* Retrieved from http://mediamatters.org/research/200810070011

Media Research Center. (2008, April 28). ABC & CBS North Carolina TV stations refuse to air anti-Obama ad. *CyberAlert, 13,* 79. Retrieved from http://www.mediaresearch.org/cyberalerts/2008/cyb20080428.asp#2

Merriam-Webster Online. Retrieved from http://www.merriam-webster.com/dictionary/uppity.

Merritt, J. (2007, May 6). Tancredo: Immigration threat to Western civiliza-tion. *Talk Left: The Politics of Crime.* Retrieved from http://www.talkleft.com/story/2007/5/6/133239/3120

Meyer, T. (2001). *Identity mania: Fundamentalism and the politicization of cultural differences* (M. Reddy & L. Hinchman, Trans.). London and New York: Zed.

Mike. (2007, December 4). *Tancredo releases newest TV ad "consequences"* [Web log message]. Retrieved from Blog 4 President.us website: http://blog.4president.us/2008/tom_tancredo/index.html

Montopoli, B. (2009, July 23). Who are the Birthers? *CBSNew.com.* Re-trieved from http://www.cbsnews.com/blogs/2009/07/23/politics/politicalhotsheet/entry5182746.shtml

Morris, D., & McGann, E. (2008, August 14). Mark Penn and Hillary: Mon-key see, monkey do. *Real Clear Politics.* Retrieved from http://www.realclearpolitics.com/articles/2008/08/mark_penn_hillary_monkey_see_m.html

Moskowitz, G.B., Gollwitzer, P.M., Wasel, W., & Schaal, B. (1999). Precon-scious control of stereotype activation through chronic egalitarian goals. *Journal of Personality and Social Psychology, 77,* 167–184.

Moskowitz, G.B., Salomon, A.R., & Taylor, C.M. (2000). Preconsciously controlling stereotyping: Implicitly activated egalitarian goals prevent the activation of stereotypes. *Social Cognition, 18,* 151–177.

Mussolini, B. (1932). The doctrine of fascism. *Worldfuturefund.org.* Re-trieved from http://www.worldfuturefund.org/wffmaster/Reading/Germany/mussolini.htm

Noon, D. (2008, October 31). Black voters strikes fear in the heart of Florida GOP chair. *Minnesota Independent: Center for Independent Media.* Retrieved from http://minnesotaindependent.com/15624/black-voters-strikes-fear-in-the-heart-of-florida-gop-chair

Nunnally, D. (2010, August 5). Obama-like target in carnival game stirs outrage. *The Philadelphia Inquirer.* Retrieved from http://www.philly.com/inquirer/local/20100805_Obama-like_target_in_carnival_game_stirs_outrage.html

Olson, K. M. (2002). Detecting a common interpretive framework for impersonal violence: The homology in participants' rhetoric on sport hunting, "hate crimes," and stranger rape. *Southern Communication Journal, 67,* 215–244.

Owens, G. (2008, November 6). N.C. State students admit to racist graffiti. *WRAL.com.* Retrieved from http://www.wral.com/news/local/story/3913132/

Paley, V. G. (1992). *You can't say you can't play.* Cambridge, MA: Harvard University Press.

Park, B., & Rothbart, M. (1982). Perception of out-group homogeneity and levels of social organization: Memory for the subordinate attributes of in-group and out-group members. *Journal of Personality and Social Psychology, 42,* 1051–1068.

Parker, J. (2008, March 11). Ferraro: Obama where he is because he's Black. *ABC News.com.* Retrieved from http://abcnews.go.com/Politics/Vote2008/story?id=4428719&page=1&page=1

Pascoe, B. (2009, July 28). Keyes, Birthers, Buckley, and Birchers, oh my. *MSNBC.com.* Retrieved from http://www.msnbc.msn.com/id/32190004/ns/politics-cq_politics/

Perry, B. (2001). *In the name of hate: Understanding hate crimes.* New York: Routledge.

Perry, B. (2003). Accounting for hate crime: Doing difference. In B. Perry (Ed.), *Hate and bias crime: A reader* (pp. 243–260). New York: Routledge.

Petty, R. E., & Caccioppo, J. T. (1986). The elaboration likelihood model of persuasion. In L. Berkovitz (Ed.), *Advances in experimental social psychology 19* (pp. 123–205). New York: Academic.

Potok, M. (2007). "Democracy Now" takes on Lou Dobbs. *Hatewatch.* Retrieved from Southern Poverty Law Center website: http://www.splcenter.org/blog/2007/12/05/%E2%80%98democracy-now%E2%80%99-takes-on-lou-dobbs/

Potok, M. (2009, Summer). Resurgence on the right (Intelligence Report No. 134). Retrieved from Southern Poverty Law Center website: http://www.splcenter.org/get-informed/intelligence-report/browse-all-issues/2009/summer/editorial

Preston, J. (2009, May 14). Mexican data show migration to U.S. in decline. *The New York Times*. Retrieved May 18, 2009, from http://www.nytimes.com/2009/05/15/us/15immig.html?_r=2&th&emc=th

Quattrone, G. A., & Jones, E. E. (1980). The perception of variability within ingroups and outgroups: Implications for the law of small numbers. *Journal of Personality and Social Psychology, 38*, 141–152.

Ray, G. B. (2009). *Language and interracial communication in the United States: Speaking in Black and White.* New York: Peter Lang.

Reisigl, M., & Wodak, R. (2001). *Discourse and discrimination: Rhetorics of racism and anti-semitism.* London: Routledge.

Rev. Jeremiah Wright's words: Sound bites vs. sermon excerpt. (2008, March 29). *The Chicago Tribune.* Retrieved from http://www.chicagotribune.com/news/local/chi-wright-transcripts-webmar29,0,5774556.story

Rhea, J. T. (1997). *Race pride and the American identity.* Cambridge, MA: Harvard University Press.

Rich, F. (2008, October 25). In defense of White Americans. *The New York Times.* Retrieved from http://www.nytimes.com/2008/10/26/opinion/26rich.html?_r=1&th&emc=th&oref=slogin

Roach, C. M. (2006). *Legitimizing cinematic hate: Understanding the birth of a nation as white supremacist hate speech through the hate stratagem.* Unpublished honors thesis, University of North Carolina at Chapel Hill.

Roberts, S. (2008, August 13). In a generation, minorities may be the U.S. majority. *The New York Times.* Retrieved from http://www.nytimes.com/2008/08/14/washington/14census.html?_r=3&th&emc=th&oref=slogin

Rohter, L. (2008, November 6). The Klan chimes in on Obama. *The New York Times.* Retrieved from http://thecaucus.blogs.nytimes.com/2008/11/06/the-klan-chimes-in-on-obama/

Rosenberg, S. L., McKeon, M. L., & Dinero, T. E. (1999). Positive peer groups reclaim rejected kids. *The Educational Digest, 65*, 22–27.

Roy, J. M. (2002). *Love to hate: America's obsession with hatred and violence.* New York: Columbia University Press.

Santa Cruz, N. (2010, May 12). Arizona bill targeting ethnic studies signed into law. *Los Angeles Times.* Retrieved from http://articles.latimes.com/2010/may/12/nation/la-na-ethnic-studies-20100512

Sapon-Shevin, M., Dobbelaere, A., Corrigan, C. R., Goodman, K., & Mastin, M. C. (1998a). Everyone here can play. *Educational Leadership, 56*(1), 42–45.

Sapon-Shevin, M., Dobbelaere, A., Corrigan, C. R., Goodman, K., & Mastin, M. C. (1998b). Promoting inclusive behavior in inclusive classrooms: "You can't say you can't play." In L. H. Meyer, H. S. Park, M. Grenot-Scheyer, I. S. Schwartz, & B. Harry (Eds.), *Making friends: The influences of culture and development.* Baltimore, MD: Paul H. Brookes.

Sargent, G. (2008a, October 16). New McCain campaign/RNC robocalls question whether Obama and Dems really want to keep us safe. *Talking Points Memo.com.* Retrieved from http://tpmelectioncentral. talkingpointsmemo.com/2008/10/mccainrnc_robocall_questions_w.php

Sargent, G. (2008b, October 16). Worst yet? McCain campaign robocall ties Obama to "domestic terrorist Bill Ayers." *Talking Points Memo.com.* Retrieved from http://tpmelectioncentral.talkingpointsmemo.com /2008/10/worst_yet_mccain_campaign_robo.php

Sassenberg, K., & Moskowitz, G. B. (2004). Don't stereotype, think different! Overcoming automatic stereotype activation by mindset priming. *Journal of Experimental Social Psychology, 41,* 506–514.

Savage, C. (2009, May 14). A judge's view of judging is on the record. *The New York Times.* Retrieved from http://www.nytimes.com/2009/05/15/us/15judge.html

Schumann D. W. & Thorson, E. (Eds.). (2007). *Internet advertising: Theory and research* (2nd ed., pp. 395–424). Mahwah, NJ: Lawrence Erlbaum.

Schwab, G. (1990). *The day the Holocaust began: The odyssey of Herschel Grynszpan.* New York: Praeger.

Scott, J. (2008, June 16). FoxNews.com. Fox News Archive Transcript. Retrieved from http://www.foxnews.com/story/0,2933,367601,00.html

Seelye, K. Q., & Bosman, J. (2008, March 12). Ferraro's Obama remarks become talk of campaign. *The New York Times.* Retrieved from http://www.nytimes.com/2008/03/12/us/politics/12campaign.html

Sinderbrand, R. (2008a, March 13). Ferraro steps down from Clinton campaign. *CNNPolitics.com.* Retrieved from http://www.cnn.com/2008/ POLITICS/03/12/ferraro.comments/index.html

Sinderbrand, R. (2008b, December 29). GOP reaction divided over controversial Obama song. *CNNPolitics.com.* Retrieved from http://www.cnn.com/2008/POLITICS/12/29/saltsman.obama.song/

Smith, A. D. (1984). National identity and myths of ethnic descent. *Research in Social Movements, Conflict, and Change, 7,* 95–130.

Smith, B. (2008, March 11). A Ferraro flashback. *Politico.com*. Retrieved from http://www.politico.com/blogs/bensmith/0308/A_Ferraro_ flashback.html

Smith, B. (2009a, March 2). Culture of conspiracy: The Birthers. *Politico.com*. Retrieved from http://www.politico.com/news/stories/0209/ 19450.html

Smith, B. (2009b, July, 31). Poll: 28% of republicans don't believe Obama was born in the U.S. *Politico.com*. Retrieved from http://www.politico. com/blogs/bensmith/0709/Poll_28_of_Republicans_dont_believe_Obam a_was_born_in_US.html

Snow, R. L. (1999). *The militia threat: Terrorists among us*. Cambridge, MA: Da Capo Press.

Sokolon, M. K. (2006). *Political emotions: Aristotle and the symphony of reason and emotion*. DeKalb, IL: Northern Illinois University Press.

SPLC. (2000, Spring). *Pagans and prison* (Intelligence Report No. 98). Retrieved from the Southern Poverty Law Center website: http://www.splcenter.org/intel/intelreport/article.jsp?pid=487.

SPLC. (2008, Winter). *Anti-Latino hate crimes rise up for fourth year* (Intelligence Report No. 132, p. 7). Retrieved from the Southern Poverty Law Center website: http://www.splcenter.org/get-informed/intelligence-report/browse-all-issues/2008/winter/hate-crimes

SPLC. (2009, Winter). Hate in the mainstream: Quotes from the right Intelligence Report No. 133, p. 4). Retrieved from the Southern Poverty Law Center website: http://www.splcenter.org/get-informed/intelligence-report/browse-all-issues/2009/winter/hate-in-the-mainstream

SPLC (2009, March 5). Tancredo: Latinos, Muslims represent "problem" cultures [Web log message]. Retrieved from GALEO website: http://www.galeo.org/story.php?story_id=0000005854

SPLC Report vol. 39, no. 3 (2009a). N.Y. county is microcosm of anti-immigrant violence, pp. 5 & 8.

SPLC Report vol. 39, no. 4 (2009b). Newspaper accounts confirm SPLC's militia report findings, p. 3.

Srull, T. K., & Wyer, S. R. (1980). Category accessibility and social perception: Some implications for the study of person memory and interpersonal judgments. *Journal of Personality and Social Psychology*, *38*, 841–856.

Stauffer, S. (2010, August 5). Outrage over carnival game with Obama like-
    ness. NBC Philadephia. Retrieved from http://www.nbcphiladelphia.
    com/news/weird/Outrage-Over-Carnival-Game-With-Obamas-Likeness-
    99991634.html
Stein, S. (2008, October 17). Palin explains what parts of country not "pro-
    America." *The Huffington Post.* Retrieved from http://www.
    huffingtonpost.com/2008/10/17/palin-clarifies-what-part_n_135641.html
Steinhauer, J. (2008, October 14). Volunteers for Obama face a complex is-
    sue. *The New York Times.* Retrieved from http://www.nytimes.com
    /2008/10/15/us/politics/15nevada.html
Sternberg, R. J. (1995). Love as a story. *Journal of Social and Personal Re-
    lationships, 12,* 541–546.
Stern-LaRosa, C., & Bettmann, E. H. (2000). *Hate hurts: How children learn
    and unlearn prejudice.* New York: Anti-Defamation League.
Strauss, A. L. (1987). *Qualitative analysis for social scientists.* Cambridge,
    UK: Cambridge University Press.
Strauss, A. L., & Corbin, J. (1990). *Basics of qualitative research.* Newbury
    Park, CA: Sage.
Tancredo, T. (2006). Islamic terrorists freely roam American borders [Video
    file]. *YouTube.* Retrieved from http://www.youtube.com/watch?v=qf3
    JunNAQQw on June 21, 2010.
Tajfel, H. (1981). *Human groups and social categories: Studies in social
    psychology.* Cambridge, UK: Cambridge University Press.
Tajfel, H., & Forgas, J.P. (2000). Social categorization: Cognitions, values
    and groups. In C. Stangor (Ed.), *Stereotypes and prejudice: Essential
    readings* (pp. 49–64). Philadelphia, PA: Psychology.
Teaching Tolerance. (1997). *Starting small: Teaching children tolerance*
    [Documentary]. Montgomery, AL: Teaching Tolerance.
Teaching Tolerance. (2000). *A place at the table* [Documentary]. Montgom-
    ery, AL: Teaching Tolerance. Retrieved from http://www.tolerance.org
Terkel, A. (2007, December 8). Tancredo to boycott tomorrow's Univision
    debate. *Think Progress.* Retrieved from http://thinkprogress.org/2007/
    12/08/tancredo-boycotts-tomorrows-univision-debate/
The Turner diaries audio book. Audio retrieved from http://www.
    youtube.com/watch?v=yl0jhD67OtQ
Thompson, M. (2009, August 19). When protesters bear arms against health-
    care reform. *Time.com.* http://www.time.com/time/nation/article
    /0,8599,1917356,00.html

Thrush, G. (2009, September 8). Rep. Schmidt whispers "I agree with you" to Birther. *Politico.com*. Retrieved from http://www.politico.com/blogs/glennthrush/0909/Rep_Schmidt_whispers_I_agree_with_you_to_birther.html

TightRope. Retrieved from the TightRope website: http://www.tightrope.cc/

Timmerman, K. R. (2003). *Preachers of hate: Islam and the war on America*. New York: Three Rivers Press.

Tsesis, A. (2002). *Destructive messages: How hate speech paves the way for harmful social movements*. New York: New York University Press.

Van Dijk, T. (1991). *Racism and the press: Critical studies in racism and migration*. London: Routledge.

Van Dijk, T. (1995). Elite discourse and the reproduction of racism. In K. Whillock & D. Slayden (Eds.), *Hate Speech* (pp. 1–27). Thousand Oaks, CA: Sage.

Vanguard News Network. Retrieved from http://vanguardnewsnetwork.com/v1/

Von Maltitz, H. (1973). *The evolution of Hitler's Germany*. New York: McGraw-Hill.

Walker, K. L., & Dickson, F. C. (2004). An exploration of illness-related narratives in marriage: The identification of illness-identity scripts. *Journal of Social and Personal Relationships 21*, 527–544.

Wallsten, P. (2008, October 5). Frank talk of Obama and race in Virginia. *The Los Angeles Times*. Retrieved from http://articles.latimes.com/2008/oct/05/nation/na-virginia5

Walsh, J. (2009, August 12). Who was that gun-toting anti-Obama protestor? On the Web, William Kostric backs Birthers, secessionists and shooting cops who bust drug dealers in their homes. *Salon.com*. Retrieved from http://www.salon.com/opinion/walsh/politics/2009/08/12/william_kostric/

Waltman, M. S. (2003). Stratagems and heuristics in the recruitment of children into communities of hate: The fabric of our future nightmares. *Southern Communication Journal, 69*, 22–36.

Waltman, M. S. (2010-a). Racist pre-Christian Paganism's call to blood and violence. In Jeffry Ian Ross (Ed.), *Religion and violence: An encyclopedia of faith and conflict from antiquity to the present*. Armonk, M. E. Sharpe.

Waltman, M. S. (2010-b). Christian identity and the faces of their hate driven violence. In Jeffry Ian Ross (Ed.), *Religion and violence: An encyclopedia of faith and conflict from antiquity to the present*. Armonk, M. E. Sharpe.

Waltman, M. S. (2010-c). Words that killed: A case study of Matt Hale and
    Creativity. In Jeffry Ian Ross (Ed.), *Religion and violence: An encyclo-
    pedia of faith and conflict from antiquity to the present.* Armonk, M. E.
    Sharpe.
Waltman, M. S., & Burleson, B. R. (1997). Explaining bias in teacher ratings
    of behavior alteration techniques: An experimental test of the heuristic
    processing account. *Communication Education, 46,* 75–94.
Waltman, M. S., & Davis, M. J. (2004). Deadly humor: How racist cartoons
    further the ideology of hate and create a symbolic code for ethnovio-
    lence. *Journal of Intergroup Relations, 31,* 3–23.
Waltman, M. S., & Davis, M. J. (2005). How to be a proper racist: Mythic
    representations in *The Turner diaries. Journal of Intergroup Relations,
    32,* 19–39.
Waltman, M. S., & Haas, J. W. (2007). Advertising hate on the Internet. In
    D. W. Schumann & E. Thorson (Eds.), *Internet advertising: Theory and
    research* (2nd ed. pp. 395–424). Mahwah, NJ: Lawrence Erlbaum.
Wardle, S. (2009, April 15). At UNC, student protestors crash Tom Tan-
    credo's party. *Indyweek.com.* Retrieved from http://www.indyweek.com/
    gyrobase/Content?oid=oid%3A388869
Weigel, D. (2009a, June 1). Tom Tancredo staffer pleads guilty to karate-
    chopping Black woman. *The Washington Independent.* Retrieved from
    http://washingtonindependent.com/45075/tom-tancredo-and-the-n-word
Weigel, D. (2009b, June 2). Tancredo, Buchanan bruised by racist "karate-
    chop": Amid aide's guilty plea in assault case, "racist" attacks backfire
    on Sotomayor foes. *The Washington Independent.* Retrieved from
    http://washingtonindependent.com/45214/tancredo-buchanan-bruised-
    by-racist-karate-chop
Weigel, D. (2009c, July 17). Birther movement dogs republicans: Ten mem-
    bers of Congress sign on to presidential birth certificate bill. *The Wash-
    ington Independent.* Retrieved from http://washingtonindependent.com
    /51489/birther-movement-picks-up-steam
Weisman, J. (2008, September 4). Georgia GOP congressman calls Obama
    "uppity." *The Washington Post.* Retrieved from http://voices.
    washingtonpost.com/44/2008/09/04/georgia_gop_congressman_calls
    .html
Wetherell, M., & Potter, J. (1992). *Mapping the language of racism: Dis-
    course and the legitimization of exploitation.* New York: Columbia Uni-
    versity Press.

Whillock, D. E. (1995). Symbolism and the representation of hate in visual discourse. In R. K. Whillock & D. Slayden (Eds.), *Hate speech* (pp. 122–141). Thousand Oaks, CA: Sage.

Whillock, R. K. (1995). The use of hate as a stratagem for achieving political and social goals. In R. K. Whillock & D. Slayden (Eds.), *Hate peech* (pp. 28–54). Thousand Oaks, CA: Sage.

White Revolution. Retrieved from White Revolution website: http://www.whiterevolution.com

Wikipedia MEChA. Retrieved from http://en.wikipedia.org/wiki/MEChA

Wilder, D. A. (1981). Perceiving persons as a group. Categorization and intergroup relations. In D. L. Hamilton (Ed.), *Cognitive processes in stereotyping and intergroup behavior* (pp. 213–258). Hillsdale, NJ: Lawrence Erlbaum.

Williamson, L. A. (2002). Racism, tolerance, and perfected redemption: A rhetorical critique of the dragging trial. *Southern Communication Journal, 67,* 245–258.

Winslade, J., & Monk, G. (1999). *Narrative counseling in schools: Powerful & brief.* Thousand Oaks, CA: Corwin.

Wise, T. (2008). *White like me: Reflections on race from a privileged son.* Brooklyn, NY: Soft Skull.

Women for Aryan Unity. Retrieved from http://wau14.com/

Wood, J. T. (1998). *But I thought you meant...Misunderstandings in human communication.* Mountain View, CA: Mayfield.

Wood, J. T. (2000). "That wasn't the real him": Women's dissociation of violence from the men who enact it. *Qualitative Research in Review, 1,* 1–7.

Wood, J. T. (2001). The normalization of violence in heterosexual romantic relationships: Women's narratives of love and violence. *Journal of Social and Personal Relationships, 8,* 39–262.

Youth for Western Civilization. Retrieved from http://www.westernyouth.org/

YouTube (2006). Jesse Helms "Hands" Ad [Video file]. Retrieved from http://www.youtube.com/watch?v=KIyewCdXMzk

YouTube (2008a). Michelle Obama: First time proud of USA [Video file]. Retrieved from http://www.youtube.com/watch?v=LYY73RO_egw

YouTube (2008b). Terrorist fist-jab [Video file]. Retrieved from http://www.youtube.com/watch?v=G_vmQrTi3aM

YouTube (2008c). Fox News' E. D. Hill apologizes for "terrorist fist-jab" [Video file]. Retrieved from http://www.youtube.com/watch?v=InahUzwRSH8&feature=channel

Zapatna, V. (2009, September 8). Rep. Jean Schmidt tells Birther: "I agree with you." *Think Progress*. Retrieved from http://thinkprogress.org/2009 /09/08/jean-schmidt-birther/

Author Index

Subject Index

Howard Giles,
GENERAL EDITOR

This series explores new and exciting advances in the ways in which language both reflects and fashions social reality—and thereby constitutes critical means of social action. As well as these being central foci in face-to-face interactions across different cultures, they also assume significance in the ways that language functions in the mass media, new technologies, organizations, and social institutions. Language as Social Action does not uphold apartheid against any particular methodological and/or ideological position, but, rather, promotes (wherever possible) cross-fertilization of ideas and empirical data across the many, all-too-contrastive, social scientific approaches to language and communication. Contributors to the series will also accord due attention to the historical, political, and economic forces that contextually bound the ways in which language patterns are analyzed, produced, and received. The series will also provide an important platform for theory-driven works that have profound, and often times provocative, implications for social policy.

For further information about the series and submitting manuscripts, please contact:

Howard Giles
Dept of Communication
University of California at Santa Barbara
Santa Barbara, CA 93106-4020
HowieGiles@aol.com

To order other books in this series, please contact our Customer Service Department at:

(800) 770-LANG (within the U.S.)
(212) 647-7706 (outside the U.S.)
(212) 647-7707 FAX

Or browse online by series at:

www.peterlang.com